THE POLITICS OF URBAN PLANNING

THE | POLITICS
OF
URBAN
PLANNING

William C. Johnson

PARAGON HOUSE
NEW YORK

First edition, 1989

Published in the United States by

Paragon House Publishers
90 Fifth Avenue
New York, NY 10011

Manufactured in the United States of America

Library of Congress Cataloging-in-Publication Data

Johnson, William C. (William Carl), 1937–
   The politics of urban planning.

   Bibliography: p.
   1. City planning—United States.   2. Urban policy—
United States.   3. City planning—Political aspects—
United States.   I. Title.
HT167.J55   1989   307.7′6   88-22539
ISBN 1-55778-054-4
ISBN 1-55778-190-7 (pbk.)

DESIGN: Stanley S. Drate/Folio Graphics Co. Inc.

CONTENTS

LIST OF FIGURES AND TABLES   *ix*

PREFACE   *xi*

1 URBAN PLANNING AS POLITICS AND POLICY   *1*

    1.1 Who builds our cities? / 1
    1.2 Five cases of planning politics / 2
    1.3 The vocabulary of planning / 8
    1.4 The vocabulary of politics / 14
    1.5 Planning in public policy / 17

2 URBAN PLANNING AS VALUE ALLOCATION—A HISTORICAL AND CONTEMPORARY EXPLORATION   *22*

    2.1 City building and political values / 22
    2.2 The esthetic values in urban planning / 24
    2.3 The functional values in urban planning / 26
    2.4 The moral values in urban planning / 29
    2.5 The social values in urban planning / 32
    2.6 Landmarks in the American planning memory / 34
    2.7 Contemporary values of space and place / 44

3 WHO DOES PLANNING: GOVERNMENTS AT WORK   *49*

3.1 The game and its players / 49
3.2 General purpose local governments / 52
3.3 Special purpose local governments / 58
3.4 Metropolitan planning agencies / 60
3.5 State governments in urban planning / 62
3.6 The federal government in urban planning / 64
3.7 The courts in urban planning / 72

4 WHO DOES PLANNING: THE NONGOVERNMENTAL PARTICIPANTS   *75*

4.1 The participants: an overview / 75
4.2 The profit-making participants / 80
4.3 Nonprofit institutions and organizations / 85
4.4 The citizen participants—organized and unorganized / 87
4.5 Summing up: the public-private network / 97

5 HOW PLANNING IS DONE   *101*

5.1 From politics to planning / 101
5.2 The goal-setting stage / 103
5.3 Making the specific choices / 110
5.4 Implementing the goals and choices / 117
5.5 Evaluation and feedback: the cycle closed / 128

6 FUNCTIONAL PLANNING   *133*

6.1 From generalists to specialists / 133
6.2 Housing: the politics of home / 134
6.3 Transportation: the politics of mobility / 142
6.4 Planning for the natural environment: the politics of trees / 149
6.5 Planning for the human spirit: the politics of culture / 153
6.6 Blending the streams: the politics of urban design / 156

7 THE POLITICAL ECONOMY OF URBAN PLANNING   *161*

7.1 The politics and economics of urban land / 161
7.2 The engines of the urban economy / 164
7.3 Where the dollars come from / 168
7.4 The politics of industrial development / 176
7.5 The politics of downtowns and uptowns / 180
7.6 High stakes and hard choices / 185

8 THE POWER TO PLAN   *191*

8.1 What the powerful have that others don't / 191
8.2 Who has the power in the community? / 195
8.3 Power structures in planning choices / 200
8.4 Planning by coalitions / 206
8.5 The ends of power: growth / 210
8.6 Planners in the power structure / 214

9 PLANNING IN AND FOR THE FUTURE   *218*

9.1 Images of urban futures / 218
9.2 Planning as anticipation / 221
9.3 Anticipating urban futures / 228
9.4 Planning as a value enterprise / 234
9.5 The end of the matter / 242

APPENDIX   *245*

GLOSSARY   *251*

REFERENCES   *255*

INDEX   *265*

LIST OF FIGURES
AND TABLES

1.1	Governmental planning decisions	12
3.1	Local governments in planning decisions	53
5.1	Sample table of contents of typical municipal comprehensive plan	106
5.2	Sketch Plan—Future Land Use	107
5.3	Zoning map, Saint Paul	118
5.4	Zoning map, Saint Paul	119
5.5	Planned-unit development	123
7.1	Structure of real estate financial market	174

PREFACE

This book, like most, is a bridge. It offers a verbal link between ideas, people, and their fields of study that merit common attention. One end of the bridge is anchored in the field of urban planning, an academic and professional discipline that is concerned with the design and function of urban built environments. It has both a technical and an ethical character, and its roots are in the city-building efforts of emperors in the early centuries of human history.

The opposite end of this bridge rests on the discipline of political science, with its empirical and normative interests in power, public policy, and the pursuit of justice. Ancient emperors and their advisers found they needed power to build their cities as well as to extend their realms. Urban planning and politics have thus been interdependent all through their evolution, and they have never been more so than in the 1980s. By repeatedly crossing this bridge, readers can grasp in a systematic fashion the political process by which modern American cities are given their shape.

I hope that among those who cross this bridge will be graduate and undergraduate students in planning, political science, public administration, urban studies, and related fields. Other audiences are targeted as well: practicing planners, administrators, and developers who seek to gain a more systematic understanding of the political context in which they work, and those "ordinary citizens" who participate in planning politics or who would if they understood it better.

Politics and planning are complementary disciplines, with different though not necessarily contradictory purposes and dynamics. Planning is concerned with anticipating urban change and commitment to certain directions of change. The focus of politics is on cooperation and conflict—on how those commitments to urban development are decided and implemented. Planning without politics is futile, but politics without planning lacks direction.

I hold three basic concepts that have both inspired and directed this book. First, *politics* stands as the essential self-steering process of a complex pluralistic society. It is the nerve system of a democracy, reflecting all of its faults as well as its strengths. Such politics must be inclusive, calling diverse interests in the public arena for their consideration and partial satisfaction. This view is basically Madisonian, as expressed by that constitutional midwife in his tenth Federalist paper.

Planning must be an element in that political process when it chooses how cities will grow. It is valuable as an ordering, holistic influence which gives political decision makers a central point of view to which they can respond. Thus it provides a "first word" about how cities can be made more humane, liveable, and just, though not necessarily the final decision. If I need a label for this perspective, it could be "Howardian," after the English father of the garden city movement who showed a dual sensitivity to how to make a living in cities and how to live well in them.

The third value is *justice*, which sets a norm for the products of planning politics. As I develop it in chapter 9, it is a dedication to the fair distribution of the benefits and costs of life in urban society. It entails a special concern for those who are currently disadvantaged by some condition of life—age, race, ethnic identity, personal disability, income, or family status. Planning politics cannot remedy all injustices, but it can mitigate some and avoid worsening conditions in others. This perspective is rooted in the Old Testament, and is profoundly influenced by the modern work of John Rawls.

These values have many interconnections—some of which are not obvious and so require deliberate attention. I assert, therefore, that such deliberation is necessary to plan and politick intelligently for cities. This text offers insights and methods necessary for such efforts.

I include several features to make this book especially helpful as a bridge. First, it makes use of much current published material. In the first chapter are five brief case studies of planning politics—from Detroit, San Diego, Warren, New Jersey, New York City's South Bronx, and the San Francisco Bay area. These are amplified later in the book and used to illustrate important points.

In later chapters I draw further examples from the contemporary professional, scholarly, and journalistic literature. While each location cited is unique, it has some features which made it typical of its group. One case never makes a rule, but many cases can suggest important patterns. This permits an inductive mode of learning, leading to concepts and hypotheses which can subsequently be tested against further evidence.

At the end of each chapter are several questions that can stimulate discussion on the themes raised in the text. There are no precise "right answers" to them, but they leave room instead for inferences and judgments.

The book closes with three additional features. An annotated bibliography lists what I judge to be the best case studies in the politics of planning. Students can use these to amplify further the themes introduced in this book. A brief essay follows on how to research and write cases in planning politics. These episodes continually emerge in every community, and there is no better way to build an understanding of planning than by firsthand investigation. Third, a glossary defines briefly the major terms that appear more than once. The languages of planning and politics are not highly specialized, but they often refer to fairly precise things.

The nine chapters of this book fall logically into four parts. In the first part, chapter 1 introduces the basic concepts and themes that will be developed later, as well as the five core cases. Chapter 2 reviews American urban planning history to find the central values and experiences that make up the collective memory that our political system works with today. It also considers the affective meanings that geographic places have for people, and how they express and defend those meanings.

The second part surveys the "cast" of participants in urban planning. Chapter 3 focuses on governments and their officials—local, state, and national—and the parts which each unit plays. In the fourth chapter, the nongovernmental participants appear, from the profit-making and nonprofit corporations to individual citizens and their voluntary organizations. Together these define the scope of cooperation and conflict and the interests at stake in each decision, and how each controversy is channeled toward certain outcomes.

How planning is done is the theme of the third part. Chapter 5 explains the procedures for making planning decisions, from the setting of goals through making specific choices to their implementation. These procedures make use of tools such as comprehensive guide plans and several forms of zoning. Chapter 6 surveys specialized fields of planning—for housing, transportation, the natural environment, and cultural amenities—and the use of urban design methods to integrate these functions into a coherent whole. The 7th chapter directs attention to the economics of planning—the financing of urban development, strengthening of the employment base, and the location of businesses and industries.

The last part looks back on the evidence already presented. Chapter 8 asks an explicitly political question, "Who has power over this?" and offers approaches to identify planning power structures. These are rarely the simple elitist or pluralist configurations so common in the literature of urban politics, but a variable pattern of coalitions that form and re-form as planning choices appear and change. Finally, chapter 9 examines how the planning process approaches the future and the values with which it can do so. I do not offer a single exclusive vision for what can or ought to be, but rather a range of options for deliberation within an open political process.

I owe thanks to more people than I can remember for their contributions to this effort. But I express special appreciation to Mike Black, former Director of Community Development, and my colleagues on the Planning Commission of Shoreview, Minnesota, for an education on the political and personal aspects of this subject that no book could really convey. Bethel College provided me with a faculty development grant that enabled me to purchase resource materials. And of course I thank my wife AnnMae and son Karl for the time away from them that I could spend in front of my Apple.

William C. Johnson
Shoreview, Minnesota

1 | URBAN PLANNING AS POLITICS AND POLICY

1.1 WHO BUILDS OUR CITIES?

We build our cities, and our cities in turn shape our thoughts, our lives, and our livelihoods. But who are the "we" who are doing the building, all of us or a few of us? And what are we building into our cities that will make us more or less humane, secure, prosperous, sociable, or just? These are the two central questions of urban planning, and of this book. These questions underlie the more visible immediate issues that civic leaders must wrestle with daily, from toxic waste disposal and housing for the homeless to job creation and recycling of obsolete warehouses. Who makes these decisions, how, and why are some choices made rather than others?

The design and building of cities is in some respects a mass action, and in others an elite process. It is mass action when people who choose places to live, work and shop, and the means to travel there, collectively determine over a period of time what areas of a city shall grow and prosper and what areas shall decline. Voters can at times choose the direction of city policy through their selection of public officials or their verdict on referendum questions. Citizens' organizations press for funding of a neighborhood improvement program or the cancellation of a highway project and at times come away with a victory. Even when it is not formally expressed, public opinion can establish the acceptable procedures and outer boundaries of decision making, which the elites violate at some danger. In such communities democracy is alive and well.

But there are other situations, often in the same communities in which mass action is significant, when decisions by a few, whoever they are, set boundaries on citizen influence. Often, these persons or organizations take the initiatives to which all other participants must respond. A few acting on behalf of all: this is a basic principle of both a representative democracy and a functionally specialized society. Those few can consist of government officials, business entrepreneurs, financiers, community social leaders, or minority-group activists, depending on the issue at hand. As a result of their choices, by whatever criteria, lower income households may have more or fewer places to live, a neighborhood may prosper or decline, or a new employer may locate on or reject a particular site. Major development schemes do not spring full grown out of public opinion, but typically take form on a planner's drawing board or a developer's sketch pad. Even popularly sought neighborhood rehabilitation efforts win serious consideration only when backed by influential and committed leaders.

This interplay between the "fews" and the many, between one small group and another, and between one bloc of the "many" and its rivals, is marked by two basic sociopolitical processes: cooperation and conflict. City building is not a game of solitaire, even for the billionaire tycoon or legendary machine boss. Some assembly of wills and resources is always necessary to make and execute a plan. But conflict is equally inevitable since wills rarely coincide perfectly, and resources can also be used by one will to oppose another. Both processes involve the use of power and influence: one person or group securing an action or outcome in a situation that would not otherwise come about. This interplay is the centerpiece of *politics,* an inescapable presence in the human enterprise of building cities. There are many ways in which to secure a desired outcome, which gives politics its fascinating diversity; these will have more thorough discussion in chapter 8.

1.2 FIVE CASES OF PLANNING POLITICS

It is helpful at this point to consider five recent cases in which urban development became a subject for both cooperation and conflict. These controversies are atypical of planning politics only in that they received attention from the national news media. The issues which they represent—industrial location, growth limitation, moderate-income housing, neighborhood redevelopment, and metropolitan transportation—arise frequently in urban communities of all sizes. They will set the stage for a more systematic discussion of the basic concepts of this study: *urban, planning* and *politics*. In later chapters, these terms will be referred to repeatedly and expanded to illustrate further points. Other cases will be added along the way to illustrate specific points.

CASE 1:   CADILLACS FOR DETROIT

In 1985, Buicks, Oldsmobiles, and Cadillacs began to emerge from a new assembly plant located on 500 acres in inner Detroit and its enclave suburb of Hamtramck. It is there because officials of the two cities cooperated with the executives of General Motors to bestow $200 million in federal and local public subsidies on that multibillion dollar corporation to locate there rather than in another city. Part of that site previously held a Dodge plant, which was closed due to technological obsolescence.

In 1980, General Motors asked officials to help it find a site for a new plant to replace two obsolete facilities elsewhere in the city. If such a site were not made available in Detroit, it could certainly be found in another city, but the 6,000 jobs would also be relocated. Mayor Coleman Young and the Community Economic Development Department did not want to lose the jobs and tax base; so they chose to acquire by eminent domain 460 acres in the neighborhood called Poletown. It was then turned over to the company without charge.

The conflict arose because 3,438 residents and 143 businesses and institutions in that multiethnic neighborhood were forced to move. Although property owners were to receive legally acceptable compensation, some reacted with a lawsuit against the project which reached the Michigan Supreme Court before its final rejection. All of their petitions and demonstrations were to no avail, since officials had made a firm decision before it was publicized.

General Motors clearly benefited from this planning action, which it virtually dictated to the cities. The latter gained $12 million annually in tax revenue, however, and 5,000 workers have jobs who might otherwise be unemployed. Detroit Mayor Coleman Young probably gained some political prestige as well.

But serious questions remain as to whether these benefits were worth the price paid for them by the displaced residents and the cities as a whole. One wonders what other benefits that $200 million could have bought. The case also raises the issue of how much control public officials really have over their land use amid pressures from a powerful corporation [Bachelor 1985; Fasenfest 1986; Jones & Bachelor 1986].

CASE 2: A HOLD ON SAN DIEGO'S GROWTH

San Diego, like most of California's cities, has grown explosively in population during the twentieth century. It spread out with little restraint over its surrounding mesas and valleys, leaving few gaps in the urban landscape. Many of its residents believe that such sprawling growth destroys the amenities of clean air and open vistas for which they moved to San Diego in the first place. In 1974, these residents, spearheaded by the Sierra Club, began to press for legal measures to slow and channel the city's growth. Their efforts began to bear fruit five years later when the city council announced new growth guidelines. Planning proceeded slowly, as planners examined the large undeveloped areas on the city's fringes for their development potential.

In 1985, the city council approved a large-scale development application from a religious organization for La Jolla Valley in the city's scenic northwest sector. That area, however, had been designated on a 1979 land use plan for "future urbanization"—that is, after 1995. In response, opponents to the project initiated, and voters approved, a ballot proposition to prevent urban development without specific voter approval on the 52,000 acres in the future urbanization zone. Although developers had spent heavily in their campaign against the proposition, the voters gave more credence to the argument that growth controls had been inadequate to protect what many of them defined as their quality of life. Growth management continues to be a political issue in San Diego County as well as the city (and indeed in much of California), and dominates debate in local election campaigns as well as planning hearings [Lindsey 1985; Stepner 1986; San Diego Planning Department 1986].

This case illustrates another facet of the elite/mass competition for control of land use: the delicate and often unstable balance of power over these choices. Planners and public officials do not always get their way if there is a determined citizen organization opposing them. It also raises the question of whom growth limitation really benefits: whose homes and jobs may be given up in order to preserve open space and scenery? What are their relative values?

CASE 3: WHO CAN LIVE IN THE SUBURBS?

Warren is a moderately affluent township in the New Jersey hills, within commuting distance of New York City and in the center of a sea of suburban growth. Since the New Jersey Supreme Court ruled in 1975 and 1983 (in the Mount Laurel cases; see section 6.2) that a city could not use its zoning power to prevent construction of homes affordable by lower income households, upper-class communities have been under pressure to allocate land for such dwellings. Many have resisted that pressure, Warren among them.

Using a court-accepted formula, Warren's "fair share" of lower cost housing was first set at 946 units. Then, however, that figure was reduced to 367 by the state's Council for Affordable Housing, a nine-member body that advises localities on how to meet the standards. Some, indeed, have been built in Warren. But that council also permits a city to "sell" part of its obligation to another; thus, Warren negotiated to transfer 166 units to New Brunswick, ten miles away, along with $4.4 million to build those units.

Citizens in most of those New Jersey suburbs have cooperated in pressures to avoid compliance with the Mount Laurel formula. Conflicts have arisen at both local and state levels between pro- and anti-open housing forces. If the obligation transfers become widespread, it will be due to their popularity with both the sending and receiving cities. But the social groups who would benefit from wider distribution of modest-cost homes lack a voice in these arenas. Given the limited enforcement authority of both the courts and the council, the local governments' decisions, whether to comply or resist, are likely to be final [Hanley 1987].

The planning process is increasingly sensitive to the questions of equity that this case poses, but has not been able to resolve all of them. An obvious issue here is the extent of any community's right

to determine who its residents shall be (at least in economic characteristics) and how many there shall be. In a large metropolitan area,
its choices affect access to not only homes but jobs and other living
amenities. Many of these suburbs are enjoying commercial, office,
and high-technology industrial development at the same time that
they are preventing many of the employees of those enterprises from
living there.

CASE 4: WHAT FUTURE FOR THE SOUTH BRONX?

The southern portion of the borough of the Bronx in New York
City has a population of about 454,000, many of them Black and
Hispanic—and poor. It has a well-documented reputation as the
most blighted large urban neighborhood in the nation; in the late
1970s, many observers wrote it off as a place without hope. Vast
areas have been cleared of buildings, and in others, the people live
in fear and despair.

But by 1988, the South Bronx had fought back, with help from
its friends. One neighborhood group, distinctively named the Mid-
Bronx Desperadoes ("we picked the name because we were desperate"), began to rehabilitate apartment buildings to provide both
homes and jobs. By 1987, it had aided about 1,000 families. One new
project, Charlotte Gardens, consists of 89 suburban style single-
family homes in a cleared slum area that sold for $50–60,000—
admittedly not for the very poorest of the populace. The South
Bronx Development Corporation established an industrial park,
called Bathgate, and by 1987 had secured seven companies with
over 1,000 employees. The "help from its friends" for these and
other projects has been substantial in the form of federal, state,
local, and private-sector funds. Government housing aid alone in the
1978–86 period came to $250 million. But the rebuilding that has
taken place is only a small fraction of what needs to be done
[Chavez 1987; Roberts 1987; Teltsch 1987].

How much more aid will be necessary to restore the South
Bronx to adequate liveability, and on what should it be spent? To
benefit whom? Here the conflict is over scarce resources between
many legitimate competitors for them. The outcomes, year by year,
will depend on who secures the greatest stock of allies and resources. This case also illustrates the vital importance of voluntary
local groups in expressing and serving the needs of the residents,
both to compete for aid and induce cooperation.

CASE 5: HOW SHALL WE CROSS SAN FRANCISCO BAY?

The San Francisco-Oakland metropolitan area is sharply fragmented by nature with two bays and two mountain ranges. What nature separated man must unite in order to carry on trade. Just before and after World War II, several bridges and freeways began to provide that unity, but they were soon crowded to capacity. San Francisco, the commercial heart of the region, is a densely populated city but houses only a small minority of its workforce. It depends on a large stream of daily commuters from surrounding counties.

In the mid-1940s, members of its business community began to plan for improved mass transportation. The orthodoxy of the 1950s among transit planners called for large-vehicle rail systems, and in 1962 state and regional public officials presented to the voters a scheme for the Bay Area Rapid Transit System (BART). It called for the sale of $792 million in bonds to finance construction of the 75-mile network. Repayment of the bonds was to come from a sales tax surcharge in the benefiting counties. The system was actually to serve only part of the region—San Francisco, Alameda, and Contra Costa Counties—since officials in Marin and San Mateo Counties, just north and south of San Francisco respectively, refused to participate.

Once the voters approved it (and by barely more than the required three-fifths majority), the district set out to map its routes and stations and select the equipment. While conflict over the voter choice was muted, it increased as the design work progressed. Observers complained that contrary to BART officials' promises that the system would serve low-income people, none of its routes went near the largest black area of San Francisco, Hunter's Point. Rather, the long line to suburban Concord and Walnut Creek indicated the cooperating business community's higher priority: to transport affluent commuters to the increasing numbers of high-rise office buildings in downtown San Francisco and Oakland [Whitt 1982, ch. 2; P. Hall 1980, ch. 5].

This case suggests that, in the light of experiences with the costs and benefits of BART, there should have been more conflict. At least, certain issues relating to distribution of service and the high-investment technology adopted needed further exploration. Perhaps conflict is the only means that a democratic society has to bring such issues to light.

1.3 THE VOCABULARY OF PLANNING

This book is about planning for American urban settlements, and more specifically about the political processes by which planning choices are made and put into effect. Thus, we must mark out the boundaries of the subject by defining its key concepts.

For the concept of URBAN, we could start with a sociologist's classic definition: Louis Wirth recognized a city as "a relatively large, dense, and permanent settlement of socially heterogeneous individuals." [Wirth 1938, 66] Although this concept identifies the major roots of planning problems, it doesn't draw a clear line between urban and nonurban. The fringes of metropolitan areas and some high-amenity regions such as Cape Cod, Massachusetts, are acquiring these characteristics, and that transitional status also calls for serious planning attention.

The Census Bureau, realizing that it also needed a more precise definition of urban places, designated as a Metropolitan Statistical Area a single city or twin cities with a population of at least 50,000, the county (or counties) in which it or they lie, and all adjoining counties that are somewhat urbanized and are socially and economically integrated with the core. Such an area may include large rural portions, but the great bulk of its population is urban by these criteria.

For the pragmatic purposes of this study, however, urban places are those which present more intense and complex planning choices than typical rural areas. A large and dense settlement poses a steady stream of options about how the land in the community is to be used. Whether a particular parcel of land is to be devoted to an automobile plant, low-cost homes, or open space concerns a great many people who live, work, or own land in the vicinity. The American political system provides multiple opportunities for such persons to influence those decisions, allowing a complex pattern of cooperation and conflict to emerge. Thus, we can include the planning for any place that is experiencing conflict about population growth or density, even if it is formally classified as rural. Cape Cod, Massachusetts, and Aspen, Colorado, may not meet all the criteria for "urbanness," but are experiencing these pressures and controversies, and so belong in this study.

PLANNING for such urban places is the process of making and implementing decisions about their land use and their space-dependent social and economic policies. This definition is narrower than a commonly used concept of planning which can be applied to long-range decision making on human services, economic development, and budgeting. Yet, this concern for planning is not sharply limited to the physical uses of land and such tangible facilities as roads and sewers, as was the focus of much of the planning profession in the first two thirds of this century.

To speak of "space-dependent social and economic policies" is to encompass within the planning process responsibilities for housing, recreation, and an array of social services that depend to some degree on specific land uses. The location and design of a juvenile corrections center or a group home for the handicapped is a planning issue, even though the nature of the treatment within the facility is decided by specialists in other fields. The same holds true for programs to increase employment in depressed areas: a factory location and the supporting utility services would be planning concerns, although a related job-training program might not be. To limit this study to land-use related issues not only makes this analysis more manageable, but corresponds to the planning profession's current definition of its field [Haar 1977, ch. 1].

Planning entails choices and control. "Plans are designed to create predictable, orderly relationships and so to establish control. The power to make and carry out plans is therefore the power to control" [Marris, 1982, 58]. Ideally, it is done by making at one point in time, and according to one set of criteria, decisions that would otherwise be made by many persons on many subsequent dates, and probably using diverse criteria. To the extent that these decisions are ratified and implemented in subsequent action, planning results in control. Thus, when General Motors first asked for a 500-acre site in Detroit, the planning began. It developed over a two-year span from a general idea to a specific design to land acquisition. That the new plant is today producing Cadillacs is evidence that the planning process was a controlling one.

We could think of planning as a cycle with three major event points. Although they are usually not distinct steps in real situations, they represent events that take place in some form. At the first point in this sequence, goals and criteria are set to guide the succeeding steps. Often these routine planning decisions simply follow previously set goals without additional thought. But when a community faces the prospective loss of jobs or can gain new ones from a plant location, it has to set a priority on economic development. Detroit and Hamtramck leaders chose job creation over neighborhood preservation in the General Motors case. The challenge is to set goals that respond adequately to needs, are financially and technically realistic, and have public support.

The second point on the cycle is the making of choices that give those goals tangible form. Ideally, these choices will conform not only to the goals set previously but are also compatible with the stream of other choices that are constantly reshaping the community. Planning decisions differ widely in the size of the area covered, commitment of resources, and time period in which they are to be controlling. The site that Detroit chose for General Motors provided a better fit to the company's demands than the others available.

Third, planning entails implementation of the choices. There is a point at which a development leaves the realm of planning: perhaps by the time that General Motors broke ground on its new plant, for example. But planning must give attention to basic follow-up actions, such as traffic management in the vicinity of the plant. Many cities have drafted elaborate master plans, but ignored them later when specific projects were considered, particularly those for which the prevailing political forces were strong enough to override any virtues which the plan may have had.

Since this is a cycle, the path back to the first point is also essential. Goal setting and choice making must be informed by what is on the ground and by the results of past efforts to program it. Planning can be a school for social learning, in which past successes and failures can be analyzed to lead to better choices and more effective control. For example, some housing complexes for lower income households failed as living environments because of improper design and location. Many of the planners who attended this "school" were able to avoid making the same mistakes a second time. Chapter 5 provides a detailed discussion of these steps.

Planning is basically a government-centered process, rooted as it is within law and accountability to legal definitions of the public interest. But the private sector is also a vital part of most planning choices, whether it be represented by a business enterprise, nonprofit institution, environmental interest group, or a lone individual. Since most urban land is privately owned, each owner is a potential party in a planning choice. Herein is the raw material for the most common type of cooperation/conflict interplay: private interests versus public accountability. In some situations, "public" interests can also be quite narrow, as we shall see later.

The governments on which this planning process is centered are predominantly local. Incorporated cities and villages and many counties have planning and land-use control powers that are specified by their respective states. School boards and special-purpose districts responsible for such functions as sewers, airports, transit, parks, and harbors plan for their own facilities, though not necessarily in coordination with the general-purpose authorities in their areas. In some metropolitan areas, regional planning agencies and councils of local governments have limited planning roles but cannot require local units to follow their recommendations. All of these governmental forms are discussed in chapter 3.

State and national governments become involved in local planning at their discretion. State legislatures can mandate, permit, or prohibit planning actions by their local units. They may also intrude upon local choices in locating a highway or state facility. The national government, likewise, enters the planning process when it locates an office building or military facility in a city or regulates the use of navigable waters. As will be seen in chapter 3, both state and national governments supply financial aid to localities for a variety of land-use related projects. Consequently, some of the cooperation and conflict in planning arises in relations between levels of government (e.g., national, state, or local) or between adjacent local units. All five of the cases just cited have such an intergovernmental dimension.

The political relationships in planning differ according to the type of decision made. It may be useful to distinguish five types, varying with the scale of impact and participation (see Table 1.1 for a comparative summary). *Type 1* is most common, in which a private source proposes to alter a building or small parcel of land in a way that requires government approval. It may be as simple as a division of one lot into two, or a request for a variance to the legal setback distance from the street. Such a choice has little or no impact on the community as a whole, though it may arouse opposition from the immediate neighbors. It can ordinarily be guided by existing policies and standards, although each case must be judged on its merits to some extent. However, if those policies are not consistently upheld in such localized cases, they could be undermined over a period of time.

TABLE 1.1

GOVERNMENTAL PLANNING DECISIONS

Type	Content of decision	Impact of decision on city/region	Conflict Potential
1	Approval of small scale private development proposal. May be residential, commercial, or institutional.	Significant only to immediate surroundings.	Low.
2	Approval of medium-to-large scale private development proposal. May be residential, commercial, institutional, or industrial.	Potentially large. May stimulate related development and require public investments.	Medium to high.
3	Governmental development project in infrastructure or service facilities.	Potentially large. Often instrumental to private development in vicinity.	Low to high, depending on scale.
4	Public-private cooperative development, usually on major scale. Similar to #2.	Probably large. Often accompanied by other public and/or private development.	Medium to high.
5	Comprehensive planning and zoning in advance of actual development. May be for first-time development or redevelopment.	Major in long run, though actual effect is probably delayed.	Low unless specific parts become controversial.

Type 2 decisions also deal with private development of private land, but they have much broader impact on the community. These may include large shopping centers, electric power plants, and apartment complexes. Concerns about noise, traffic, drainage, and visual impacts may be major. The process of making choices of this type is more intricate and consumes more time than in Type 1. More participants will seek to influence the outcome as the stakes are increased in importance. The community itself may have to rethink its goals and decide whether it really wants to become more industrial, or multifamily residential, for example. This may call for another turn in the planning cycle noted above.

In *Type 3* planning decisions, governments embark on development projects of their own. Many of these are infrastructure investments, the basic support facilities that traditionally are the province of the public sector. Among them are public utilities such as sewage disposal and water supply, parks, libraries, hospitals, and the many facilities that support movement of people and goods: streets and highways, parking garages, airports, harbors, and mass-transit lines. Educational buildings, from preschools to universities, also fall into this group. Other major projects such as sports stadiums, convention centers, and museums are built to strengthen the city's economic base and cultural life.

Many Type 3 projects are built according to a capital development plan, for which the construction and funding are mapped years in advance. It is common to borrow money for these through the sale of bonds, though funds also come from local, state, and/or national revenues. In most local government units, issue of general-obligation bonds must be approved by the voters, and the election becomes a judgment on the project itself as well as the tax increase it entails. Although such decisions do not formally involve the private sector, they may draw serious lobbying from those who stand to gain or lose from it, particularly business and labor interests and residents of the areas to be most affected.

Type 4 decisions are marked by formal cooperation between one or more government units and a set of private sector partners. The initiative for the project may come from either side, but a complex working relationship appears in the goal-setting stages. This type is common in efforts to renew a deteriorated central business district or inner-city neighborhood such as the South Bronx, in which it is necessary to attract large-scale commercial or industrial enterprises. There is such intense competition among cities for major investments that they will pay handsomely to win them away from other bidders. General Motors received precisely what it wanted from Detroit because, with its employment and tax potential, it would have had no shortage of bidders for its plant.

The process of Type 4 planning can become very complex. There must be the forecast that the project will be of such benefit to the community as to justify the public subsidy, an assumption that can spark popular opposition at the beginning. Then the government officials negotiate a development contract with the private partners, covering matters of design, financing, construction, and operations. Often, a public agency acquires the land on the chosen site, whether by voluntary sale or condemnation. The project's approval may require several stages of assent by different bodies, which allows its opponents more than one chance to defeat or modify it. Subsequent changes in conditions, such as increased interest rates or slumping markets, may also force renegotiation or even cancellation.

Finally, *Type 5* planning generates or alters comprehensive plans, intended to guide decisions in the first 4 types. It could be a total plan reformulation or revision for a city, or a more limited strategy for improving traffic circulation, rehabilitating a neighborhood, or attracting industrial investment. This type also includes comprehensive zoning and rezoning programs. The choice of the San Diego voters for a development moratorium is in this category. On some occasions, this package is chosen at one time, while in others planning policies may come together piecemeal. These decisions do not appear on planners' agendas as regularly as the previous types, but might be mandated by a state law or by such changed local conditions as a sudden spurt of population growth or the departure of a major employer.

A major challenge is to coordinate local comprehensive plan making among adjoining and overlapping governments. A typical metropolitan area has several counties, dozens of municipalities, several school and special districts, and various state agencies responsible for such functions as highways and natural resources. In the 1960s, Congress placed legal and financial pressures on metropolitan areas to engage in comprehensive planning, and much activity resulted, though of varying effectiveness. Regional urban plans for transportation, waste management, and parks frequently result from bargaining among all parties with a stake in it. Cooperation is essential to their formulation, but it only takes place (if at all) against a backdrop of potential conflicts over the application of specific provisions to areas that oppose them. Chapter 3 will survey this picture also.

1.4   THE VOCABULARY OF POLITICS

The distinctly political feature of planning is its interplay between conflict and cooperation. But what is the unique purpose of politics which sets it off from other social enterprises? The political scientist David Easton [1953, 129] has characterized politics as "the authoritative allocation of values for a society." The three key terms in this abstract but widely cited definition require closer attention.

Values consist of the benefits people seek as they engage in social activity. Some values are material: present income, the prospect of future income, and the security of one's property. They may relate to the essential means of life: health, education, safety, and nutrition. Others are less tangible: identity with one's community, enjoyment of attractive surroundings, and the personal gratification gained from controlling events or influencing other persons. Still others relate to a public cause one identifies with, such as protecting a forest or securing shelter for the homeless. The list of valued things is as long and diverse as individuals want to make it. In chapter 2, values will be discussed as qualities which people seek in their built environments.

Allocation is the process of distributing these valued things among the members of the society. Where a particular value is inherently scarce relative to demand, such as money, most people have to be denied as much as they want while a few may be satisfied. To be sure, these values can be supplied by many institutions in society, not just government. But the policies of government can shape that value flow in many ways, indirectly as well as directly. General Motors as a private corporation supplies income to its workers, but whether it supplies that income to workers in Detroit or elsewhere is dependent partly on the city of Detroit's willingness to support its new factory location there. In the same action, the opportunity to live in a particular neighborhood is ordinarily a private matter, but the 3,000-plus Poletown residents whose homes were taken were also the objects of governmental value allocation.

Value allocation becomes *authoritative* when it is decided by the highest source of legal power in the society. Government may deprive a person of life, liberty, or property when acting by constitutional standards, and it can certainly channel lesser values for a lawful public purpose. When the New Jersey courts ruled that communities must provide land for lower income dwellings, it took away their power to zone land exclusively for other purposes. The concept of authority implies moral as well as legal rectitude; thus prudent officials take care that policies and actions conform to widely accepted standards of public good and benefit.

Cooperation and conflict both contribute to this authoritative allocation of values. Many benefits are widely shared, and those who expect to benefit have every reason to advocate or defend them. The South Bronx development is backed by a loose coalition of groups and enterprises whose aims would be served by it. Some values can only be obtained by large-scale, long-term action. Such open-housing laws and subsidized housing stocks as exist were won by a very persistent movement comprising minority groups, lower income persons and their allies against determined opposition and uninterested neutrals. This illustrates an essential facet of politics: the effort to secure joint action among persons and groups who have partially conflicting goals and interests.

Conflict stems from the basic fact that values are scarce, they mean different things to different people, and the allocation of a benefit to one denies that or a different value to another. The South Bronx is a maze of contradictory values and interests. The new homes in Charlotte Gardens, as plain as they are, cannot be afforded by those who were displaced from the tenements that once stood on that site. Jobs that new industry creates in the area may be taken by those who live elsewhere. The sense of "turf" is strong in many neighborhoods, and stimulates defensive attitudes and actions against the tides of change that continually sweep through cities.

Virtually every action that authoritatively allocates values must do so out of some kind of conflict and by means of some level of cooperation. Politics consists of the social processes that combine the two in the production of public policy, and all of these are found in urban planning. General Motors won aid for its plant by direct, formal negotiation of its demands with the cities of Detroit and Hamtramck and state and national agencies. The opponents were simply overridden by that powerful public-private coalition. But San Diego denied development rights to landowners in La Jolla Valley because the verdict was submitted to that most ancient of democratic rites, popular election. Modest cost housing was to be promoted in New Jersey by a third political means: a judge applying a provision of the United States Constitution to a dispute between two contending parties.

The South Bronx illustrates a more pluralistic means of allocation. It is a large enough area to accommodate many kinds of development—industries, shops, parks, and homes for various income levels. As redevelopment proceeds, different areas will be devoted to each use, as specific neighborhood groups, investors, and public agencies choose. There may be confrontations over specific sites, but such a division of the area minimizes the likelihood of massive struggles over the future of the South Bronx as a whole. No single plan will control the area's development, but rather a mosaic of blueprints with many designers. This also means that some parts which no one singles out for investment will remain neglected.

Another aspect of allocation makes urban planning a political concern: the age-old questions: Who gets what? when? and how? [Lasswell 1958] It is obvious that some persons and groups consistently get more of the valued things they seek than others do. Further, these groups can use their advantages to dominate the allocation process to gain even more in the future. There is a close correlation between being poor and politically inactive and living in a neighborhood where housing is inferior, the crime rate is high, and pollution is most prevalent. Since politics from the time of Plato has been concerned with justice, these concerns have to be part of its study.

Unfortunately, in most real-world planning choices, the questions of who gets what, when and how lack clear-cut answers. General Motors certainly gained much from the destruction of Poletown; so did the workers employed there. But who lost jobs as a result? Did all who had to relocate get poorer or more expensive housing? Where are the "hidden" gainers and losers? A project as complex as that one has a heterogeneous mix of outcomes over a span of time, which permits no simple measurements of justice or injustice. And who are the lower income persons most likely to live in Warren should homes be constructed for them? Presumably they will be employees in the offices and industries in that suburban area, not poor emigrants from Newark or the South Bronx. Planning necessarily entails the allocation (and deprivation) of benefits, whether specifically intended by policy or as a by-product of the results. Thus a key source of conflict is the demand of the deprived and the cost bearers (or those who perceive themselves as such) to reallocate valued things more to their advantage. That they must also cooperate among themselves and possibly compromise with their adversaries completes the political scenario.

1.5   PLANNING IN PUBLIC POLICY

Urban planning is one form of public policy, but we have seen that it is not exclusively *government* policy. Planning decisions of Types 1, 2 and 4 involve the private sector to such an extent that its choices have great effect on the community. In a broad perspective, "a public policy is any policy whose fundamental impact is a binding allocation of values for a significant segment of society." [Nadel 1975, 33] This conception holds that nongovernmental or "private" policy can be binding upon the persons affected by it when government either endorses it or does not act to the contrary. For example, when lending institutions refuse to extend credit for purchase or improvement of homes and businesses in depressed neighborhoods, they effectively condemn the area to continued decline.

The private sector also provides initiatives to which government policy and action respond. Its ownership of most urban land and its central role in maintaining property values and employment make it a central planning actor. Assume that a chamber of commerce of a city has a policy to foster growth in the downtown area. If the city council adopts that goal (and it would rarely choose not to), it typically responds with supportive programs such as improved parking, better mass transit, and financing. This cooperative process will be surveyed in chapter 7.

Because planning policies are complex bundles of governmental and private efforts, participants must take care that they are indeed compatible and mutually supporting. Many policies have failed because not all of the relevant efforts moved toward the same purpose. Where a school district allows its buildings to deteriorate, the residents to whom education is important, and who are able to relocate, simply move out and so contribute to the neighborhood decline with which the city government must cope.

What public policies constitute planning, as defined here? Recall that the term focused on the use of land and space-related aspects of other policies. Some governmental responsibilities in the following list are fully in this category, and others are partly so.

1. *Secure orderly use of the community's land resources.* This is a central purpose of planning, so intensively practiced in most urban areas that it could be thought of as "land budgeting." As a community contemplates the future use of vacant land and possible changes in the use of already built areas, it makes basic decisions on the amount of space to be devoted to residences, industry, commerce, recreation, transportation, and other applications, and on how the different uses shall relate to one another (e.g., residential land adjacent to factories).

2. *Provide for mobility of persons and goods.* This is also a major planning concern, encompassing the location and design of public streets and highways, airports, bus stations, transit facilities, ports, and vehicle storage. How people and goods travel and where they stop affects all other uses of land, so planners have learned they must integrate these in a single perspective. The design of BART has been criticized for its lack of attention to the full range of its social impacts.

3. *Protect and enhance natural resources.* Many policies are necessary to relate the built environment to the natural in order to prevent degradation of wetlands, wooded areas, steep slopes and shorelines; to maintain water quality in lakes, streams, bays and underground aquifers; and to protect scenic views and require landscaping in new developments. This purpose was certainly in the minds of promoratorium voters in San Diego.

4. *Assure satisfactory residential environments.* The allocation of most homes is left to the private sector, operating within the building and zoning codes. Much time of planners is taken up with proposals for new dwellings and requests of individual homeowners for changes to their premises. However, the planning process must at times go beyond these to address the housing needs of low-income households (as in New Jersey), the handicapped, and the elderly.

5. *Promote economic development and employment opportunities.* This is of growing importance to the governmental sector of planning, as cities try to retain and nurture their industries and attract new ones. To do this, they establish industrial parks with necessary support facilities, reserve choice land for offices, laboratories, and factories, and finance land acquisition and new construction. Without the income and tax revenue that these employers provide, the community is hampered in supplying its public services. What Detroit did for General Motors is being duplicated on smaller scales throughout the country.

6. *Assure safety of life and property.* While the planning process does not take in police and firefighting operations, it is concerned with safety-related features of new construction, such as vulnerability to fires and floods and access by emergency vehicles.

7. *Isolate or recycle wastes safely.* This becomes a planning concern in a choice to extend a sewer line to serve a new development or to locate a storage or processing area of household refuse or

hazardous wastes. Landfills are increasingly unacceptable in urban areas, and long-term plans must emerge for processing what can no longer be "thrown away."

Other responsibilities of government in urban areas have some relation to planning: location of parks, schools, libraries, and health facilities; drinking water supply and quality; television antennas and cables; and energy production and consumption. The typical comprehensive guide plan that a city or county adopts is intended to integrate policies on all of these within its land budget. Neighborhood renewal schemes must consider all of the area's institutions and resources, from schools and churches to employers and small shops, to insure that public actions benefit as many as possible and strengthen their contributions to community life.

Here, too, the need for cooperation and the potential for conflict are evident. Even when limited to the built environment and space-related issues, planning is so multifaceted that it requires the collaboration of specialists in safety, transportation, housing, and the other functions listed above. That same diversity is likely to engender conflicts in values, interests, and professional ambitions. When and if these conflicts are dealt with by cooperative efforts, their resolution is binding on all who are affected by it.

In this book, the author takes the overall perspective that the political process is central to planning, and not only *is* but *should be*. Democratic society has institutionalized conflict and cooperation as the engines of policy making, rather than the centralized decision making of authoritarian regimes. Conflicts over policy are not simply impediments to wise or timely decision making, as some might claim. Land is the common heritage of all citizens, and these "stakeholders" have the right to be considered in choices about it. Planners must marshal all of the knowledge and expertise of their trade to inform the public and enlighten the process. Political leaders, however, must blend these with the raw and considered views of all other stakeholders. No one can predict how this synthesis will look in any given case, nor does the most just, efficient, or popular decision always emerge. But for the long run, a democratic society must protect the political process or it will lose control of it.

This book demonstrates the interplay of cooperation and conflict in real situations. There is much evidence that democracy is limited in most decisions: "government by the few" was clearly the rule in Poletown. A *political* process is not necessarily a *democratic* one. But citizen participation can affect policy in many ways, as was shown by voter action in San Diego and the San Francisco area, popular resistance to housing integration in New Jersey, and grass-roots activism in the South Bronx. No one can describe these processes simply; perhaps a genius of democracy is that people find many ways to get things done. If readers find it hard to draw many clear-cut conclusions by the end of chapter 9, they have probably grasped the real situation.

People who cooperate or disagree over the authoritative allocation of values have set ideas of what the planning process ought to do, and possibly an image of what kind of city should emerge from it. These mental images are individual but when they are shared by many influential people, they can dominate that value allocation. American cities embody in their visible presence a host of intangible values to which we have given such names as beauty, efficiency, productivity, community, and opportunity. To understand how these values have shaped the built environment and have been shaped by it in return is the goal of the next chapter.

QUESTIONS FOR DISCUSSION

1. Why is it important to plan consciously for urban growth and renewal? Why is it difficult to do?
2. What is likely to happen when there is no "planning" as defined here?
3. Why does urban planning engender conflict?
4. Why is cooperation necessary in urban planning?
5. Could urban planning ever be nonpolitical? Why or why not?
6. What would urban planning be like if it were not subject to a democratic process?

2 | URBAN PLANNING AS VALUE ALLOCATION—A HISTORICAL AND CONTEMPORARY EXPLORATION

2.1 CITY BUILDING AND POLITICAL VALUES

City building has always served human ends, whether of the few who rule or the many who have the opportunity to decide for themselves. From the kings who planned Paris to suit their own concepts of grandeur and majesty to the small shopkeepers who placed their booths in the most convenient parts of the local marketplace, the shapes of cities have been a mirror of people's ambitions and of the civilization that constructed them.

City building has also been a political process. Clearly, Louis XIV had the authority to construct a wall or boulevard or palace in the Paris of his time. The shopkeepers' choices were more personal, for they wanted to avoid government interference in their businesses, but their very freedom to decide was protected or allowed by the local authorities. In the past century, city environments have taken shape under the increasingly watchful eye of governments and sometimes as a result of their initiatives. Thus, urban development becomes a political issue whenever a governing authority engages in it to alter the value allocation that would otherwise occur. In so intervening, it creates conflict and stimulates cooperation to influence its outcome.

This chapter surveys the experience of American urban planning, with emphasis on the past 100 years, to examine the general values that guided decisions as to how valued things were shaped and then allocated. This history is not simply a "past story" but a living public memory. It is a collection of images of how things have been done, for better or worse, and how American cities evolved through a chain of choices that began in the distant past. Because it is living memory, it continues to shape choices. This history is embodied in many forms: laws of all levels of government, procedures for making decisions, popular expectations of governmental action, the norms and sense of expertise held by professional planners, and above all in the built environment itself.

What is a *value?* Generally, it is a good that people seek, a quality in an object or situation that makes it valuable. In the previous chapter, a political value was defined as a benefit that one seeks in life, whether tangible or intangible. In the context of urban development, that benefit is one which can be derived from the city's built environment and the activities it supports. Cities embody many kinds of such goods: beauty, security, economic opportunity, and so on. Choices to build one thing or another emerge from the definition and pursuit of these values. What is "on the ground" provides visual evidence of a variety of intertwined planning values. A new high-rise, high-tech office building in Chicago or New York overlooks a century-old cheap hotel inhabited by destitute elderly men and families; their proximity contradicts one another and poses questions of which interest is to be served in which locations.

As government struggles to reconcile these incompatible urban values, it typically plays the role of problem solver of last resort. This nation has relied on the private sector to solve many problems, whether profit-making businesses, nonprofit institutions, or voluntary associations. But as the demands of a complex industrialized society multiplied beyond the capacity of those organizations to solve them, national, state, and local governments were again and again called on to deal with them. Certainly the Depression of the 1930s demonstrated the need for better homes and society's inability to provide them in the conventional way; and the Wagner-Steagall Housing Act of 1937 was a result.

But when government did enter the arena, it was not to assume full control of the particular problem area. As in housing, the participation of the national and city governments was piecemeal, partial, and experimental. In allocating values, it had only a limited impact. If the private sector with its resources and expertise could not deal with a difficult new problem, there was no assurance that, even if it spent more money, government could solve it. Thus, in so many of government's new challenges, there was a strong possibility of failure. The nation's housing needs had multiplied so much during the depression and later, after four years of war, that the task the nation faced post-1945 would have required an enormous sum of money and massive organizational skills. To keep government's role in urban planning a limited and fluid one, cooperative rather than dominating, is itself a central American political value. This ambivalent attitude toward government's role underlies the history which follows.

2.2 THE ESTHETIC VALUES IN URBAN PLANNING

Four basic groups of values have traditionally influenced planning decisions in the political system. They have not had equal impact overall, but each has made its unique contribution. These values have been closely tied to other political and intellectual movements of their time such as the Progressive Era, the "business culture" of the 1920s and later, and the civil rights movement of the 1960s and 1970s.

First, there is a cluster of *esthetic* values that relate to the visual and sensual properties of the built environment and their impact on the inhabitants of the cities. It was widely held by civic leaders in the late nineteenth century that the quality of the physical and visual environment had a profound impact on the morals, life styles, and views of the world held by city dwellers. This concept of environmental determinism was believed to be particularly applicable to the "lower classes," those who lived in the most squalid circumstances and held the most menial jobs the society provided. An immigrant from a muddy Russian village who passed through Ellis Island into a filthy tenement and a job making trousers in a dark sweat-shop was not expected to fit into "normal" American culture because of those surroundings.

The answer advocated by many planners over the years, but particularly by the City Beautiful movement just before and after the turn of the twentieth century, was to recast public spaces according to the genteel values of beauty, dignity, and order that the upper classes already enjoyed at their own expense. As Boyer [1983, 45–46] described it,

> the municipal art, city beautiful, and civic improvement crusades grew as piecemeal efforts that aimed to convert a city built primarily for utility into an ideal form through artistic street signs, well-designed municipal bridges, using color in architectural elements, and improving public squares and buildings. In similar manner these crusades were aimed to express the fullness of the human spirit: the ordering of material objects so that they elevated from the commonplace, the embedding of social ideals in public buildings, statues, bridges, street ornaments, and objects so that the better impulses of the most elevated men would soon become common to all.

This was indeed a crusade, for these attempts at beautification sought nothing less than

> a new conception of public life and civic loyalty, a restoration of a lost community ethic through the enhancement of public spaces, decorating them with monuments, beautiful street vistas, majestic and classical architecture for public buildings, and allegorical murals in public places.

There is no doubt that these values had been neglected in the explosive growth of nineteenth century American cities. The ambitions of a laissez faire industrial civilization had been in control, and the ugliness and disorder left in their wake had made those cities depressing places for many to live in, particularly those who lacked the means to escape it on vacations or furnish their own homes and workplaces in more pleasing ways. Yet it was some of those upper-class members who became the advocates of esthetic values on behalf of the ones who were apparently least sensitive to them.

What the realms of private enterprise had made ugly, however, it was now the duty of government to beautify. While it was still in the power of businessmen to erect more attractive buildings, only the city governments could begin to control the street vistas or provide the "allegorical murals in public places." However, even the public authorities had little legal power to regulate the development of land in private ownership. A city might construct a Greek temple as its city hall, but it probably could not prohibit a slaughterhouse from locating next to it.

One expression of this drive for esthetic values was the "back to nature" movement that sought more land for parks and open spaces amid the increasingly crowded cities. The city improvers, as Boyer relates, offered urban parks as

> points of contact between the afflictions of congested dwellings and a curative natural environment, between uncouth masses and the social values of an ideal rural order. . . . They saw a need to revitalize and restore the balance between urban dwellers and nature, even if at government expense.

Frederick L. Olmsted, who designed New York City's Central Park, and other reformers [Boyer 1983, 33–34] held that

> a civilization of cities would not survive if it was cut off from nature. Nature held the power to uplift the downtrodden and instill in man the best ideals from America's rural past. Thus islands of nature had to be inserted into the artificial urban milieu; a synthesis had to be forged out of the rural landscape and the commercial and industrial order.

Indeed, many urban parks were created as a result of this movement with landscaped boulevards, gardens, semiwilderness areas, lakeshores and river banks, sports facilities and children's playgrounds. A twentieth century leader in this field was Robert Moses, who spearheaded the acquisition and development of state parks and beaches in the New York City metropolitan area [Caro 1974].

One event that portrayed these esthetic values in tangible form was the World's Columbian Exposition in Chicago in 1893. Its creators believed that it "would stand as a promise and pledge that the fullness of the human spirit could come to fruition in this new art of city making." [Boyer 1983, 46] The Great White City that stood in the former swamps of Jackson Park demonstrated to many observers the purity, light, and nobility that could be embodied in cities built according to the highest esthetic standards of Western civilization.

2.3 THE FUNCTIONAL VALUES IN URBAN PLANNING

The second group of values that can be allocated through urban planning are *functional.* In contrast to the esthetic, these guide the practical uses to which urban land is put, above all the accumulation of wealth and the means necessary to carry on productive enterprises. Certainly these have been most prominent in the broad sweep of planning choices, due to the connection of land with wealth and the opportunities to increase it.

One functional maxim is that land should be devoted to its "highest and best use." This means that any given parcel should be allowed the most intensive (and profitable) use appropriate to its site and surroundings. Central business districts are proper locations for high-rise offices, not for single-family homes, and industry is best located next to railroad lines or freeway interchanges. Basically, this optimal use at any given time is to be determined by the marketplace, supplemented by such government regulations as are needed to protect the public interest. Since the values of the marketplace change due to many factors, what is "highest and best" may also change frequently and so cause headaches for planners and investors who try to forecast them.

A second principle is that property values should be preserved to the maximum extent possible, especially those in residential areas. A home is the largest investment that a typical household makes, and to protect the value of it is a prime economic and political goal. If an "incompatible use" such as a noisy or smoky factory were located next to a residential area, those homes would become less pleasant for the residents and would sell for reduced prices as a result. Many of the early efforts at zoning city land were to keep commercial and industrial uses away from residential areas, including the case from Euclid, Ohio, that led to the definitive ruling by the U.S. Supreme Court in 1926 [*Village of Euclid v. Ambler Realty Co.*]. (See the discussion of zoning's origins in section 2.6 below.)

Related to the above principle (but at times in opposition to it) is the landowners' right to use their land for their greatest benefit. The Ambler Realty Company sued Euclid because the city zoned for exclusively residential purposes a parcel of land it had previously bought for commercial development. It claimed that the zoning deprived it of income that it would have received if it had been allowed to build as expected. This, in its view, amounted to "taking" private property without just compensation, contrary to the Fourteenth Amendment to the U.S. Constitution. While the Supreme Court rejected that interpretation, courts elsewhere have placed limits on governments' powers to reduce land values where no clear public benefit is produced. City governments are also sensitive to the need to preserve land values and developmental opportunities because of the property tax revenue they generate. A deteriorating neighborhood or business district with falling land values produces less real estate taxes to support the services it consumes and tends to spread its blight to surrounding areas.

Yet another functional value is transportation related: accessibility of locations and speed in movement of people and goods. Early in the twentieth century, the City Beautiful movement waned as immobility replaced ugliness as the chief evil. Narrow streets were clogged with horses and wagons and increasingly the noisy new horseless carriages. Workers had difficulty in reaching workplaces from their homes, and freight movement to and from docks and railroad stations slowed. The crusaders for esthetic values had advocated wide boulevards because they were beautiful, but the "functionalists" favored them as more efficient for moving large volumes of traffic.

By 1910, writers on planning were emphasizing that city government's prime duty was to provide streets wide and direct enough to carry the traffic volumes that would permit continued commercial and industrial expansion, particularly in the central business districts and near the railroad depots. While street railways and rapid transit lines were privately owned, the cities were expected to coordinate their development so as to make sure all areas were adequately served. Consolidation of railroad passenger and freight terminals to reduce transfer time was another priority.

As the century went on, these values were increasingly served with the construction of urban freeways, government assumption of mass transit services, and public construction of airports, harbor facilities, bus terminals, and parking garages. Few argued that this was an improper role of government in view of the size of investments required and the dependence of the entire private sector on its means of mobility.

Functional values were also evidenced in concern for human needs. It has been long recognized that poor housing, education and health care weakens the contributions that individuals can make as part of the work force. Some of the turn-of-the-century reformers advocated tenement regulation, better sanitation, recreation opportunities and access to schools, not so much for the benefit of the individuals as for the well-being of the local economy. Slum areas were often looked upon as cancers that would spread their ills to adjoining healthy neighborhoods. The expense of dealing with those ills would then have to be carried by the more prosperous taxpayers. Urban blight was thus bad business and a drag on economic growth that government was expected to prevent or remedy.

2.4 THE MORAL VALUES IN URBAN PLANNING

Moral values constitute the third category, probably a less coherent one than the first two. On one hand, they refer to the character of urban citizens and the influences that shape their abilities to obtain a fair share of the city's benefits and contribute to its well-being. A second facet points toward the ideal of justice, the fair distribution of what advantages and disadvantages an urban society has to offer.

The United States has always had a moralistic culture due to its deep Judeo-Christian heritage and the expressions of it that developed in the nineteenth century. The antislavery and prohibition movements were its major products, but parallel to them and more urban in nature was a vigorous social reform crusade. Its purposes were several: to provide better living conditions for unfortunates who deserved them, to give children a better start on the way to becoming decent citizens, and to strengthen the moral fiber and character of those persons so they could become better Americans. The assumptions of environmental determinism were articles of faith for this group of reformers. The Social Gospel movement had emerged in urban Protestant groups by the 1890s, and taught that these reformist and charitable impulses were at the core of Christian faith and practice.

One expression of this was housing reform. An early movement led in 1867 to the first law regulating tenements in New York and Brooklyn, and in 1879 to a requirement that each room have an outside window. Laws quickly accumulated in other cities as well, spurred on by research showing the extent of disease and crime in the neighborhoods inhabited by the poor. While this concern had the "functional" character mentioned above, there was also a genuine compassion for the urban poor, many of whom were viewed by the middle- and upper-class reformers as honest, hard working and potentially worthy citizens.

Housing quantity and quality remained on the agenda in the twentieth century. The Great Depression spurred reformers to seek national, as well as local, government action, and the programs set up in that decade have survived, though with modifications, into the 1980s. To expand the supply of decent and affordable homes for all persons has become a responsibility of government in general, although disputes over how to accomplish it and how much to spend on it have at times obscured that goal.

Parallel to the pressures on government to intervene in housing problems, private philanthropists entered the scene out of a sense of *noblesse oblige* to promote what they conceived as "civic betterment." For example, Elgin R. L. Gould, a political scientist and municipal government specialist, published a study in 1895 of the housing efforts of European cooperative societies and private industry. He advocated that wealthy American investors construct "model tenements" for the urban working class on a limited-dividend basis. A year later he formed a company in New York City that built apartments and cottages, but which were not, unfortunately, within the incomes of the average tenement dweller [Scott 1969, 8–9]. Such philanthropic efforts were woefully inadequate; there were too many slum dwellers for the limited resources they could marshal, and it was not profitable to build a decent home affordable to those who most needed them.

The moral reformers around the turn of the century also stressed efficiency and honesty in municipal administration and participatory democracy for the citizens. There was no doubt that corruption of businessmen and public officials went hand in hand, maintained by the political machines of the day and the practices they used to stay in power. Such collusion affected land use in that what little power city government could exercise over it was "bought" with bribes and political pressures to the financial benefit of the officials and land developers alike. The moralists' purpose was thus to "return" control of land use to the upright.

Reform, in this context, aimed to restore honesty and public accountability through nonpartisanship in local elections, the opportunity for voters to legislate directly through the initiative and referendum, and the use of primary elections to nominate party candidates. More directly related to planning, citizen participation in land use decisions increased through the rise of lay planning commissions. Voluntary groups appeared first, composed of the same social stratum that produced the urban reformers. Hartford,

Connecticut, established the first official planning commission in 1907; by 1927, 390 cities had such bodies to advocate and advise on the city plans that were rapidly being formulated [Scott 1969, 249]. These commissioners were viewed as politically independent, objective and able to make decisions in the community interest alone [Catanese 1984, 18].

One more expression of moral values was added to this mix beginning in the 1950s. The concern for the civil rights of blacks and other minorities had been very low-keyed as the nation struggled with blight, depression and war. But with the swelling of post-World War II affluence, it became apparent that prosperity and social dignity need not be limited to whites only. When the U.S. Supreme Court ruled in the case of *Brown v. Board of Education of Topeka* (1954) that segregated schools were inherently unequal and thus unconstitutional, some major principles of land use regulation as well as educational policy were about to be overturned. When Rosa Parks refused to go to the back of the bus in Montgomery, Alabama, in 1955, and the little-known Baptist minister, Martin Luther King, Jr., organized a boycott of the buses, the civil rights movement was on its way to seek by political means what the Supreme Court ruled was already its rights.

The civil rights movement injected a more advanced concept of justice into the traditional moral values. What the reformers of a half-century earlier advocated out of a sense of compassion, King and his supporters sought as a basic human right, guaranteed by the Constitution. A landmark ruling on urban planning was secured in *Hawkins v. Town of Shaw* (1971) when the Fifth Federal Circuit Court of Appeals ruled that a city may not discriminate by race in providing such essential municipal facilities and services as street paving, sewers, and drainage.

Civil rights organizations raised the issue of how comprehensive urban plans contribute to racial integration and expansion of opportunities for minority citizens for homes and jobs. For example, the Chicago Urban League criticized the 1966 Comprehensive Plan of Chicago for its insensitivity to black concerns. In its view, the plan placed a higher priority on retaining the white middle class than on providing more housing opportunity for its black middle- and low-income people. Overall, the city had not encouraged participation by civil rights groups in the physical planning process. The league was not opposed to the use of "the tools of urban renewal" as such in planning. However, "the powerlessness of the Negro community to define, within the political process, how these tools will be utilized and what priorities should be emphasized, makes the application of these tools harmful to the Negro." [Chicago Urban League 1968, 17] Since then, Chicago, Detroit, Los Angeles and other large cities have elected black mayors and council members and many minority organizations have learned to be effective in planning politics, but their appeals are still couched in moral terms in many cases.

2.5 THE SOCIAL VALUES IN URBAN PLANNING

Finally, *social* values have played a major role in planning choices. These likewise have several aspects: solidarity, identity, and mutual responsibility among citizens, along with the means by which they could take part in the decisions affecting their lives and neighborhoods. They are deeply rooted in American culture; early communities were laid out around common grounds and meeting spaces in which citizens could intertwine their lives. As villages grew into large cities, the challenge was to retain those values in the face of pressures to become anonymous and unsocial. Nineteenth century cities had grown largely by in-migration from rural villages in this country or Europe, and their residents were compelled to weave new social fabrics for themselves and establish new identities with the places in which they lived.

By the 1890s, social reformers were establishing settlement houses in lower class neighborhoods, not only to provide the health, educational, and recreational services needed, but also to supply a focal point to enable residents to identify with one another and with their geographic neighborhood. These settlement houses did not, at first, have major impact on land use planning. However, in 1907, the Civic League of St. Louis proposed that each neighborhood in the city have a common center in which a school, library branch, playground, settlement house, and all the other institutions necessary for its common life would be placed. This arrangement, in the league's judgment, would center the residents' interests on the neighborhood, foster pride in it, and stimulate them to participate in its governance [Scott 1969, 72–73].

During the 1920s, Clarence Perry developed the neighborhood unit concept as a planning device to give expression to these social values. Concerned that the automobile was destroying social life in the traditional neighborhood blocks, he argued that a new land use design with lower housing density, more open space, and reduction of traffic on residential streets would enable self-contained communities to flourish. Within these surroundings, people would be more inclined to take responsibility for them and their neighbors and participate in political life. He intended this to work for lower income as well as middle-class populations [Perry 1924; Silver 1985]. Thus, he proposed an ideal neighborhood for approximately 1,000 residents with its own park, local shops, a school and gymnasium, and a separation of pedestrian from vehicular traffic. It would have an identifiable boundary to separate it from adjoining areas and give it a character that its residents would have a stake in preserving.

By the 1960s, the federal Model Cities program, and others which stressed citizen participation in formulating and implementing neighborhood renewal plans, added a more explicitly political dimension to these social values. Residents' identity with their area and neighbors was seen as essential to mobilizing for political action to secure aid and defend them against outside forces that would reduce the area's liveability. "Community control" became a popular slogan, though never fully realized in fact. This was not a prescription for any particular land use design, since by that time Perry's norm for the size of an ideal community was no longer accepted. But it was a call for neighborhood-based planning and for city administrations to respect and support locally generated priorities in spending for improvements and in zoning decisions [Silver 1985].

It is obvious that the specific values in each of these four categories can be defined in many different ways according to one's interests and culture. That fact makes it difficult for political systems, and their business and civic coparticipants, to take clear action on allocating specific values to particular social groups. Sometimes, it is a zero-sum exchange, in which a benefit provided to one group deprives another of what it seeks. To build a freeway to increase mobility and possibly economic opportunity for some inner-city residents may also destroy a healthy residential community and its social institutions that lie in its path. To spend generously on attractive parks may indeed increase its residents' enjoyment and physical fitness, but if less money is thus available to renew its streets and subways, what is the net gain or loss? Where precise

measures of benefit and cost are lacking, the door is open to allocation by political argument and pressure, shaped by those who are
best organized and have the readiest access to decision makers.
Although the functional values have exerted the most influence on
large-scale urban development, it is essential that we seek a rea-
soned balance between all four. In section 9.4, we will return to
these value categories for a future-oriented look.

2.6 LANDMARKS IN THE AMERICAN PLANNING MEMORY

Earlier we saw that the planning memory exists in laws, procedures, the values held by the participants, and in the built environment itself. It has grown incrementally rather than by any
grand design, in steps that were each shaped by the time in which
they were taken. At each point, the participants perceived the
problems and needs before them, identified their opportunities to
shape the urban scene, and acted within the existing legal, financial,
and cultural constraints. In many cases, action lagged well behind
the need for it; while slum clearance was more imperative in 1900
due to the lower quality of housing, it was much easier to accomplish in 1950 when public acceptance was greater. The following
landmarks and turning points deserve study because of their subsequent impact on planning thought and practice.

Early City Plans

The earliest city plans of colonial days offer insights into the
dynamics of frontier community development. One of the first systematic plans was sponsored by William Penn for Philadelphia in
1682. It featured a gridiron street pattern with rectangular blocks
between the Delaware River on the east and the Schuylkill River on
the west. A public square was at the center and four other blocks
were devoted to parks. This type of configuration was ideal for
subdivision and sale of individual parcels of land. Thus it was widely
copied as the frontier moved westward, even where the land was not
as flat and suitable for straight-line streets as in Philadelphia. Much
of San Francisco was laid out in this fashion, even where the streets
plotted on the map had to climb excessively steep grades.

When Congress decided to place the United States capital on

the swampy banks of the Potomac River, a French designer, Pierre L'Enfant, was commissioned to integrate the best of European concepts into an appropriately grand and dignified design. He superimposed on the gridiron plan a system of diagonal boulevards radiating from major squares, to provide distant views of the government buildings. Taking seriously its situation on the river, he planned open malls running to its banks from both the "President's House" and the "Congress House." Although some parts of his plan were ignored in the city's later development, the malls exist largely as he laid them out, and those diagonal streets and squares remain to channel the flow of the automobile traffic that he could not foresee. That design proved to be highly influential on the City Beautiful movement which sought to capture that grandeur and harmony with the natural environment for other cities.

Pullman and the Planned Industrial Towns

Some industrialists took up the challenge of planning whole towns in fine detail; the "company town" of Pullman on the South Side of Chicago is best known and its buildings remain to this day. George Pullman wanted a clean and wholesome living environment for the workers in his railroad sleeping car plant, that would maximize their productivity. In the spring of 1880, work began simultaneously on his new factory and the employees' community adjacent to it. Within five years, Pullman consisted of homes for 8,500 people, a grand arcade that served as a community center, a market house, church and school. All horses in the town even had to be kept in one stable. Although the streets followed the gridiron pattern, the buildings were architecturally innovative with significant ornamentation. All homes and business spaces were rented, enabling the company to maintain close supervision over the community.

George Pullman himself was a conscientious, methodical person and these traits permeated the concept of the community. He later stated,

> The working people are the most important element which enters into the successful operation of any manufacturing enterprise. We decided to build, in close proximity to the shops, homes for workingmen of such character and surrounding as would prove so attractive as to cause the best class of mechanics to seek that place for employment in preference to others. We also desired to establish the

place on such a basis as would exclude all baneful influences, believing that such a policy would result in the greatest measure of success from a commercial point of view.

[Buder 1967, 42–43]. His philosophy thus enlisted esthetic values in the service of his functional values.

The community's philosophy of organization was ultimately discredited by the labor unrest that led to a violent strike in 1893, caused in part by the company-as-landlord's refusal to reduce rents when it cut wages. By 1910, all of the property had been sold and Pullman was just another industrial neighborhood within the Chicago city limits. Other company towns failed sooner or later, when inadequate maintenance or the paternalistic control by company officers made them undesirable to residents who had other living options.

Burnham's Plan of Chicago

With the turn of the twentieth century, the making of large-scale city plans came into fashion. The architect Daniel Burnham was a pioneer at this, becoming known for a comprehensive update of L'Enfant's design for Washington in 1900–02. He followed that with a plan for the reconstruction of San Francisco after its earthquake and fire in 1906.

But Burnham's apogee of accomplishment was the Comprehensive Plan of Chicago, commissioned not by the city government but by the Commercial Club, a leading business organization. Published on July 4, 1909, it continued in the City Beautiful tradition in that it envisioned an elaborate park and boulevard system throughout the larger metropolitan area and wide radial avenues within the city converging on a grand civic center. The lakefront was to be reclaimed from the railroads with landfill and transformed into a complex of parks and lagoons for its entire length [Burnham & Bennett, 1970].

However, this plan of Chicago departed from the exclusive concerns with esthetic values of earlier plans. Enough motor vehicles were now on the streets, with more expected, to require serious attention to traffic circulation. It included schemes for elevated, surface, and subway transportation in its central business district, consolidation of railway freight and passenger facilities, and expanded harbors at the mouths of the Chicago and Calumet Rivers. As he stated it,

> The plan frankly takes into consideration the fact that the American city, and Chicago preeminently, is a center of industry and traffic. Therefore attention is given to the betterment of commercial facilities; to methods of transportation for persons and for goods; to removing the obstacles which prevent or obstruct circulation; and to the increase of convenience.

[Burnham & Bennett 1970, 4]. This is a clear statement of functionalist values, which Burnham intended to marry happily to the esthetic ideals.

It is important that this plan was for the entire Chicago metropolitan area, not just the city proper. Burnham recommended that the city project uses of undeveloped lands certain to be added to the city in the foreseeable future. Even more, he hoped that the entire urbanized region would be ultimately placed under a single metropolitan administration, with powers to implement this plan for parks and highways in the developing fringe area [Scott 1969, 106–107].

This plan made no provision, however, for housing or for other conditions of the everyday lives of Chicago's working class. It was drafted for the downtown business community and leading industrialists and reflected their esthetic and functional values. Even though the novelist Upton Sinclair had just graphically portrayed the poor working and living conditions of the mass of Chicagoans in *The Jungle* [1906], and housing reformers and settlement house workers had been active there for decades, Burnham's plan was somehow "above" those mundane concerns. His only reference to slum conditions was a recommendation for "remorseless enforcement of sanitary regulations." [Burnham & Bennett 1970, 108] A famous aphorism of Burnham's was "Make no little plans;" the plan of Chicago was grand indeed, but his successors came to realize that the "little plans" were also needed where the daily life of ordinary citizens was concerned.

The Garden City Movement

While Burnham and his school of planners were studying the experiences of Paris and other great European cities, more holistic planning influences were also crossing the Atlantic. Ebenezer

Howard [1965], an English social reformer, published in 1898 a design for a planned city that combined the benefits of both town and country living for a population of no more than 32,000. It was to be self-supporting, with its own industries and farms, and separated by a greenbelt from other cities like it. Basically, he sought to synthesize the prevailing individualist/functionalist ideal, with its emphasis on production and enterprise, with what he saw as the social ideals of fair division of wealth and holistic community well being. All land was to be owned by the municipality, and leased to residential, commercial and agricultural tenants. These rents would pay all of the city's expenses.

Howard formed a corporation which obtained 3,800 acres north of London and in 1903 began to build the town of Letchworth according to his principles. It stands today, not in full accordance with the Garden City model, but a viable and attractive community. One element of its construction was a design competition for "cheap cottages" for working-class families, showing sensitivity for moral as well as functional and esthetic values.

A group of American churchmen and financiers, including Elgin Gould, enlisted Howard's assistance in forming the Garden City Association of America in 1906. But its aims of advising industrialists on planning new communities were not fulfilled, and it never sponsored any development of its own. Even so, these design principles had wide appeal, and soon appeared in Forest Hills Gardens, a middle-class home development in New York City's borough of Queens [Scott 1969, 90].

In 1929, the Garden City concept was linked with Clarence Perry's neighborhood unit principle in the design of Radburn, New Jersey. A suburban community without industry, its architects reserved much of the land for gardens and parks. Further, it separated automobile traffic as much as possible from the living areas, and enabled residents to walk through most of the area without crossing a street. Although it too failed to address the housing needs of the poor, it drew considerable attention and its features have appeared in numerous later community plans [Scott 1969, 59–60].

Zoning

While the more imaginative planners sought to put new Letchworths and Radburns on vacant land, most had to occupy themselves with the less inspiring tasks of improving what already existed. It took until 1900 just for many cities to obtain the legal powers to control street locations. Owners of property strongly resisted efforts of municipalities to assert the public interest in regulating the uses of that land, and the courts were sympathetic to them. But gradually the property owners themselves discovered that government authority could protect their investments as well as restrict their freedom. Thus, they gradually came to accept *zoning* as a proper land regulation device.

In its simplest sense, zoning is the division of land into distinct use categories, permitting specified ones and excluding others. Implicitly, it requires a calculation that the restriction it places on a given group of property owners provides a net benefit to those persons and/or to the city as a whole. It is a management technique to control or prevent the evils resulting from incompatible adjoining land uses or the "wrong" uses of certain lands.

Boyer [1983, 164] found one of the rationales for its adoption in the 1910s and 1920s to be the Scientific Management movement inspired by the engineer Frederick Taylor. In his view, industrial production should be rationally organized by distinct functions, each developed to its highest level of efficiency.

> Zoning, the practice of boundary management, depended upon the separation of conflicting functional uses that took place in the same environment. Its main procedures were based upon defining land-use districts in a manner analogous to the steps of scientific management, steps that separated a job into elementary movements before synthesizing these operations into the correct sequence of timing and motion for performing the task. The basic value was one of economic utility: achievement of a perfectly efficient and functional machine.

In New York City, the drive for zoning also had more immediately financial motivations. Owners of high-class shops along Fifth Avenue were alarmed as garment factories and skyscrapers were erected next to them, introducing hordes of workers whom they deemed incompatible with their clientele. This, together with growing traffic congestion and fears of property value degradation, moved the city to pass the nation's first zoning regulation in 1916. It established three categories of land use districts, residential, commercial, and unrestricted, five building-height districts, and five areas with different sizes of yards and courts. Among other things, it forbade future factory locations in central Manhattan north of Twenty-third Street. Residential streets were placed in districts that allowed only homes, with businesses restricted to the ends of blocks and main thoroughfares [Scott 1969, 153–158].

The purpose of New York's zoning effort was entirely functional. The Fifth Avenue merchants had won allies among the insurance, banking, real estate, and general commercial interests, and the law was drafted narrowly to be acceptable to the courts. Housing reformers, social workers, and some civic groups, with greater concern for moral and social values, requested that the ordinance include measures on housing quality and sanitation. But the business community rejected these appeals, not only because their own interests were not served thereby, but also out of fear that they might lead to judicial invalidation of the entire law [Scott 1969, 155].

This zoning effort was not part of an overall plan for the city; indeed any detailed comprehensive plan even for Manhattan would probably have been impossible. Thus, the zones were set up to serve narrowly specific interests, and often to protect a certain status quo against likely change. Scott [1969, 160–161] concludes,

> The New York zoning resolution was in some respects a setback to the city planning movement because it contributed to the widespread practice of zoning before planning and, in many cities, to the acceptance of zoning as a substitute for long-term planning. . . . The allocations of the land resources of cities under these enactments were preposterous, often providing for population densities and uses beyond any reasonable prospect of growth. Most cities also continued the New York practice of permitting so-called lesser economic land uses, such as residential developments, in zones of higher economic use, such as commercial and industrial districts, thereby perpetuating many of the frictions of earlier periods.

Zoning was quickly embraced by many cities forced to deal in the 1920s with rapid growth in both population and motor vehicle use. Intensive land uses in central business districts created even more intense traffic jams that threatened large cities' commercial growth. Yet, where zoning was not linked with long-range planning or serious forecasting of traffic levels, population growth, or land needs for various uses, it was typically reactive, dealing with yesterday's problems. The private market in each city essentially planned the land use, and the zoning ordinances simply etched those choices into the body of law, subject to change on demand by the politically powerful.

While zoning as a practice did not explicitly espouse social values, land use segregation fostered social and racial segregation as well. Middle-class residential neighborhoods benefited in particular from the zoning walls that excluded not only business and industry but also the kinds of structures inhabited by the poor. Atlanta established racial zoning in its 1922 plan: black families were excluded from white-zoned areas, and vice versa [Boyer 1983, 167–168]. Even where no explicit racial or class criteria were stated in the codes, social custom supplemented the lot size and building standards that tended to stratify residents by income.

Le Corbusier and The Contemporary City

While zoning became a pragmatic solution to very pressing problems, more visionary ideas continued to flow from Europe. In the 1920s, Charles-Edouard Jeanneret, an architect who practiced in Paris under the name of Le Corbusier, published his dramatic city plans featuring high-rise buildings and wide open spaces between them. His Ville Contemporaine (Contemporary City) design would house three million people in eight-story apartment buildings and single-family garden cities. The commercial center consisted of a transportation hub and 60-story office buildings. Most of the city's land was reserved for parks to link people with nature and give an open, uncongested feeling. Subways moved commuters about easily and quickly. Residents collectively owned their homes, which were allocated according to a person's status in the hierarchy of production and administration.

Behind Le Corbusier's design lay a unique blend of esthetic, functional, and social values. He rejected the nineteenth century city, dominated by unrestrained greed and exploitation of both man and nature. Rather, human rationality would take control from these self-seeking economic forces and embody the common good in every detail of the plan. Ideally, this would build a society in which interclass conflict would be unnecessary because all values would be fairly distributed. Therefore, it would also be a society without politics. The cities would be administered (not "governed") by an elite of industrialists, scientists, and artists whose technical expertise would insure order, prosperity, and beauty. The ordinary citizens would not have to be concerned with public affairs, but simply with the productivity of their jobs and enjoyment of the abundant living amenities [Fishman 1977].

In many respects, Le Corbusier's designs were utopian and revolutionary. They incorporated a philosophy of the industrial revolution that popular thinking neither understood nor sought. To him, houses were "machines for living," just as the skyscrapers were machines for communication and trade. Yet his designs, apart from his philosophy, or perhaps subtly incorporating that philosophy, have been widely accepted. High-rise structures, surrounded by open space and accessible to rapid transportation facilities, dominate most major city centers and the suburban rings served by freeways. The stark Stuyvesant Town housing project in New York City and Robert Taylor Homes in Chicago are concrete expressions of Le Corbusier's designs, though they are far from his social philosophy. Contrary to his hopes, political conflict has not been banished from these sites, because they allocate values in ways that many persons and groups continue to perceive as unfair.

The Urban Renewal Movement

The last of the planning landmarks surveyed here has been a logical culmination of all of the developments in this chapter and an attempt to blend the four value groups to solve increasingly pressing problems. By the 1930s, many major cities' population growth virtually ceased. Most of their buildings were a half-century or more old, in more or less deteriorated condition, and often unsuited to their sites and the land uses that had evolved around them. For them, planning had to address the reuse of space and the replacement or rehabilitation of structures and public facilities. Thus, "urban renewal" and its related terms rose to the top of those cities' political agendas and at the same time secured major attention from the President and Congress.

The problem presented by center-city decay and slum proliferation has both economic and social dimensions. Renewal can take place under private auspices, but only in conditions set by the market. A decaying tenement building or an abandoned factory continues to stand because it does not represent an attractive investment opportunity to an entrepreneur. The site may not be appropriate for a new dwelling or commercial structure, or the price to be paid is too high compared with the expected return.

Planners also recognize the larger social and economic costs of blight, of *not* renewing an area. As the nineteenth century reformers learned, poor health, crime, and social disorder tend to cling to slum housing, which acts like a sink for public funds and services. An empty factory not only represents lost employment and production opportunity but also missing tax revenue, a safety hazard, and possibly a resort for criminal activity. It was estimated that the city of Cleveland spent $2 million in 1934 to support services in a slum that produced only one eighth of that amount in revenue [Boyer 1983, 244].

This condition also pointed to a deficiency in the urban planning process. Harland Bartholomew, a leading planner, told the National Planning Conference in 1931 that too much effort had been devoted to the business centers and the fast-growing suburbs, to the neglect of the districts which were suffering the greatest population loss and physical decay. To rehabilitate the latter areas was now the greatest planning challenge of the future [Boyer 1983, 214].

The Depression of the 1930s, while it aggravated these problems with a decline in private construction and increased human misery, also stimulated new action on a broad front. The combined burden of housing renewal and unemployment relief far exceeded the capacity of local governments, private business and charities to cope with it. Clearly, only the national government had the financial resources to fill the gap, and with Franklin Roosevelt's inauguration to the Presidency in 1933, this alternative became realistic. Even so, the lack of planning was evident as it proved difficult to coordinate aid to the unemployed with home construction. Not until 1937 was it possible to pass a national housing aid act, and the funds appropriated for it were far from adequate to meet existing needs.

Much of the problem of selecting action strategies for urban renewal lay in the lack of experience with it. New York City's Housing Authority reported in 1934 that it had 17 square miles of slums, of which 10 were so unfit for habitation as to require immediate evacuation [Boyer 1983, 252]. Thus, nothing less than an areawide strategy would be sufficient, for a partial renewal effort would be futile if the blighted blocks around it remained. No standard blueprint for action existed, any programs would have to be understood as experimental, and there was a high risk of failure.

By the end of the 1930s, three leading methods had emerged: public housing, in which local government built, owned, and operated the dwellings; government incentives to limited-dividend private corporations to undertake redevelopment; and joint public-private action to rehabilitate declining areas that did not warrant total clearance [Scott 1969, 379]. Public housing had already been instituted under the support of the Wagner-Steagall Housing Act of 1937. The second alternative received legal sanction in 1941 when New York State permitted private redevelopment corporations to acquire property through condemnation if they had already obtained 51 percent of the designated project site. The incentive for this action was a freeze on the assessed value of the land for property tax purposes for ten years, amounting to a subsidy from local revenues. Other states quickly followed [Scott 1969, 380]. The third approach showed some success with a neighborhood improvement district in the Waverly area of Baltimore in 1939 [Boyer 1983, 252–253].

Private renewal on a large scale appeared in New York City in the early 1940s with Stuyvesant Town, a project of the Metropolitan Life Insurance Company. It encompassed 61 acres and was designed to house 24,000 persons in 13-story buildings. The city's subsidy included not only the tax exemption but also the contribution of street and school lands and construction of new facilities nearby. Controversy arose over what some observers considered an excessive population density and the fact that no blacks would be accepted as tenants [Scott 1969, 421–423].

One final problem had to be surmounted before the urban renewal programs that multiplied after World War II could stand on a firm footing: their constitutionality. It was legally permissible for cities to take private land (with due compensation) to serve public purposes for streets, schools, hospitals, and housing. But urban renewal programs typically turned the land so acquired over to a private developer for residential or business purposes, and judges in some states struck down condemnation action on this ground. In 1954, the Supreme Court ruled in *Berman v. Parker* that properties may be taken in blighted areas for rebuilding if they are part of a long-range general plan. In so doing, the Court gave to legislative bodies the broad leeway to determine the public interest that had been allowed them in planning and zoning generally. Discussion of more contemporary experiences with urban renewal follows in chapters 5 and 6.

2.7 CONTEMPORARY VALUES OF SPACE AND PLACE

What urbanites value today is a legacy of these and many other memories and experiences. They exist in the mind-sets of people whom the city serves, frustrates, enriches, and endangers. Kevin Lynch [1984, 359–372] reviewed several surveys of what people want in their cities, and one can find each of the four value categories discussed above represented in the responses: beauty and abundant natural features, accessibility and the means to make profits, opportunities for all to choose homes and jobs, and social freedom within a sense of mutual responsibilities. Often people speak of specific services and facilities they value: schools, police and fire protection, orderly land use, parks, shopping, and ease of travel. The tangible desires mix with the intangible in many minds, the former representing and supporting the latter.

Esthetics, functionality, moral qualities, and social opportunity are very generalized values that can be applied to cities as a whole. But the meanings which they can have "on the ground" to particular persons can vary widely. Planning must be concerned with the ways in which the South Bronx teenager, the Warren homeowner, and the Detroit autoworker view their own urban environments and what they expect of them. One needs insight into the personal, subjective values that people hold which relate to the locations in which they live, work, play, and travel.

This divergence between the "macro" and "micro" perspectives could be expressed as the space/place dichotomy. *Space* is abstract; it is an area, as viewed by an outsider, for a site on which to put a condominium, highway, or Cadillac plant. It can be described as "blighted," "transitional," or a "prime commercial site." A realtor catalogues it by its extent, land uses, market value, topography, and distance from the nearest freeway. Treated as a commodity, one space could be interchangeable with another for the intended use.

A *place,* on the other hand, is a unique location with which a person has established an emotional connection, a source of security and identity. Each place has qualities to a person that no other one has. Yi-Fu Tuan [1974, 9] has referred to this relationship as *topophilia,* defined as "the affective bond between people and place or setting." When understood as personal experience, this concept is vivid and concrete, including "all of the human being's affective ties with the material environment" [Tuan 1974, 93]. These feelings may be very warm and positive, but they can also be negative, filled with fear, antagonism toward one's neighbors, or a sense of hopelessness.

For example, the deepest such relationships are often with the places one lives in. "Home" is a place in this sense; contrast that with the impersonal, space-linked concept of "housing" [Ravetz 1980]. Home may be a single room in a decaying hotel, but it can be the only source of security a low-income elderly person has. That home can be extended to one's neighborhood: the single block in which one lives, a district of several hundred people, or an independent suburban village on the edge of a large city. It has meaning for many reasons: one has grown up there, one's friends are there, or it is regarded as beautiful, safe, or congenial. Areas of natural beauty, such as a park or tree-lined boulevard, and of historical significance are also such places.

The concept *valued environment* designates a place that holds such meaning for a group of people. Derek Hall [1982, 172] stated,

> An environment can be considered 'valued' if its residents can show recognition of an empathy with their local social and physical environment, a milieu that in turn serves to buttress their own preferred life-styles. In this sense, the word 'value' acquires a mirror-like quality in which residents recognize attributes in their local environment which are themselves reflections of the residents' own scale of preferences.

These values are not static; they change with the residents' life situations and the condition of the area, but there is enough consistency to enable them to be recognized and acted upon.

These place-based values are important to the planning process in two ways. Actions that change the built environment of cities also manipulate valued environments for better or worse. Successful plans organize important aspects of human lives: their space, their use and concepts of time, whom they are likely to communicate with, and the meanings they find in that environment [Rapoport 1977]. We have already seen how any plan imposes values of some kind. But they are not imposed in a vacuum; they always impinge on some places and the values that people already attribute to them. In the encounter between General Motors and Poletown in chapter 1, the meanings and values that the residents had invested in their neighborhood were subordinated to the more abstract functional value of economic development. This is not to claim that localist place values are necessarily superior to the larger scale benefits. Rather, the planning process should be open to compare them and consider every reasonable synthesis.

Valued environments are also politically significant. The strength of these attachments usually becomes evident only when they are threatened, as with a major redevelopment project or a highway bisecting a neighborhood. Gold and Burgess [1982, 2] said,

> Large-scale environmental change, not instigated by the inhabitants themselves and outside their control, often seems disturbing, disruptive, and divisive. Increased demands for active involvement in environmental decision making, the burgeoning growth of pressure groups, and widespread suspicion of policy-making bodies together reflect a belief that political decision-makers cannot and will not do enough to protect our environmental interests.

We have already observed the politically active groups that formed to contest the destruction of Poletown, slow the uncontrolled urbanization of San Diego, and garner funds for rehabilitating South Bronx homes. Though their conditions were very different, each had a sense of "turf" which called for its protection or enhancement and sparked joint action by persons who would otherwise have little in common.

Planners must be sensitive as well to the process of creating place values in newly redeveloped areas. When whole neighborhoods were demolished as substandard and new dwellings were built in their place, the residents had to begin to form new environmental identities. But it was difficult for many of them, especially families with small children, to regard the new high-rise apartment structures as home and acquire a sense of responsibility for them. The characteristics of the buildings themselves, designed more for economy than for liveability, frustrated these residents. As a result, those who were able to leave did so, and left behind the poorest and the antisocial elements, who were free to turn the project into a battleground. One result of this was the demolition of the Pruitt-Igoe homes in St. Louis in 1976, which had failed totally as a living environment because of this insensitivity [Meehan 1979].

As the role of government in urban value allocation was growing, the controversy also grew over which level of government should take the lead. Municipal governments were involved first, but as time went on the responsibilities broadened to include county and regional authorities and the state and national governments. Local responsibility was still strong—but within what legal and financial framework? Cooperation and conflict go on not only between government and the private sector but also between units of government that adjoin and overlap one another. To this pattern the next chapter turns.

QUESTIONS FOR DISCUSSION

1. In what ways can values come into conflict with one another?
2. What are the limits to the private sector's ability to resolve urban value conflicts? How is government limited in this?
3. What is the political process that injects some values (or certain interpretations of them) into public policy more than others?
4. What major lessons for today stand out from the shaping of the American planning memory?
5. What is the linkage between perceptions of valued environments and political action?
6. In what ways do all of these values put requirements and restraints on the planning process?
7. How important have racial and economic biases been in American planning choices?

3 | WHO DOES PLANNING: GOVERNMENTS AT WORK

3.1 THE GAME AND ITS PLAYERS

To identify the participants in the planning process might not seem much harder than listing the cast of a play: a finite number of actors, arranged in order of their appearance in predictable acts and scenes. And one could certainly provide such a cast of the significant actors in the saga of Detroit and General Motors. But planning as conceived here is very unlike a stage production in some ways. Any given decision is but one link in a chain of related decisions from the distant past into an uncertain future, so there are no opening or closing curtains. There is not one play but many—several on one stage going on simultaneously, and actors may jump from a production on one stage to one on another. Finally, there is no clear distinction between actors and the audience, since the latter is free to assume spontaneous and unrehearsed roles. Obviously, a "planning critic" has a harder job than a drama critic.

This theatric analogy points to the lack of consistent boundaries in the patterns of conflict and cooperation in planning—either of what the issues are or of who gets involved. E. E. Schattschneider [1960, 18], speaking of how politics differs from a football game, wrote, "Many conflicts are narrowly confined by a variety of devices, but the distinctive quality of political conflicts is that the relations between the players and the audience have not been well defined and there is usually nothing to keep the audience from getting into the game." Very few players were initially involved in the General Motors plant location choice described in chapter 1, and their intention was to relocate the residents and businesses away from Poletown in a quiet and orderly manner. Only one issue was on the table then: to provide a site for that corporation in the city. But the "audience" of Poletowners chose to add another issue—whether a viable neighborhood was to be preserved or eliminated—and joined in the conflict itself.

The example of the San Diego referendum shows that the size of a conflict can be enlarged to the point of defeating the plans of the original collaborators. Schattschneider [1960, 4] pointed out that "conflicts are frequently won or lost by the success that the contestants have in getting the audience involved in the fight or in excluding it." This is because every change in who and how many participate is likely to change its ultimate outcome. Thus one side in a planning controversy may well seek to keep the matter as private and localized as possible, with no publicity, while the opposition, sensing likely defeat, tries to broaden the context by enlisting allies. Those who spearheaded the San Diego zoning moratorium did not believe that the city council and hopeful land developers shared their concerns for the quality of life in that northwest sector.

The purpose of this chapter and the next is to provide a generalized "cast" of potential participants in planning decisions and to describe the conditions in which they are likely to become involved. Some are consistently in the midst of the process by legal mandate or financial necessity, while others are involved only sporadically or peripherally. The content of the specific planning choice tends to define the immediate participants: owners or users of the land involved, those who propose changes, officials whose approvals are required, and others with a direct or secondary interest in the issue.

Whether these individuals or groups become actual participants at any given time also depends on other variables: their perceived stake in the issue, the amount of publicity devoted to it, and where the particular contest is in the long sequence of decisions that must be made on it, from the initial proposal to final ratification (of which more will follow in chapters 5 and 8).

As used in this book, *planner* will have the rather limited meaning of one who has professional education and credentials in the field and/or is employed as a specialist in urban planning. Such positions can be found not only on local governments but also in state and federal agencies, private firms that do planning by contract, and private architectural and development enterprises. This term also covers nonprofessional members of planning and zoning commissions.

This definition distinguishes such a person from one in a professional post in human services, public works, or finance, and from generalist executives and legislators who are elected or appointed directly by elected officials. Granted, this distinction is not sharp in that "nonplanners" may also have planning expertise and influence. However, this definition highlights one crucial role among many in the planning process. It is not a controlling role in most planning decisions and may be only marginal in some, yet it is a centerpiece role in this book.

Chapter 1 presented planning as a government-centered process. This is so in two ways. First, Type 3 land use choices are initiated by some unit of government due to its responsibility to provide public services and facilities. Many of these were noted at the end of the opening chapter. The amount of discretion allowed to public officials varies with the object: street routings tend to be routine, but a sports stadium permits much leeway, both in whether to build it and where it shall be located.

Government is also at the center in that all land use choices by the private sector are subject to some kind of legal controls. They require positive approval by some jurisdiction before they can be put into effect, from the billion-dollar commercial complex to a homeowner's addition of a porch. In general, this role of government conforms to its traditional *police power,* the broadly conceived responsibility to guard the health, safety, morals, and general welfare of the public. Courts have ordinarily upheld the government's position in disputes over zoning and other land use regulation as long as its action was a fair and reasonable exercise of this power.

This chapter surveys the governmental participants in the planning process. For ease of identification, they are divided into six categories. In actuality, they are interdependent and major planning choices often involve officials from two or more categories. This is further evidence of the fragmentation and decentralization that usually prevails in making and executing urban plans. American urban governance is marked by the devolution of decisions to the smallest local units practicable. Most citizens resist intrusion of large area governments into local land use decisions.

The large number of small area and population jurisdictions and special districts further complicates planning choices, particularly on problems that cross municipal boundary lines and require voluntary cooperation between two or more units to solve. No other industrialized nation has so complex a system for local governance in general and for land use planning in particular. It is a judgment call whether this characteristic, by itself, results in better or worse policies, but the system is doubtless harder for the average citizen to understand and may be less accountable to the public as a result.

It is important to see these governmental units not as neutral arbiters or technical managers of planning choices and conflicts, but as value-oriented participants in themselves. As we will see in chapters 7 and 8, each jurisdiction represents one or more constituent interests, and so may clash with other players in the game. Obviously, public officials in Detroit sided with General Motors against the Poletown residents. Governments are automatic contestants in the games that Schattschneider described, but they can choose whose side to play on, and switch sides at will.

A government's participation can be complicated by internal division, however. A mayor might seek one outcome, while the city council opts for another. More often, a planning department or commission urges (or opposes) a particular program, and the elected officials choose the opposite. If internal deadlock arises, a government may not be able to play any clear role, and a decision falls to others by default. Observers must be sensitive to the values of the participating governments, and how they influence the choices that emerge. This issue is addressed repeatedly throughout the remaining chapters.

3.2   GENERAL PURPOSE LOCAL GOVERNMENTS

The front line of government's urban planning runs through the counties, cities, villages, and urban towns and townships of the nation. These are called general-purpose governments because they are responsible for a wide range of public services and regulations. Land use control is always included with these, for it is considered within the police powers noted above. The laws of each state specify the powers that its local units have and the procedures by which they can exercise them, although there is much similarity from one

TABLE 3.1

LOCAL GOVERNMENTS IN PLANNING DECISIONS

Unit	Planning role and powers
City (village, borough)	Primary land-use decision maker for incorporated urban areas; extensive powers to initiate and regulate development.
County	Same as cities in many unincorporated areas; variable otherwise. May have no powers where all of its land is in incorporated cities.
Town/township	Similar to cities in unincorporated areas in some states. In other states, may have minimal powers or none.
School district	Controls use of its own properties with local government approval.
Special district/ authority (non-school)	Varies with function: those which control essential urban services and facilities (e.g., transportation, natural resources, parks, sanitation) have extensive powers therein and a high degree of autonomy.
Metropolitan planning agency (council of governments)	No direct authority over land use; advisory and coordinating role only.

state to the next. See Table 3.1 for a summary of these local governments and their planning roles.

Cities, boroughs (except in Alaska), and villages are legally termed municipalities. The 1982 Census of Governments counted 19,083 of them. They were generally created at the will of their residents to provide the services and regulations needed by an urban population. They operate with powers granted by general state law or under their own home rule charters.

Most counties (or which there were 3,041 in 1982) are rural, but county governments in metropolitan areas have increasingly taken on urban functions, with planning powers. Their powers are likewise state granted or derived from charters approved by their voters. Los Angeles County, California, acts as a municipal government for several hundred thousand residents in areas that are not incorporated in any municipality. Counties on the fringes of metropolitan areas or in high-amenity growth areas face especially serious planning challenges but may lack the planning capacity and power to cope with them. Mercer County, New Jersey, for example, has taken legal action to slow the pace of office development in the corridor between New York City and Philadelphia that centers on Princeton

University. Its own powers to control such growth are quite limited [Lueck 1985].

There are 16,748 townships and towns in 21 northern states, and most are rural units with few powers. In New England and a few other states, however, they exercise important planning functions. Warren, New Jersey, in the case in chapter 1, is a township like many of the suburban communities facing the modest-cost housing challenge. The town of East Hampton, New York, on the eastern tip of Long Island, adopted a new zoning code in 1984 to curtail the building of homes and preserve its scenic open space. Prior to this, it experienced a political struggle over whether to maintain its own planning department or rely on outside consultants [Woodhams 1983].

Planning policies and methods also vary between local units, depending on their size, form of organization, and political climate. In one type of city or county, authority is centered in a strong chief executive who is directly elected by the people. The legislative body, whether a city council or county board, has power to pass the annual budget and make the laws, including the zoning ordinances and other planning-related legislation, but not to direct their administration. This form most resembles the separation-of-powers model of the national government, and the political conflicts between mayor and council tend to echo those of the President and Congress. The Detroit city government, in which Mayor Young dominated the General Motors decisions, is organized in this manner. Mayors who are strong politically and personally can also dominate the city's legislative function. Often, they can gain popular acclaim when they take the lead in planning enterprises, and this gives them the base of support they require within the government structure as well.

A second type of city or county government is focused on a strong legislative body which hires a professional manager to oversee the administration. It resembles a business corporation, its officers corresponding to a board of directors and the chief executive officer. The job of the legislature, in addition to lawmaking and budgeting, is to hold the manager accountable for all parts of the administration. Thus it has a potentially larger role in planning than in the strong-executive type of government. The city of San Diego has this form of organization; so the referendum described in chapter 1 was aimed at that council's control of zoning.

Most smaller cities and counties use a third type in which the elected council or board has many direct administrative as well as lawmaking powers. There is often, in this and the second type, a person with the title of mayor, who presides over council meetings and may be a focal point of accountability to the public, but this person has no administrative powers.

A fourth type of local government is the commission, used in a small number of cities. The members of its elective commission double as legislators and as individual administrators of municipal departments. This form is declining in use, due to its lack of a focal point for accountability. It also has a mayor, but that office typically has little power.

The planning specialists in these local governments are of two types: full-time professionals with credentials in planning, engineering, urban design or a related field; and planning and zoning commissions composed of lay citizens or (less often) generalist local officials. The relationships between them and with the elected authorities can vary with the specific structure used. Medium-sized and larger cities and counties have a department of planning and/or community development that has responsibility for all of the types of planning decisions described in chapter 1. The larger the department, the more specialists it is likely to have in such fields as transportation, housing, recreation, neighborhood relations, and economic development.

In one kind of system, the planning commission is appointed by the mayor and/or council (or the corresponding positions in a county government) and it supervises the planning department. Both operate in a staff role, separate from the line departments which carry out its decisions. Once quite popular, its semi-independent status is less acceptable today. Other models retain the independent commission as an advisory body, but place the planning department with the other line and staff agencies under the authority of the mayor, manager, or council.

Each form of organization for planning poses some authority questions. According to one observer, "The planning department can be susceptible to the experience of serving two masters simultaneously. It is subject to the oversight of the chief executive in day-to-day affairs, but it is also subject to the advice and influence of the planning commission" [Spencer 1979, 72]. This "two masters" dilemma is common throughout local American governments and owes much to public demands for checks and balances on officials.

The typical planning department is headed by a director, who is appointed by the mayor, council or board, manager, or planning commission, depending on the particular structure. This office has considerable potential for leadership on planning-related policies (see section 8.6 for its alternative roles). Basically, this director must not only oversee the operations of the department and motivate its staff, but also provide leadership to the city or county government on planning-related policies. Two-way communication with the citizens and development-related interests is equally important. Ultimately, the success of the department and its director and of the planning commission depends on their ability to induce the legislative body, operating agencies, and private-sector participants to complete the planning cycle and put the plans into effect.

The planning commissioners, anywhere from five to twenty-one in number, are part time and serve with little or no pay. The better educated and higher income homeowners, male and female, predominate in their membership, although in large cities they tend to be broadly representative of the ethnic and social groups. In most decisions, they function in an advisory role, in which they study the significant planning choices to be made by that government and recommend action on them to the legislative branch. Smaller communities without their own planning staff rely heavily on their commissions, since any professional advice they get is from outside consultants who are retained as needed. Although these commissioners are ideally independent of political influences and thus able to represent the full spectrum of community values, they often carry with them personal business and real estate connections which make them vulnerable to conflicts of interest.

Larger cities and counties often have a separate zoning board which hears appeals from the land use regulatory decisions of the administrators. It may be asked to grant variances from the regulations in unique instances of hardship and examine requests for rezoning. Such quasi-judicial boards are structured similarly to the planning commissions. In other cities, the planning commission itself may sit as a board of appeals and adjustment.

Some cities also use design review boards (the exact title varies) made up of local citizens and/or design professionals. Their mission is to evaluate the esthetic qualities of development proposals. Some have the power to reject designs of proposed buildings, while others have only an advisory role. New Orleans set up one of the first of these in the Vieux Carre Commission (1936) to protect the unique qualities of that district, popularly known as the French Quarter. While this review function is performed elsewhere by planning commissions, some cities see an advantage in drawing upon design specialists who can apply professional criteria. Proposals to create or expand the powers of such boards have been controversial in many cities, since property owners and architects instinctively resist such control. Even so, Cleveland's Fine Arts Committee secured the political support necessary to compel the redesign of the Sohio Tower [Zotti, 1987b].

Other city or county departments take part in aspects of planning. In many larger cities, a separate department of housing and/or redevelopment directly operates programs in these areas and so makes key land use choices. Because it is delegated considerable power to receive federal and state grants, borrow money, and acquire land, it can operate quite autonomously from other municipal agencies. The San Francisco Redevelopment Agency was able in the 1970s to use its legal powers to initiate the hotly disputed Yerba Buena redevelopment project with minimal review by the Planning Department and Board of Supervisors [Hartman 1984].

Additional agencies are responsible for sanitation, drainage, transportation, building inspection, parks and environmental quality. Their cooperation is essential to the fulfillment of any plan. To keep these separate agencies working compatibly is no easy task in a large city or county with myriad demands and constraints. Long-range plans are often bent or ignored under pressure of other political or bureaucratic priorities. For example, a public works department, by its action or inaction on a neighborhood drainage problem, can determine the future of development there, regardless of any plan statements. Much depends on the power and will of the administrative mayor or manager to direct such agencies.

Some cities have semiautonomous departments that play a major role in development finance. Saint Paul, Minnesota, is typical, using its Port Authority to sell bonds to finance private commercial, industrial, and residential construction. Acting through Type 4 planning decisions, it has backed a number of large-scale projects; by 1982, its bonded indebtedness exceeded $435 million [Alperin 1983, 17]. The choices of such authorities to fund specific projects clearly affects the planning capacities of the cities in which they operate.

Since much of the planning examined in this book is done by these general-purpose units, this discussion leaves them for now. The remainder of this chapter focuses on the governments that are less direct or less frequent participants, though no less important.

3.3   SPECIAL PURPOSE LOCAL GOVERNMENTS

Urban communities are also overlaid by jurisdictions that are responsible for only one or a few related functions and are usually independent of the general-purpose units. Many of them participate in land use planning to some degree, though their role varies widely. Their names also vary: district, board, commission, and authority are most common. They can be assigned any legitimate function of government, but most commonly they deal with education, water supply, housing, waste management, drainage, parks, hospitals, transit, and transportation terminals. The 1982 Census of Governments found 43,765 such units in the nation (15,032 of them school districts), and their number has increased steadily over the years, a testimony to their flexibility and usefulness.

Separate school districts exist in nearly every state, and they are the most visible of these special governments. While their function is to provide educational services from preschool to the community college level, they are also major owners and developers of urban real estate. Their choices to build new schools or to close others parallel the planning by municipalities. A disused school building is an opportunity to create a community center, housing complex, or business facility.

Of the other special purpose governments, many affect land use only marginally or sporadically. Nevertheless, a choice by a park district to acquire land in an urban fringe area not only removes that parcel from development but may also increase the residential attractiveness of the surrounding area and raise traffic counts on nearby streets. A watershed district may veto a building project in a wetland because it would increase the potential for flooding or reduce water quality.

In metropolitan areas, however, such special districts have often been created to finance improvements in public facilities. They can borrow money for investments in their functions, such as water and sewer facilities, streets and roads. Since cities and counties in their service areas are often limited in their power to take on further debt, these districts offer an opportunity to expand infrastructures when they are needed. New Jersey, Florida, Texas, and California use these extensively [Porter 1987].

However, a group of larger units are major planning participants due to their responsibility for extensive land-related public services and their ability to finance private development projects. The giant of these is the Port Authority of New York and New Jersey, a multifunction district in the New York City metropolitan area. In its ownership are airports, bridges, tunnels, bus and ship terminals, a subway line, and the World Trade Center towers. Since it controls much of the transportation infrastructure of the region, its planning efforts are basic to the land use choices of the many municipalities which it overlaps [Danielson & Doig 1982]. In 1984, it expanded its realm to establish a $50 million development bank to finance road, sewer, and waste treatment improvements, and to expand the region's employment base. It also has given financial support to the Bathgate Industrial Park in the South Bronx.

Two problems stand out in considering the role that the major authorities play in the local planning process. First, they are relatively independent from the citizenry and their accountability is thus tenuous. While some of their governing boards are elected by their constituents, most are appointed by the executives or legislative bodies of other governments. The twelve member board of the Port Authority of New York and New Jersey has divided accountability: six each are appointed by the governors of the two states.

Much of the public authorities' independence grows from their status as business enterprises, drawing most or all of their revenue directly from their operations. Many lack power to levy taxes and so need not submit to the legal scrutiny that is focused on the use of tax monies. They have thus much autonomy in their decisions as long as they operate within their legal powers. Most of the agencies which Robert Moses headed in his expansion of the New York metropolitan region's parks, bridges, and freeways were of this character [Caro 1974].

These features make them vulnerable to the criticism that they often act contrary to the overall interests of their city or region. Of this, Walsh [1978, 6] asserted,

> Because of their insulation, they overemphasize financial returns and reflect or accept the viewpoints of banking and business participants. They bias government investment in favor of physical infrastructures for short-term economic return. . . . The financing of public authorities through the private tax-exempt bond market determines priorities of public planning, shapes criteria for selecting new pro-

jects, and affects the pace of public investment. This method of financing encourages higher rates of borrowing, spending, and construction than are possible for programs that must run the gauntlet of the political marketplace.

This characteristic makes them natural allies of the major development interests in the region, an issue to which chapter 8 returns.

A second problem arises from the lack of coordination between the special districts' plans and those of the general-purpose units. For example, the unincorporated area around Houston is served by a number of water and utility districts. These serve their constituents by selling them ground water for household use, with the fees paying off the bondholders who initially financed the system. But their extensive pumping has contributed to land subsidence in the region, increasing the dangers of flooding and salt intrusion into wells. The districts have generally refused to cooperate on any remedial plan, and the general-purpose local governments cannot compel them to do so [Perrenod 1986].

3.4 METROPOLITAN PLANNING AGENCIES

Although metropolitan areas constitute geographic, economic, and social wholes, their governance is fragmented between one or more counties, many municipalities, townships (in some states), and special districts and authorities. Although some civic leaders in Boston recognized as early as 1910 the need for a comprehensive metropolitan authority, political forces have prevented the establishment of such units anywhere until the few city-county consolidations of the 1960s. Metropolitan service districts have proliferated since the 1920s (the Port Authority of New York and New Jersey was created for this purpose in 1921), but their presence only added to the fragmentation. Central-city and suburban leaders alike fear that such a reform would transfer authority from them to a body whose actions and purposes could not be foreseen.

Yet, the need for serious integrated planning grew with the metropolitan areas and could not be totally ignored. The first governmental regional planning agency was the Los Angeles County Regional Planning Commission, created in 1922. Although very active and professionally competent, it was unable to plan far enough ahead and with sufficient authority to keep up with the region's booming growth of that decade [Scott 1969, 206–209]. More public and private agencies appeared in subsequent years, but lacked the legal and political power to control the key decisions that shaped both the central cities and their suburbs.

In 1962, the initiative for regional planning shifted to Congress. It realized that the six-year-old interstate highway program had begun billions of dollars worth of urban freeway construction without any systematic planning for its relationship to land use, mass transit, housing, or other land-related factors. Thus it mandated that after 1965, highway grants would be made only to those metropolitan areas that had a comprehensive transportation planning process. In response, the local governments, transit agencies, and state highway departments quickly organized such processes.

Congress took a further step in 1966. It stipulated in the Demonstration Cities and Metropolitan Development Act that applications by local units for federal funds must be reviewed by an areawide planning agency. That agency was to comment on whether the proposed project was consistent with the plans of the surrounding communities and with such comprehensive metropolitan plans as then existed. These projects included hospitals, airports, libraries, facilities for water and sanitation, transit, highways, and open space acquisition. The comments of the reviewing agency were not to be binding on the federal office that provided the funds, but to enable the latter to judge the merits of the application within an areawide perspective. This became known as the A-95 review because its guidelines were stated in a circular with that designation issued in 1968 by the U.S. Bureau of the Budget (renamed in 1970 the Office of Management and Budget).

In response to those federal stimuli and in order to do the planning that was required, voluntary interlocal cooperation took the form of councils of government (COGs). These are bodies in which all municipalities and counties are, or can be, represented, and they maintain a staff for research, planning, and exchange of information. It is typically financed by a combination of membership dues and state and federal grants. By 1970, more than 300 of these existed. Some COGs prepared metropolitan development plans that integrated all of the region's land use concerns. But since participation is voluntary, a COG must confine its planning to matters on which a consensus already exists. Currently, with federal grants at a low ebb, their level of activity is much reduced in most areas [Wikstrom].

The most comprehensive response to the metropolitan planning challenge was taken in the Minneapolis-Saint Paul region. In 1967, the Minnesota legislature transformed an ineffective metropolitan planning commission into the Metropolitan Council, with increased authority over the seven-county region's land use and physical development. Over the years, it established a metropolitan development guide with policies for transportation, waste management, airports, regional parks, housing, and environmental quality. But unlike a council of government, it has authority to alter the plans and capital budgets of the regional operating commissions responsible for sewers, airports, and transit. It also has virtual veto power in the area over highway planning by the Minnesota Department of Transportation. Finally, it can compel all of the municipalities, counties, and townships in the region to conform, in their own comprehensive plans, to its regional systems policies. A general goal has been to restrict expansion of the service infrastructures, particularly sewers, on the urban fringe in order to induce infill development on vacant land already served by those facilities [Harrigan & Johnson 1978]. Recent studies show that the Metropolitan Council has had some success in implementing the development guide, although its planning influence is clearly limited by the major economic and political forces that foster development in the metropolitan area.

In the mid-1980s, such metropolitan planning as is taking place is quite incremental and low-keyed. There is no question that the general-purpose governments have retained the authority to conduct their own planning, subject to such constraints as the state and federal governments impose. The flow of federal grants that fueled the regional planning efforts has greatly diminished. In some areas, central-city and suburban business leaders have responded with linked efforts, not only to secure commercial development, but also to induce local and state authorities to supply public services and facilities without regard to city or county boundaries.

3.5 STATE GOVERNMENTS IN URBAN PLANNING

The role of state governments in planning has expanded steadily over the years. First, state legislatures empower local units to control land use, and set the conditions within which they do this. They can mandate comprehensive planning for parts or all of the state and specify the elements which they must cover. California requires that local plans deal with open space protection, seismic safety, and scenic highways in addition to the more familiar land use and housing regulation.

Second, the states may mandate the content of local plans. Minnesota requires that new building lots adjacent to many of its 10,000-plus lakes be of a minimum size, in most cases 15,000–20,000 square feet. The intent here is to control the intensity of development along increasingly expensive and urbanized shorelines to protect water quality.

Some state governments have expanded their involvement further into a broadly applicable land use plan of their own. Florida provides that a "critical area" designation may be given to

> an area containing, or having significant impact upon, environmental, historical, natural, or archeological resources of regional or statewide importance; an area significantly affected by, or having a significant effect upon, an existing or proposed major public facility or other area of major public investment; or a proposed area of major development potential, which may include a proposed site of a new community. . . .

[Finnell 1976, 37–38]. The state administration makes these designations, the local governments concerned make the initial decisions on regulating the areas, and the State Land Planning Agency approves the regulations.

California's regulation of its coastal zone illustrates the intricate relationships that can result. This is a state-local partnership in which cities and counties prepare local coastal plans that maximize public access to shorelines, protect agricultural lands and scenic areas, and encourage coast-dependent industry to locate in developed areas—all within the one-half to five-mile wide strip (depending on location) designated by the state as the coastal zone. The State Coastal Commission oversees the local planning processes and adjudicates disputes arising in specific cases. As of 1986, it had not been fully implemented due to intense political pressures on local units and their consequent inability to adopt final land use plans and zoning regulations. There is enormous conflict potential between the environmental and economic interpretations of coastal development, which far exceeds the political capacity of the cities and counties (and indeed the state) to resolve quickly or cleanly [Fawcett 1986; Fischer 1985].

Finally, state governments participate in land use planning directly through their own operations. Departments of transportation play a major role in their decisions about highways, airports, and in a few states, rail service. A department of natural resources has power to protect urban rivers, lakes, and shorelines, control drainage of wetlands, set rules for disposal of wastes, and establish state parks and wildlife areas in urban regions. Other state agencies do locally specific planning when they place a prison, office building, or hospital in a particular community, or approve the application of a private utility to build an electric power plant.

However, when there is inadequate communication between the state agency and affected local communities, such actions may disrupt established local plans and impose costs that residents are unprepared for. Indeed, part of many communities' political efforts must be aimed at securing, modifying, or preventing state planning actions that will affect them in some way. Section 8.3 includes examples of this related to state highway location. This task of intergovernmental diplomacy applies equally to the actions of the national government.

3.6 THE FEDERAL GOVERNMENT IN URBAN PLANNING

Washington's impact on the content and processes of planning has been substantial, particularly since the mid-1960s. Its influence upon metropolitan planning, reviewed in section 3.4, is but part of a larger endeavor in which Congress and several federal agencies responded to the demands of urban-based interest groups by mandating reforms in both land use choices and socioeconomic policies.

This federal participation has taken four major forms. First, as with the states, the everyday operations of its departments and agencies impinge on the planning choices of cities and counties. In many metropolitan areas it is a major landowner, and where its facilities generate much traffic or otherwise have impact on their surroundings, local planners must try to integrate and control these relationships. The federal agencies involved, however, may fail to cooperate and even take initiatives contrary to local wishes.

Second, federal regulatory policies affect local land use choices. Section 404 of the Clean Water Act requires anyone who proposes to place materials into open waters or wetlands to obtain a permit from the Army Corps of Engineers. The Environmental Protection Agency (EPA) may veto such a permit if it judges that filling would endanger wildlife or water quality and if there is a reasonable alternative to that action. When the Pyramid Companies applied for such a permit in 1983 to construct a shopping mall in Attleboro, Massachusetts, and thereby fill in most of Sweeden's Swamp, it proposed to replace it with a new and larger wetland elsewhere. Although local planners and the Corps of Engineers accepted that substitution, EPA denied the permit, holding that Pyramid did not fully explore other possible locations [Bachman 1987].

Federal water quality regulations have also compelled many local communities to build or expand sewage collection and treatment facilities. In cases like these, the effects on urban planning may not be directly intended, but are by-products of policies to achieve other benefits. Still other regulations, more scattered in their application, are designed to protect floodplains and historic buildings and secure safety in residential construction.

By far the greatest impact of Washington has come by means of its grants in aid to state and local governments, which encompass the third and fourth means of participation. The third, aid to the local planning process itself, reflected Congress' view that municipal authorities needed financial aid and legal incentives to build their expertise. The Wagner-Steagall Housing Act of 1937, which first provided direct grants to cities for slum clearance and construction of new dwellings, stipulated that responsibility for designing and developing each project would rest with local agencies whose officers were selected by mayors and/or city councils. But it was not until 1954 that a housing act specifically supplied grants and technical assistance for planning. Section 701 of that act authorized grants for general planning to cities with populations of less than 25,000 and to official metropolitan planning agencies. Other grants were made to help cities develop the urban renewal programs also funded in that act.

This planning assistance coincided with a growing popular awareness of suburban sprawl and the costs arising from uncontrolled growth. As Scott [1969, 504] observed,

> The urban planning assistance program, which was independent of urban renewal or other federal aids, was intended mainly to help suburban communities and metropolitan areas that were undergoing

explosive growth. As it called for matching state and local funds and for the disbursement of federal funds by state agencies, it encouraged the states to pay more attention to local planning and to increase their support of local planning and development agencies.

An explosion in plan making resulted, both by local and regional agencies and by private consultants who enjoyed a booming market. However, as with earlier and later efforts, the mere generation of a plan did not insure than an effective planning process came into existence, nor that the cycle would be completed to the critical point of implementation. By the time of its termination in 1981, Congress' appropriations for the 701 program totaled $1.014 billion [Feiss 1985, 182].

The fourth means of federal participation is the most obvious: the hundreds of grant programs that have financed the housing, urban renewal, airports, highways, mass transit facilities, and other physical developments that changed the face of American cities in the past 50 years. The 1937 Housing Act was the first major step. It was both a political response to the high unemployment rates of the Depression and a humanitarian response to wretched slum living conditions. But it also bestowed financial power on planners and other local leaders who had sought serious housing reform since the turn of the century. The act required that local authorities tear down at least one substandard dwelling for each new unit of public housing constructed: testimony to its emphasis on slum clearance.

The Housing Act of 1949 went further, declaring that housing quality was thereafter to be a matter of national, not simply local, policy. Congress declared that the general welfare and security of the nation required a remedy for the serious housing shortage and elimination of substandard dwellings through the clearance of slums and blighted areas. Together with the Housing Act of 1954, it expanded grants for urban renewal programs, enabling cities to purchase blighted land, clear it, and sell it to a private developer at a below-market price. But it stipulated that grants could be awarded only to cities with a redevelopment strategy that conformed to a comprehensive plan for the entire locality. The 1954 act added demonstration grants to encourage pilot projects from which all communities could learn. In many ways, the outcomes of the earlier acts were disappointing in terms of the numbers of dwellings actually built compared with those demolished. Congress hoped that more research and experimentation could make local planning a better learning experience.

Highways have also exerted great influence on urban planning, both in the location of the roads themselves and their many land use and social effects. Congress made a modest commitment to urban road building in 1944 when it created a national system of interstate highways. The National Defense Highway Act of 1956 had much more impact, however, for it increased the federal share of construction costs from 25 to 90 percent. What resulted, of course, was the network of urban freeways that greatly accelerated suburban growth and destroyed or transformed many inner-city neighborhoods and central business districts. In the 1953–62 period, the amount of federal aid spent on urban highways was approximately ten times that devoted to urban renewal [Judd 1984, 295].

The 1960s witnessed the maturing of the civil rights movement and the inner-city violence due to the rising but frustrated expectations of black people, which turned public attention away from the suburbs' problems. In 1965 Congress established the Department of Housing and Urban Development after years of lobbying by urban interests, recognizing the increased claim that cities had on federal policy and financial aid. The Demonstration Cities and Metropolitan Development Act of 1966 advanced the urban renewal policy to the point of targeting federal funds for social services as well as physical redevelopment of neighborhoods judged to be in greatest need. A significant provision of this act was the requirement that residents of the areas served be included in the planning for projects carried out there. This was not at first effective in most places, but had some longer term consequences to be noted in section 4.5.

The federal impact shifted again after 1974, with the passage of the Housing and Community Development Act. First, because it consolidated seven narrow categorical grant programs into a single block grant, it gave local officials more leeway in allocating funds to meet their unique needs. The spending simply had to promote "community development," broadly defined to include urban renewal, housing rehabilitation, water and sewer facilities, parks, and human service projects. This act preserved the earlier requirements for locally generated plans and for citizen participation in that process. A 1977 amendment added the Urban Development Action Grant program, which gave economically depressed cities funds to loan to private developers for projects that would not otherwise be undertaken. Funding for this was terminated in 1988.

Ronald Reagan's election to the presidency and the Republicans' control of the Senate in 1981–86 marked another turning point in federal-local interactions. His predecessors believed that while state and local governments bear primary responsibility for urban development and renewal, federal aid is instrumental in helping them fulfill that task. Reagan's position, by contrast, was that Washington should take the lead neither in urban policy making nor in financing. He and key conservative members of his administration viewed the private sector—business and nonprofit institutions—as the dynamic forces of urban change, which should be relied upon to finance it as well. One innovation he supported was the urban enterprise zone concept, which would designate highly depressed areas for tax reductions and relief from certain regulations to business investors who would locate there. Although several states adopted this idea in some form, Congress did not respond favorably. The major outcome of the Reagan policies for urban planning was the significant reduction in the dollar volume of federal grants for development efforts. Private business investment has filled the gap in some cities, particularly in the more prosperous Sunbelt, but not in such declining industrial centers as Detroit.

To identify the net effect of 50 years of federal endeavors on urban planning is difficult. Their effects have varied widely from one locality to another; how can one rate New York City's experience as equal to (or higher or lower than) that of Orlando or East St. Louis? Also, the impacts have not been the same for different population groups within each city, and no statement would be complete without their varied experiences. Yet, it is helpful to offer certain impressions, limited in this chapter to federal programs for land use control and physical urban development.

First, the planning process, by whichever level of government that engaged in it, became much more one of intergovernmental bargaining. As chapter 2 showed, early city planners held the ideal that their decisions should reflect a rational understanding of what was best for the community as a whole. They admitted that compromises might be necessary, but only with the political, economic, and social forces within that city alone. But now the planning bargains have taken on national scope. This is partly due to the legislative origins of the programs. City officials and their private-sector allies joined in coalitions to convince Congress of the grass-roots demand for them, and agreements had to be made and remade in the process of bill writing. Once passed, the laws were open to various interpretations, and individual cities and states sought to adapt the regulations to particular local conditions. Cities competed for project grants, those awarded to support specific endeavors, not supplied automatically by a set formula. On some issues, particularly, highway locations, bitter struggles entangled federal and state highway officials, mayors and local planners, and civic and neighborhood organizations. For example, popular protests in New Orleans defeated a proposal for an interstate freeway that would have run between the French Quarter and the Mississippi River [Baumbach and Borah 1981].

In a bargaining situation, it is not enough to be rational or virtuous; an official or government must have power resources sufficient for success. The federal government did have the money to grant or loan, and it had the authority to stipulate how the cash was to be used, but it was also compelled to spend it somehow and show the best results for it. Further, it was pressed by a network of financial, construction, and social interests to "strengthen our cities"—particularly their major wealth- and job-producing enterprises. Local forces organized in the 1930s to pool their lobbying efforts through the National League of Cities, United States Conference of Mayors, and associations of specialized officials in such fields as housing and redevelopment, planning, transit, water, and sewage treatment. For each aid program, a coalition of private interests also appeared to augment the influence they exerted through their geographic constituencies.

The bargains that these contestants struck were always temporary. They returned to the table annually to review what had happened with the previous agreement and make adjustments to reflect changed conditions and power alignments. The varied fortunes of the federal housing programs summarized above demonstrate this process well. Each decision shaped a new situation to which subsequent agreements had to respond.

As a second effect, local planning activity greatly increased after 1954, and metropolitan planning programs began to flourish in the mid-1960s. The establishment of the Department of Housing and Urban Development in 1965 was an artifact of this surge and gave it a further boost. More significant, the planning that was being done broadened in scope, transcending the narrower land use focus that the profession had maintained since its birth to encompass a wide range of social and economic problems of cities. Planning teams were often composed of persons from a variety of fields: social work, public health, anthropology, and economics as well as the more traditional planning-related disciplines. When the members of the American Institute of Planners met in their 1967 annual meeting, they altered its constitution to endorse a comprehensive approach to planning which integrated social and economic development with the physical development of cities [Scott 1969, 617]. The flow of federal funds supporting research, citizen participation, and plan making directed the attention of the urban political systems toward the many prospects for central-city renewal, suburban growth control, and human services development that remain on their agendas today.

Was there a concomitant increase in localities' ability to implement their ambitious new plans? Comprehensive data on this are not available, but impressionistic evidence suggests that there was. Congress' basic reason for providing the aid was to achieve its substantive goals in housing, transportation, urban renewal, open space preservation, and pollution abatement. Clearly, the cities, counties, and special districts received far more money for these projects than before, but their activity had to be targeted to federal priorities. In fiscal year 1978, for example, New York City received $224,775,000 in Community Development block grants alone, and other large cities were awarded proportional amounts. For every dollar that the city of Cleveland raised from local sources, it received 68 cents from federal aid [Hale & Palley 1981, 131–133]. Much of this funding supported programs related to the cities' planning processes, although the precise amounts cannot be calculated due to their division into many different fund categories.

This is not to say that these federal priorities conflicted with local objectives; indeed the local interests' influence in Washington shaped those priorities to a great extent. Even so, the process of transmitting funds and rules from Washington to the city halls was complex, lined with innumerable forms and regulatory details. For the cities in the greatest fiscal distress, the federal aid enabled them to do what they could not have done otherwise, but it naturally made them more dependent on those dollars. As those funds were reduced in the 1980s, even greater distress threatened where they could not be replaced.

The impact of federal programs upon the physical shape and arrangement of metropolitan areas has also been great, although they usually reinforced prevailing trends. Mortgage guarantee programs enabled households to buy homes of their own; most vacant land suitable for home building was on the urban fringes, of course, but the Federal Housing Authority and the private lenders through which it worked showed preference for suburban locations over central cities. The federally aided highway efforts supplied freeways on which the new suburban residents could travel to their central-city jobs, and also aided residents of the entire metropolitan area to journey more quickly to fast-growing suburban offices and factories. Federal water quality funds enabled those new municipalities and special districts to lay sewer lines and build treatment plants to serve the growing populations.

Some city centers have also benefited from federal programs, however. The urban renewal schemes since the 1940s have subsidized construction of many office buildings and public facilities. More recent use of community development grants and tax-exempt bonds has stimulated downtown rebuilding at an unprecedented pace. The same urban freeways that enabled the suburbs to expand, and disrupted the fringe of many downtown areas, also permit commuters to reach the central business districts in most cities in reasonable travel times. The centers of such cities as San Francisco, Atlanta, Chicago, and Baltimore are also more accessible by new or expanded rapid transit systems that were financed in large part by Washington. Residential development has even come to some down-towns; more than 13,000 dwelling units were built in and close to Chicago's Loop from 1979 to 1986, although not all of these benefited from direct federal aid. This offers clear testimony to the influence of a complex of economic interests which still value central business districts; these will be further analyzed in section 7.5.

Perhaps the least benefited (or most harmed) by such national programs has been certain inner-city neighborhoods that have experienced decline in housing quality and employment opportunities. Often, they are inhabited by the poor and racial minorities. Large public housing projects and smaller scale rehabilitation programs have supplied mixed benefits, but for many cities the pace of deterioration has overwhelmed the limited public and private resources available. Many of the federally supplied benefits simply did not reach them.

A final impact of federal programs, though somewhat delayed, has been the rise of citizen and neighborhood organizations in many cities. The mandated citizen participation in the Model Cities, Community Development Block Grants, and other programs disappointed many hopeful observers. In some cities the political leaders resisted any threat to their supremacy, and in others the disadvantaged residents lacked the skills and experience needed to take charge of their own neighborhoods' planning. A study of Community Development Block Grant spending in Milwaukee and Baltimore found that it primarily served the goal of economic development and through that the political purposes of their mayors and other elected officials. Very little went toward redistributive programs that benefited low-income residents directly, who were not able to exert sufficient power [Wong & Peterson 1986]. But through the 1970s and into the 1980s, the descendants of these committees and boards in many other cities came to grasp their opportunities and developed into effective participants in the planning process. Their present activity is reviewed in the next chapter.

3.7   THE COURTS IN URBAN PLANNING

The state and federal courts have been major actors in the urban planning process due to their role as authoritative dispute settlers. Because land use regulation deals with government interaction with private parties on a one-to-one basis, it is natural that conflicts arise in interpretation of law. If they cannot be settled by informal negotiation, the courts become the obvious recourse.

Most cases related to planning originate in the state court systems, because it is typically an interpretation of a state law or constitution that is in contention. Each state has a network of city, county, or district trial courts that bear the major burden of interpreting land use regulations, and most controversies are settled there.

Occasionally, major policy questions are also resolved in the court system. When the Southern Burlington County chapter of the National Association for the Advancement of Colored People sued the Township of Mount Laurel, New Jersey, for its zoning that discriminated against the poor, it went first to the New Jersey trial court. The final ruling on the issue was announced by that state's Supreme Court in 1975, and reinforced by a further decision in 1983 [*Southern Burlington County N.A.A.C.P. et al. v. Township of Mount Laurel* and *Mount Laurel II,* 1983]. While rulings by state supreme courts are not binding elsewhere, some have been adopted by federal and other state courts.

Some disputes are taken directly to the federal district courts on grounds that relate to federal law or the U.S. Constitution. When Renton, Washington, required in 1981 that theaters showing sexually explicit films be located at least 1,000 feet from any home, church, park or school, a theater owner sued the city in the federal district court in Seattle, claiming the ordinance violated his First Amendment right to freedom of speech. The U.S. Supreme Court took the appeal and the justices decided by a 7–2 vote, on February 27, 1986, that local governments may use their zoning laws to restrict location of adult-clientele theaters [*City of Renton v. Playtime Theatres*]. The U.S. Supreme Court may also consider appeals from state court systems, but does so only where there is a substantial federal question at stake. When it does refuse to consider an appeal, the last decision made stands as the final one.

During the twentieth century, a substantial body of case law on planning has accumulated by means of these state and federal court rulings. In general, local governments have substantial powers to legislate land use controls as long as they do not violate the constitutional guarantees. Courts will generally uphold municipal actions as long as they are consistent with their own laws and are not "arbitrary and capricious" in their application to individual situations. Yet, as a recent collection of cases shows, court responses to new and hotly contested zoning issues are unpredictable. A 1987 U.S. Supreme Court decision asserted that when a local government prevents an owner from using his land temporarily, even for a valid reason, it may have to pay compensation [*First English Evangelical Lutheran Church v. County of Los Angeles*]. Attorneys skilled in land use law can have great impact on the outcome of such controversies [Babcock & Siemon 1985, ch. 13].

The overall effects of broadening governmental involvement in planning has been to expand the scope of conflict by introducing new interests and values. State and national legislation has, in effect, told the localities that their decision making criteria are too narrow in some cases. Local autonomy and responsibility are still valid principles, but in matters of housing, transportation, and environmental protection, the dominant political forces in these areas can overlook concerns that a state or nation as a whole may have. There is thus a "ladder of involvement" on which state and/or national legislators and administrators may intervene, reflecting of course their own dominant interests. Often, this intervention has supported social or moral values in an effort to modify the heavy local emphasis on functional value. Chapters 5 through 8 provide abundant evidence of this.

The governmental participants in any planning process are fairly recognizable. But the second cluster of participants may not be so easily identified or categorized. These are the many private-sector agents for whom the planning is done in many cases and who are in any event deeply affected by it. They are the subject of the next chapter.

QUESTIONS FOR DISCUSSION

1. What factors affect the scope of conflict in planning issues? Can that scope be either too narrow or too wide?
2. How does the fragmentation of American local government affect planning politics and outcomes?
3. How closely should local government planners work with elected officials? How can they balance their professional objectivity with the need for political power?
4. What hinders metropolitan planning agencies from guiding regional urban growth effectively?
5. Why do governments have to bargain with one another over planning choices? What kinds of choices result from it?
6. As the federal government reduces its financial and policy involvement in urban planning, what influences have replaced it? Has local planning capacity been reduced as a result?

4 | WHO DOES PLANNING: THE NONGOVERNMENTAL PARTICIPANTS

4.1 THE PARTICIPANTS: AN OVERVIEW

Planning decisions are typically confined to a single unit of government, although the previous chapter showed how other units can be drawn in. But there are virtually no boundaries to participation by nongovernmental groups and individuals. Schattschneider's observations on the scope of conflict cited at the beginning of chapter 3 apply most of all to this group of contestants.

A key question for identifying these contestants is, "Who are the city's *stakeholders*?" This term implies ownership, but it is more than that. Stakeholders are those affected by actions taken in a realm of which they are a part. This entails a right to petition, to be consulted, and to have one's concerns treated seriously. Thus, a person who owns a home in a neighborhood scheduled for major rehabilitation has the right to be informed and heard on that program. This right also belongs to a renter of a home in the area and a person who operates a business there. But what about one who lives miles from that neighborhood but shops or works in it? Or a resident of another part of the city whose taxes or services will be affected by what happens in that area? The larger the number of stakeholders, naturally, the smaller is the amount of influence that the average one can exert and the greater the possibility of conflict over the choice.

Obviously, the circle of active stakeholders has a vague perimeter. In many cases, they are self-selected; some are regularly involved in planning issues in which they are interested, while others who have as much or more at stake pay no attention to them. The purpose of this chapter is to survey that circle to understand who takes part and for what reasons.

Since not all participants operate at the same level of intensity and influence, it is helpful to categorize those levels. In a study in Syracuse, New York, which included some land use decisions, Freeman [1968, 41–42] discerned several "layers" of community leaders. On top were the *institutional leaders,* the heads of the largest and most active business, political, professional, educational, labor, and religious organizations. Their impact depended on the influence which the organization had and on the individual's reputation for competence and power.

A second group in the Syracuse study were the *effectors,* who represented the institutional leaders in many actual decision situations, or acted on their own but in general conformance to the organization's interests. For example, it may be a bank manager or union shop steward who gave visibility to that group's presence. Below them were the *activists,* the leaders in the voluntary organizations, neighborhood groups, and service clubs. These lacked the prestige and power base that the above persons may have had due to their positions. Yet they could be very committed to their cause and so have a major impact when they chose to.

In addition to these leaders were the occasional participants and followers. They may speak out at meetings, make suggestions or threats, join and pay dues to an *ad hoc* group concerned with planning, or simply take part in community discussions of issues. But as spectators or peripheral players in the game, most have the option to step up their involvement, as Schattschneider described it, and so are potential effectors or activists.

A group of planning participants that overlaps with the leaders described above consists of the initiators of development. Recall that Types 1 and 2 planning decisions (presented in section 1.3) begin with the proposal from a private owner or developer, and those in Type 4 often do as well. Their involvement is formalized from the beginning, complete with legal rights to fair treatment. Of course they may not get what they apply for, which depends on the criteria which the government officials use in their decision and on the influence exerted by other public and private parties who join in later. General Motors enjoyed an unusually advantageous position in the case described in chapter 1, but the religious organization in San Diego whose intention was frustrated by the referendum lacked the ability to exclude the additional participants.

Whatever the group involved, it is much more likely to take political action on relatively specific decisions than on general policy matters. Thus, a city council or planning commission may discuss a municipal policy to increase the supply of apartment units for lower income households and draw little public attention. But should it establish such a policy and consider actual sites for that housing, support and opposition mobilize quickly to debate its implementation. Type 5 choices, concerning comprehensive plans, are too abstract for many participants to grasp unless they state concretely what is projected for specific areas.

Another way of categorizing these nongovernmental participants is by their linkage with the official decision makers. At one end of a spectrum are those who regularly and effectively intervene in planning choices, and who enjoy a close, ongoing liaison with key officials. Davidson [1979] characterized this as an *insider* relationship, in which the official grants access and information in return for what the official or the city needs: development initiatives, political support, and important viewpoints. The business leaders who initiated BART used their insider relationships to win governmental backing for it. These do not have to be the exclusive property of business interests, but can be obtained by any person or group who recognizes what is required and invests time and money to obtain it.

Outsider status characterizes those whose participation is only limited or very formalized (as in speaking at public hearings) and does not aim at cultivating an on-going and mutually beneficial relationship. Their power resources are quite limited or simply not used. Success is not always denied to them, however, for they can mobilize mass support and persuade elected decision makers to back their position. But it is difficult to maintain such efforts consistently. Even the activist South Bronx residents have been limited to this role, and so the support they have secured for redevelopment has been sporadic. One can also stand between these two extreme positions, and move in either direction from time to time.

Evidence from cases in local politics has sustained an extended debate over the nature of community democracy. To oversimplify this debate, on one side of the argument are those labeled "elitists" who perceive that a small, cohesive group, generally drawn from the socioeconomic upper class, controls decision making on public issues to its advantage. These persons are able to make it difficult or impossible for others to influence those choices significantly. In the opposing camp are several kinds of "pluralists" who hold that the system is relatively competitive, allowing representatives from differing groups to enter the arena and shape the choices to serve their interests, in part at least. Neither side perceives participatory democracy to work consistently, but the latter is more sanguine about the prospects for representing all of the stakeholders in decisions. Chapter 8 considers this debate more fully in the light of the planning politics discussed in the intervening chapters. It is sufficient for this chapter to identify the cast of influentials.

These participants rely on eight major tactics for exerting influence [Sayre & Kaufman 1965, 482–496]. Most visibly, they express their views on planning decisions in public hearings before city councils and other lawmaking bodies, planning commissions and similar advisory groups, state legislatures, and administrative agencies. This tactic is most relied upon by outsiders, who lack effective access by other means. If these expressions are not augmented by other forms of political action, they probably have little effect by themselves.

Second, extensive informal consultation with public officials is the special province of insider interests. An understanding between a developer and a planner reached over a cup of coffee may not become a final decision, but at least sets the context within which that choice is made. Because it takes place away from public view, it is more conducive to complex negotiations that can turn confrontation into agreement.

Third, interest groups provide advice and service to policy makers. It can take place when group representatives sit on a city advisory committee on economic development or environmental protection. They contribute their expertise free of charge, but in the process make recommendations which incidentally advance their interests. Such organizations also do research and propose solutions to problems, augmenting the limited resources of most governmental planning organizations.

Fourth, a group may intervene in electoral politics. Pro- or anti-development interests have occasionally promoted the election of mayors and legislators sympathetic to them. They can endorse candidates and contribute campaign funds, though they must be careful that voters do not perceive them as "buying" officials. By means of petitioning for initiatives and referenda and campaigning in them they can have a direct policy impact.

A fifth strategy is to file a lawsuit on a planning conflict. This is increasingly common and used not only by wealthy corporate interests but also by concerned residents of a neighborhood and individual landowners. The aim may be to establish a legal principle as well as to obtain a favorable judgment on the given controversy. An interest group may give legal and financial aid to the plaintiff or defendant when the outcome may affect its broader concerns.

A sixth method is also more common among outsiders: arousal of public opinion. This works well when a decision with potentially broad public effect is about to be made quietly. An opposition group, fearing defeat, takes Schattschneider's observations seriously (see section 3.1) and calls to the sidelines for new contestants to enter the game. It will use the news media, mass demonstrations, boycotts, petitions, and door-to-door canvassing to recruit support.

The seventh tactic also broadens the conflict: forming coalitions among interest groups for mutual support. Several neighborhood or business organizations may ally by agreeing to back each other's causes. Most such alliances are temporary, lasting as long as the threat or opportunity exists. Section 8.4 provides further insight into this highly important process.

The final involvement could be called implementive participation [Johnson 1984, 168–169]. This occurs as plans are taken off the drawing board and put into effect by concrete actions. Developers and their associates accomplish this in their financing and construction actions, while individual homeowners who choose to participate in a rehabilitation loan program are crucial to the success of such programs.

This chapter posed the question, "Who are the city's stakeholders?" From a pragmatic (and perhaps cynical) political perspective, one might answer, "Whoever wants to be." That is, regardless of any ethical or legal criteria for certifying stakeholders, the benefits of ownership really flow to those who not only "want to be" but also intervene in the choices that make the city what it becomes.

4.2   THE PROFIT-MAKING PARTICIPANTS

The use of land has high stakes. While the values identified in chapter 2 all have tangible and intangible dimensions, their lowest common denominator is eminently quantifiable: money. The sheer volume of urban land values is one facet of this. Perhaps more significant is the amount at stake in major development projects. New York City's Battery Park City, nearing completion on 92 acres of fill along the Hudson River shoreline, encompasses some 8 million square feet of homes and offices and has a price tag of $1.5 billion. A just-cancelled project in that city, the Westway, a six-lane freeway along the Hudson River, was estimated at two billion dollars. The stakes in these and all other projects include not only the direct private and governmental expenditures, but also those dollars that change hands in transactions that are stimulated by the original one. Such development in the immediate Battery Park City area would certainly spread to investments on adjacent lands. On the other hand, when one part of a city secures improvements, other parts may be deprived as a result.

The most visible private participants are the land development professionals, including developers, realtors, architects, and construction firms. "Developer" is a broad term that includes those persons and companies that put the whole package together for a given project, including the design, financing, governmental approvals, and construction. Most do not own the land they develop but work in partnership with the owner. While they may engage in any of the tactics listed above, their role is most distinctive in the informal consultation at the beginning and the implementive participation at the end.

Many major enterprises are built on land development. The Battery Park City project is an undertaking of the Reichmann brothers of Toronto, through their Olympia & York Enterprises, Ltd., the largest commercial landlord in New York City. The Reichmanns control more than 50 million square feet of commercial and residential space in major cities of Canada and the United States [Warson 1986]. Donald Trump and Trammel Crow are also among the nation's top operators, and like the Reichmanns, have the financial strength to apply their plans on virtually any parcel of land in the country.

Better known personally is James Rouse, whose firm, the Enterprise Development Company, has specialized in renewal of such historic structures as Boston's Faneuil Hall and Baltimore's Harborplace and smaller inner-city commercial developments around the country. Most of these have taken place in public-private partnerships and have an excellent record of financial success as well as popular appeal. The new city of Columbia, Maryland, was also his creation [Catanese 1984, 171–2; Mouat 1984]. Collectively, these large and medium-sized developers take the initiatives that most strongly influence the shape of central cities and their suburbs, including the Type 4 public-private partnerships, because they have the entrepreneurial incentive and skills to make them work. They can apply any of the political methods listed above to secure the official approval and possible subsidies which may be necessary.

Thousands of medium-sized and small developers also make vital choices and exert influence that shape the built environment. They may choose to convert a potato farm in New Jersey into a 50 home subdivision or a California orange grove into a convenience shopping center. A single project may not be controversial or have great impact on the environment, but taken together, such "minor" developments can transform a suburban community into a new metropolis. Many towns in Suffolk County, New York, on Long Island, have had such weak land use controls that virtually any proposal by these developers was approved. The result was often inefficient land use, poor quality homes and developments, and inadequate open space [Gottdiener 1977, ch. 5]. On the other hand, the many large and small developers active in San Diego have divided over the issue of growth control. While some oppose such restrictions, others have supported them, perceiving good opportunities in the limited space that is designated for development in that fast-growing region.

Since major development firms operate nationwide, much of a city's growth is likely to be based on choices by outsiders. Rouse is based in Baltimore, and the Reichmanns, like several other megadevelopers, are Canadian. Whether a given city's particular interests are overlooked in this cosmopolitan development market is open to debate. While some put up the same buildings whether the site is in Hartford or Hong Kong, others, like Rouse, are more sensitive to local environments and their historic character.

Architects, realtors and construction firms are integral parts of these development efforts. Their financial stakes are high, and profits are not assured in volatile markets. Overestimation of the demand for offices and homes can leave a pool of vacant buildings for years, as in Houston and Denver in the mid-1980s. An architect's creation may be radical or conventional, but once enshrined in steel and glass, it has a public presence for all to see in decades to come. A rough approximation of the law of supply and demand operates here, but the market tends to work in spurts and slumps. Individual choices are often subjective and based on limited information, and swayed by political and economic forces at the national and local levels.

Attorneys who advise on land use issues and aid in litigation of them constitute an ambivalent category. Many of these handle a case for a client without a personal interest in the outcome. But others are committed to certain planning values, perhaps historic or environmental preservation, and so play an advocacy role in planning politics. In either instance, the outcomes of legal battles over zoning and other planning issues can depend heavily on the quality of the attorneys' preparation and argument of their cases. Richard Babcock and Charles Siemon [1985, ch. 9], themselves nationally known land use attorneys, described how Alex Polikoff, of the American Civil Liberties Union, has battled since 1969 to expand the supply of public housing for Chicago's poor. Using a variety of political as well as legal weapons, he sought, largely in vain, to get the Chicago Housing Authority to place its dwelling units in predominantly white neighborhoods against bitter opposition from the residents.

Those who finance urban development constitute another vital category of participants. These include commercial banks, savings and loan institutions, mortgage firms, insurance companies, pension funds, and other enterprises that make and manage real estate investments. At the end of 1983, these had more than $1.1 trillion dollars of their funds in real estate, about a quarter of their total assets [Downs 1985, 316]. Their directors, by deciding whether and to what extent to finance a proposed project, can of course regulate the developers' own activity. In many cases, these financial institutions are direct partners in major projects, shaping their locations and design. Usually, they are constrained by law as to the nature of investments they make, but they also consider their internal goals on profitability and risk, and the stake which they wish to have in particular cities and communities. A broader survey of sources of development financing follows in section 7.3.

A sensitive social as well as economic issue is the extent to which a bank or savings institution deliberately invests (or refuses to) in particular neighborhoods. Its refusal to grant business loans or home mortgages in a certain area because it is designated as risky or deteriorated is known as *redlining*. Widely practiced a few years ago, it is now reduced in extent under legal and political pressures. On the other hand, a lender may "greenline" an area, targeting it for loans to stimulate its renewal. The South Shore Bank, in a changing neighborhood on Chicago's southeast side, abandoned redlining in the mid-1970s for a deliberate policy of upgrading the area, now 98 percent black in population. Half of its $74 million loan portfolio is invested locally, and it has attracted deposits from 700 individuals and corporations that choose to aid the bank in its renewal efforts [Phillips 1986].

Land speculators, which may include any of the above, are another source of planning influence. Sensing abundant profits as suburban areas expand, these persons purchase land in the path of growth and hold it until the demand rises to the expected level. At some point, they may request a rezoning of the land to the use expected to yield the highest price. They also exert influence on the routing of highways, sewer lines, and other services that would enhance the value of that land. Much controversy has attended their activities. Gottdiener [1977, 104–8] argues that in Suffolk County, New York, at least, they share responsibility for unwise urban sprawl, having promoted development of land that should have been left open or developed in another manner. Local officials, of course, permitted this and so bear some of the blame.

Beyond these are businesses of all kinds that participate as current or prospective landowners, tenants, lessees, and users of related facilities. If they are large (relative to the size of the community), the sheer size of their buildings, employment, and tax payments give them major influence, as the General Motors case in chapter 1 amply illustrates. They can thus secure the zoning changes, subsidies, street improvements, parking facilities, and other benefits that enhance their own investments and maximize the efficiency of their operations. Since most large corporations operate facilities in many cities, their corporate headquarters, based perhaps in New York or Tokyo, makes decisions affecting the success and failure of plans in other cities. The political processes of those cities have little or no ability to reach into their boardrooms.

By their choices to maintain their existing properties or allow them to deteriorate, such businesses shape and limit the planning choices of a community. A major retailer on a shopping street can strengthen the entire district by investing in improvements. But by neglecting the property the retailer can make it unattractive to customers and neighboring merchants as well. Landlords of relatively low-rent apartments in high land-cost areas have a strong economic incentive to replace those buildings with more profitable structures, thus compounding the steady loss of homes for lower income persons in central cities.

The planning process also draws in interest groups and trade and professional associations that represent collective business interests. These participants tend to have policy concerns that are broader than specific site decisions. Chambers of commerce (or similar groups by other names) are located in nearly every city, and there are separate groupings of downtown and neighborhood businesses. Just about every kind of skill and specialty employed in the planning process also has an association that speaks for it. It is common for these progrowth coalitions to intervene in Type 3 and 4 decisions where they see potential for improvement of the city's commercial prospects. For example, the first impetus to the construction of BART came from the Bay Area Council, an organization of leading corporations based in downtown San Francisco. One key aim it had was to maintain property values in that business district by improving its accessibility to suburban commuters [Whitt 1982, 42–44].

Such groups are able to mobilize planning expertise and thereby shape public decisions directly. When the city of Denver sharply reduced its planning department and eliminated any capability for long-range planning, an advisory role was filled by the Denver Partnership, a group of 130 business executives. Through its subsidiary, Civic Ventures Inc., it became the *de facto* planning agency for the central business district and has designed a new zoning ordinance, established a transit mall, and coordinates public and private efforts for new development and renewal of historic structures [Foster 1983]. Basically, Denver's downtown planning was led by those who stood to benefit the most financially from it.

The news and information media have the ability to play a role in planning choices. First, by choosing to publicize (or not) a given issue, a newspaper or television station can define its terms in the public mind and shape the size of the conflict over it. The media in each community play an obvious role in this. Nationally, the television networks and news services decide which events and conditions in one urban region are publicized elsewhere. As Warren and Rosentraub [1986, 44] put it,

> If the residents of diverse cities believe that the physical structure of many cities is about to crumble, that Houston is managed efficiently without zoning regulations, it is, in large part, because of media reports which contain these pictures of reality and reinforce them through repetition.

Home-owned media enterprises that depend on local advertising, and thus on the economic health of their area, are naturally inclined to back the development initiatives of the business community. A media company may participate in development as an entrepreneur itself. The Minneapolis Star and Tribune Company was a major advocate of construction of the Hubert H. Humphrey Metrodome on its present site. It was also the largest investor in a development consortium which secured from the city exclusive development rights in a 50-block area surrounding the stadium site. Charges were made that its advocacy biased its own editorial policy and coverage of the stadium controversy. The area has yet to reach its full potential and some of the plans went awry, but the newspaper company remains an important booster of development there.

4.3 NONPROFIT INSTITUTIONS AND ORGANIZATIONS

A cluster of groups with interests that do not provide direct profits to their members also participate in planning choices. First, labor unions may choose to back or oppose certain projects. In such cities as New York, Detroit, and Chicago, labor leaders are active in many public decisions. In most cases, their interest is job creation for members. Thus, they have a natural affinity with developers and business interests in new construction and rehabilitation. Unions also have good reason to present a united front with business to convince prospective employers that their area has a favorable labor market. Friedland [1983, 119–21] found that while unions retain some potential to mobilize central-city votes and provide essential support to candidates, their overall influence on urban development issues is much less than the profit-making groups in the previous section. In the General Motors case in Detroit, the United Auto

Workers rarely appeared in the proceedings. If that politically powerful union had any role in it, it was probably quietly supportive [Jones & Bachelor 1986].

A growing and diversified cluster of foundations and not-for-profit organizations is having a major impact on planning and land development. Since financing of certain kinds of construction, particularly homes for lower income households and restoration of historic structures, is difficult to obtain due to the lack of potential profits, these "nonprofits" have a wide latitude. Sometimes, a profit-making developer spins off a foundation to support socially worthy goals. James Rouse, the developer mentioned in the preceding section, created the Enterprise Foundation in 1981. Its treasury, nourished by his company's profits and other business gifts, has dispensed loans and grants to neighborhood housing improvement groups in many cities. The foundation's planning impact lies in its ability to help cities fulfill renewal plans for which funds are lacking [Mouat 1984].

More common are local nonprofit corporations that receive grants from various sources and direct those funds to planning and implementing projects they deem socially and economically worthy. Ten neighborhood groups in the South Bronx were selected by Mayor Koch in 1987 for aid to rehabilitate one thousand city-owned housing units. One of these was the Mid-Bronx Desperadoes noted in chapter 1 (now known as the M.B.D. Community Housing Corporation), which has also cultivated ties to local merchants and worked to upgrade police protection [Teltsch 1987]. Such groups necessarily build political influence while they carry out self-help projects, gaining visibility at city hall as well as in the neighborhood.

Churches and religious organizations have also established a presence in planning politics. They have learned how to lobby on social and moral issues that touch land use choices. One congregation may advocate that the city close down an adult theater in its vicinity, while another may protest the lack of action to house homeless persons. Churches have long had the power in most communities, formally or informally, to veto the grant of liquor licenses within a certain distance from their property. As major owners of land free of property taxation, their choices of how to use it also enter into city plans.

If a church building is also a historic structure, as many are, its congregation can pose special planning problems. St. Bartholomew's Episcopal Church on Park Avenue in New York City has sought to replace its Community House with a 59-story office building in order to secure income to maintain its own activities. The city's Landmarks Preservation Commission, which must approve the project if it is to proceed, faces the question of whether the architectural significance of the church outweighs the congregation's right to make its own development plans [Dunlap 1984].

Religious institutions also act in ways similar to the nonprofit corporations above. In Brooklyn, New York, clergy from several Protestant and Catholic congregations formed the East Brooklyn Churches in 1980. Within five years it became an independent and politically influential lobby for its area, able to mass popular support for its aims. But its best known endeavor is the Nehemiah Project, which as of mid-1985 had sponsored construction of 384 homes for middle-income persons on large areas previously cleared by urban renewal. It has attracted gifts from denominational offices, and secured major support from the city government. By providing an essential rehabilitation service, it has established an insider relationship instead of the outsider status which those ministers and their parishioners had before.

4.4   THE CITIZEN PARTICIPANTS— ORGANIZED AND UNORGANIZED

Citizen is a broad term, covering a great variety of actors in planning decisions, and no clear line separates them from the profit-seeking and institutional influentials in the two preceding sections. Basically, one can define as a citizen participant a person whose aims are rooted in relatively individualistic interests or those of the social community with which he or she identifies. Those interests may have a financial dimension, as when a homeowner seeks to protect the value of a home from the degrading effect of a nearby waste disposal site. The interest could also be ideological (e.g., to prevent government control of a person's land use choice), esthetic (to protect a woodland or historic structure from alteration), or social (exclusion of a housing project likely to bring "different" people next door). Certainly they are not altruistic in most cases; vigilant homeowners can be as selfish as huge developers in their own realms.

This citizen involvement also differs from the previous forms in that the participants' personality is likely to be a more intense ingredient of the political contest. Imagine a city council meeting in which a developer seeks approval for an apartment building next to a neighborhood of single-family homes. The attorney, architect, and engineer representing the developer present competent but dispassionate evidence for the project, aided by a dozen professionally drawn maps and sketches. Then the residents next to the proposed project stand up, one after the other, claiming that it will degrade their property values, flood their backyards, increase their traffic, endanger their children, and violate their sense of beauty. Unless unusually well prepared, they present few hard facts that a court of law would find persuasive. Yet, they argue with a passion that draws the sympathies, if not the support, of the council members who realize that the protestors are also voters. Planning politics is thus more volatile in entangling one's emotions in the choices that have to be made. This is why the scope of conflict is so susceptible to expansion.

Among the citizen organizations are those broad-based associations at the city or metropolitan level that have explicit interests related to planning and other public issues. They have a long history, since some were instrumental in putting planning on the agendas of many American cities in the late nineteenth and early twentieth centuries. Societies supporting parks, the arts, and better planning in general appeared then in Philadelphia, Baltimore, Cleveland, San Francisco, and uncounted others. Often made up of personally or institutionally influential citizens, these groups came to enjoy insider status and saw many of their aims realized through the City Beautiful movement [Scott 1969, ch. 2]. Later groups advocated metropolitan-area planning in the New York, Los Angeles, Minneapolis-Saint Paul, and other regions, though with less success. A recent example is the San Diego chapter of the Sierra Club, which spurred serious consideration of growth control in the 1970s. Ordinarily concerned with wilderness protection, this group adapted well to its urban environment.

Such groups are as diverse in their aims as in their membership. Their interests may be broad or narrow, innovative or defensive, or concerned with the needs of the "have-nots" or those who "have" to one extent or another. Some are based in a particular ethnic group, perhaps black, Hispanic, or Vietnamese. COPS (Communities Organized for Public Service) was formed in San Antonio in 1974 to speak for the interests of its many Mexican-American residents. Its first objective was to demand public services for the neighborhoods inhabited by its members and to mobilize their voting power to gain strength on the city council. But in the process, it also worked to halt a major development on the "Anglo" north side, fearing both pollution of the water supply and a further diversion of the city's resources toward that area [Babcock & Siemon 1985, ch. 5].

Another common group theme is environmental protection. People for Open Space works to preserve farmland in the San Francisco Bay area by persuading local governments to grant protective zoning to agricultural areas in the path of urban expansion. It also seeks to aid farmers to keep their land in production and so be able to resist temptations to sell out to speculators and developers. A lobbying group allied with it, Greenbelt Congress, has active chapters in the nine Bay area counties [Henderson 1985]. Preservationist organizations generally have a middle-to-upper class membership with above average education, and are often able to form insider relationships with officials they seek to influence.

Civic associations are influential in many communities and metropolitan areas. Leagues of Women Voters are found across the country, and frequently take part in planning-related issues. While they are nonpartisan and avoid endorsing candidates for office, they provide the information and awareness on controversies that individual members can use in their own activity.

Broader-base civic organizations have established themselves as serious contributors to planning debates in certain areas. The Citizens League in Minneapolis-Saint Paul has functioned for more than two decades to research and make recommendations on public issues. Its member-constituted committees have examined such matters as transit, downtown renewal, highways, parking, development finance, and housing, and their findings have been accorded much respect by local and state officials. The league's socioeconomic orientation is business and professional, though politically progressive in a well-established Minnesota tradition.

A much larger number of citizen interest groups exists at the neighborhood level in medium-sized and larger cities. In those with more than 100,000 residents, the machinery of government appears more distant and less responsive than in smaller ones. Thus, politically aware residents in many of their subareas find an intermediate organization necessary to embody their sense of place and represent its special concerns to higher authorities.

The term *neighborhood* is open to many definitions, depending on what causes people to recognize boundaries to their valued environments. For some, it is their immediate residential area, perhaps a block or a similar district with boundaries which the residents agree separate them from other areas. For others, it can be the relationship with a particular institution—a public school, church parish, or police precinct. Still others are designated by the local government as service areas or election wards.

The actual organization most often takes place in response to a perceived threat, perhaps steady physical deterioration, or a single event such as a redevelopment proposal or highway routing. It is not unusual for even a Type 1 planning decision to mobilize a neighborhood if it is publicized sufficiently. Whether the people remain organized after the threat is defeated or acceded to depends on their leadership and perceptions of their opportunities and further threats.

Urban territorial units are natural bases for political organizations, according to Crenson's research on neighborhood associations in Baltimore [1983, 15]. "If physical force is regarded as the hidden engine that drives political systems, physical space is seen as the traditional and singular medium in which this energy source achieves tangible expression." That people have to live and do business in close proximity creates political concerns that set up both cooperation and conflict. These concerns are both internal to the area and link it with the larger politics at city, state, and national level. Thus, Crenson [1983, 17] asserted, "the residents of a neighborhood do not constitute a private group at all, but a miniature 'public'—more like citizens than like members of a private association."

Neighborhood organizations have many interests which they seek to promote, but their general character is shaped by which of two basic strategies they choose to promote them. One strategy is direct political action, in which the neighborhood's goals require action and support by governments, businesses, and other institutions that have some control over the area. The organization mobilizes its members to use their political resources—votes, pressure, money—to secure that action. This approach is particularly identified with the Industrial Areas Foundation, begun in the 1940s by the community organizer Saul Alinsky. It has aided in the creation of community groups across the country that enable lower income and minority groups to build political influence. COPS in San Antonio, mentioned above, is based on such neighborhood units.

The second strategy is community development, by which the association becomes an economic enterprise and gains benefits for the people through its revenues, jobs, and the physical renewal which it initiates. Basically, it operates as a business, drawing capital from the financial community as well as government [Ventriss & Pecorella 1984, 225]. It is not impossible for a particular group to combine both strategies, but the kind of leadership required for each differs sharply, and one is likely to take precedence over the other. The first strategy requires persons who are good at community organizing, raising issues, and lobbying. The second, by contrast, calls for financial and managerial skills, to negotiate with officials rather than confront them.

The East Los Angeles neighborhood, which is primarily Hispanic, poor, and plagued with substandard housing, has two powerful organizations, one dedicated to each strategy. The United Neighborhood Organization (UNO) pursues the former course, stressing mass member involvement and a confrontational approach to city officials. Among other victories, it has persuaded the city to begin a housing rehabilitation program. The East Los Angeles Community Union, by contrast, has secured diverse financial backing for its own programs in housing and business development. It has a much larger budget and professional staff than UNO and has had to learn to be a sophisticated financial manager. On the other hand, its active member involvement is much lower, and it has developed closer ties to the governmental and economic institutions of the city [Ventriss & Pecorella 1984]. The choice of strategy has much bearing on whether an insider or outsider relationship develops.

Many neighborhood groups pursue primarily preservationist goals. The Midtown Citizens Association in Wichita, Kansas, is active in a predominantly white district just north of the downtown area that has small, older homes and some businesses. It was formed in 1972, when some residents became concerned that city neglect and the changing land use market would reduce their area's quality of life. It has intervened in decisions on zoning, street traffic, a proposed freeway loop (defeated), park improvements, and other municipal projects. Its strategy is clearly one of direct action, but its tactics have been confrontational only as needed. With maturity and official recognition, the group has found more cooperative tactics to be effective [Cunningham & Kotler 1983, 27–33].

The Southeast Community Organization (SECO) in Baltimore is one of the largest and most sophisticated groups oriented to community economic development, although exerting political pressure has also been a vital part of its strategy. Founded in 1970, it is actually a coalition of more than 70 block clubs, neighborhood improvement and civic organizations, churches, and senior citizens' groups, and has a complex governing structure that represents its diverse constituents. Initially, it focused on pressure action on such issues as truck traffic routing and school location. But its leadership gradually moved SECO toward community development, having concluded that government was in no position to provide much of what Southeast needed. With a Ford Foundation grant, SECO created a subsidiary, Southeast Development, Inc., to aid in commercial and residential property renovation, a land bank, and several industries. Later, SECO became a general contractor for lower income housing [Cunningham & Kotler 1983, 71–81]. Because it is a federation with decentralized governance, it can pursue both the pressure-politics and community development strategies, although both have been the source of internal conflict within its leadership and between the constituent groups.

The citizen groups already described are entirely private, with no formal recognition or access to the government's planning processes. But there is a logic in drawing such organizations into the system in order to make those processes more realistic and responsive. To choose representative citizens and endow them with a quasi-legal status, access to information, and a right to be consulted on defined planning issues could yield major benefits for the local political system, argued the Advisory Commission on Intergovernmental Relations [1979, 61–62]. Basically, it would improve the quality of the planning choices, stimulate resident responsibility for their neighborhoods and city, and reduce the political alienation that is so widespread in larger cities.

This logic was first persuasive in the early part of this century in the transformation of many unofficial citizens planning associations into the planning commissions that now have legal status. Their upgrading was relatively easy in that the would-be commissioners were often persons of high standing in the community and enjoyed insider relationships with officials. But that argument was picked up by Congress in the 1960s to serve another end: empowerment of the poor and politically disadvantaged. As cities received their grants, they were mandated to set up advisory boards and committees made up of the constituencies to be served by the programs. This requirement was continued in the 1974 Community Development Block Grant (CDBG) program and remains today in various forms.

Cities varied widely in the influence granted these committees. Some were simply created to satisfy the "Feds" and were allowed no meaningful role. At the other end of the spectrum, a few were major participants in shaping programs. Several evaluations of CDBG efforts found that although cities were generally meeting the minimum participation requirements, there was much popular dissatisfaction over the meager involvement of lower income groups and the insensitivity of public officials to citizen concerns [Advisory Commission on Intergovernmental Relations 1979, 144]. Rivalries between politicians, administrators, city departments, and neighborhoods often turned this consultation process into guerrilla warfare.

The citizen groups themselves varied widely in their capacity for influence. Their ability to build coalitions, gain information and technical assistance, and use their formal powers depended upon consistent and effective leadership. What happened subsequently, however, was that groups which did find such leadership blossomed on their own. Both their successes and frustrations in Model Cities and CDBG convinced enough community activists that power flowed to those who exercised it. For them, the pressure politics strategy was the logical first step, both to assert their presence in the planning process and to mobilize residents into a credible and coherent force.

Many cities have given formal recognition to neighborhood organizations. Washington, D.C., as required in its Congressionally granted home rule charter of 1974, granted legal status to 36 advisory neighborhood commissions. Some commissions are more active than others and their concerns differ with the kind of area they cover. The Du Pont Circle Commission, in an affluent district, seeks to preserve its diverse residential character, while the Adams-Morgan Commission, with an ethnically mixed constituency, works to protect and expand lower income housing opportunities. Each commission can make recommendations to the District of Columbia government on zoning and public services, and must be notified before an official decision is made that would affect the neighborhood. Since their role is only advisory, what influence they can exert depends on their political effectiveness and the quality of their recommendations [Cunningham & Kotler 1983, 115–122].

Saint Paul, Minnesota, established a network of 17 district councils in 1975, with members elected periodically by residents. Each one employs a community organizer, paid by the city, and a person from the city staff is assigned to each district to provide planning expertise. It receives notification of all development applications for its area and has the opportunity to favor or oppose each before the city planning commission and the city council. Each council generates specific proposals for capital spending in the neighborhood, both from the city's funds and CDBG grants, which are consolidated by a committee that represents each district. The mayor and council have generally followed these recommendations.

When Saint Paul revised its comprehensive city plan in 1977–81, each district council prepared a general district plan as the first step. Then they were incorporated into an overall city plan by the planning commission and city council. Most district-generated choices were accepted, and when they were not, the councils played an effective role in negotiations over the final outcome. The system is now politically popular, able to handle conflicts over the substance of policy rather than its own existence. Local observers claim that city council members sometimes use the district councils as political shields on controversial matters, adopting neighborhood positions as their own [Johnson 1984, 182–183].

Another category of citizen organizations comprises the candidates for office, political parties, and campaign organizations that produce elected officials for all levels of government. Elections for most local governments are legally nonpartisan, but groups of all sorts (including the established political parties) are free to take part with endorsements and campaign help. These electorally oriented groups can influence planning choices directly if there is a live controversy at the time of election. Then, a pro- or anti-development movement may secure victory of a candidate favorable to its side. Housing issues have dominated local election campaigns in many of the New Jersey suburbs since the first Mount Laurel decision in 1975, and candidates apparently have won most with pledges to limit or block the mandated rezoning for modest-cost homes.

The San Diego and BART cases in chapter 1 illustrate another method of citizen involvement: direct policy making through the initiative and referendum. The initiative is a process of lawmaking by voters, and takes place in two stages. Although procedures vary with state law and local charters, the first step requires circulation of a petition with the proposed ordinance. If it obtains the signatures of a set percentage of the registered voters (typically 5–10 percent), it is formally presented to the local legislative body. Should the council not act in a certain period of time, an election takes place at which a simple majority of those voting can enact it. Such an initiative may be used, for example, to rezone a parcel of land.

The referendum comes in two forms. One is a repeal of an ordinance already passed by the council, and takes place in much the same manner as the initiative, beginning with a petition. The action in San Diego was of this kind. The other is required to approve borrowing of funds by the local government through general obligation bonds. In that process, the city council, school board, or special district may plan street improvements, a new park, a new school building, or rapid transit system and choose to finance it by selling the bonds. While the voters are called upon to approve the increase in the public debt, they also rule on the particular project that is planned and the method of repaying the bonds. Such a vote was necessary to initiate San Francisco's BART system.

These legal procedures may be used in many ways to serve local aims. In 1976, the U. S. Supreme Court, in *City of Eastlake v. Forest City Enterprises* upheld a local charter provision that requires a referendum on every land reclassification, with a 55 percent majority required to overturn it. In Hawaii, a beachfront lot was rezoned by referendum to negate its newly approved resort classification, even though construction had begun [Callies 1981, 293].

In these uses of voter power, interest groups and influential individuals play a vital role. They take the lead in defining the issue to be brought before the public, and must draft a legally valid ordinance in the case of an initiative. Further, they circulate the petitions and publicize them. If an election is called, they mount a campaign pro or con, and in larger cities may spend major sums of money on media advertising, mailings, and billboards. The San Diego growth moratorium described in chapter 1 pitted the ample resources of the development professionals against the environmentalists' organization and publicity.

Individual citizens, not organized in the ways already described, play more sporadic roles in planning politics. They can speak at hearings, sign petitions, write letters, or discuss an issue with neighbors, but unless they cross the line into a leadership or mobilizing role that collects support, they have little effect. To file a lawsuit takes only one person, of course, and can be a route to victory, but even these are typically joint efforts. Yet, because these individuals are always potential members of the above efforts, even just as voters, prudent decision makers are sensitive to their concerns.

Citizen participation in politics, in all of the above forms, has been repeatedly defended as a counterweight to the biases of the business interests, a democratic expression of "the people" as opposed to the rich, the powerful and the self-seeking. But in speaking of government by the people, one must always ask, "Which people?" Several problems appear in evaluating these participation methods.

First, one must ask how representative the particular group is of those for whom it purports to speak. Repeated studies have shown that those who take part in citizen planning efforts are typically of middle to upper income, above-average education, and business or professional occupations, along with home owners and long-term residents of the area. There are proportionally fewer women, racial and ethnic minority group members, and persons under the age of 30 and over 65. The willingness to participate and the capacity to do it effectively depend on personal qualities and skills that are cultivated by, and lead to success in, higher education, high-status occupations, and ownership of property. Citizens who lack this status tend to believe they can have no influence whatever, and so do not even try. Knowing this, those who seek the sense of the public on planning choices must be alert to who is *not* participating.

A second problem is apparently the opposite of the first: many and varied citizen voices on an issue. This can happen when several organizations represent one neighborhood, as in the Uptown district on Chicago's North Side. As of 1979, four groups expressed different viewpoints in that diverse and rapidly changing area, plus a host of block clubs, some independent and others affiliated with a larger association [E. Warren 1979, ch. 4]. That can be an advantage if they actually represent all of the perspectives that such a neighborhood contains. However, when citizen opinion is divided, city officials may have a freer hand to make decisions according to criteria of their own choosing.

Questions also arise over the quality of this citizen participation. A professional planner with years of experience or a mayor who seeks to serve the holistic needs of the city may believe the often self-serving demands of community groups and individual landowners to be a hindrance to reaching a sound decision. Some citizens may have unrealistic expectations of a project or insist on undue control. When the choice is to locate a needed community facility that residents do not want near their homes, such as a waste management operation or halfway house for criminal offenders, the NIMBY response (Not In My Back Yard) will block any action if citizen opinion is taken seriously. Some cities and private foundations have sought to improve the level of citizen expertise with education and information programs or through close liaison between neighborhood groups and planning staffs, as Saint Paul has done.

These concerns are not limited to citizen activism, of course. Participation by developers and other business firms and individuals is also subject to bias and distortion. When the conflict over a particular issue widens in the manner that Schattschneider described, the best that one can often hope for is a balanced process, in which every possible viewpoint is pressed by someone, and the public decision makers thus gain the information they need for a suitable decision.

4.5 SUMMING UP: THE PUBLIC-PRIVATE NETWORK

What conclusions can be drawn from the evidence in this chapter and the preceding one? It is helpful to distinguish the processes typical of the different types of planning decisions. A major variable, as surveyed in this chapter, is the number of stakeholders in the decision. This breaks down into the stakeholders who actually take part, and the remainder who are affected by it and could take part but do not for some reason.

Type 1 choices are so highly localized that the likelihood is small of expanding the scope of conflict beyond the applicant, the planning officials, and possibly a few neighbors. Yet, several of them that are together perceived to be important, perhaps converting single-family homes to multiple residency, have caused neighborhood organizations to form.

Type 2 decisions on large-scale private developments are much more likely to draw in organized support and opposition and possibly other units of government than the one in direct control. A developer from outside the city or region is likely to encounter more obstacles than one from within the community, other factors being equal. The scale and complexity of such choices makes it harder for an individual "outsider" to exert influence.

In the third type, government officials take the initiative and such capital plans are proposed and debated years in advance. The process is thus much more public and there is greater citizen opportunity to seek a park improvement, for example, or influence the location of a highway. Organized community and business groups can compete here on a more or less equal footing. A problem can arise, though, if such capital investment decisions are not considered within the overall land use planning process of the city. In some governments, there is weak coordination between the location of streets, schools, and sewers and the control of private development. This can fragment the attention of interest groups concerned with them.

The partnership decisions in the fourth type are more variable in their politics. If government has taken the initiative, as with a housing rehabilitation project, there may be much publicity and debate beforehand. But if a major developer does the planning and then enlists a city's backing, the process can remain relatively closed. Complex negotiations over land assembly, funding, and design are often done in secret. After commitments are made by both sides, opponents are at a serious disadvantage even if they mobilize support.

Type 5 comprehensive plan choices offer serious opportunities to groups that know what they seek and persist in their efforts. Although planning commissions and legislative bodies publicize these efforts in various ways (and must hold public hearings at crucial stages), few individuals pay attention. Comprehensive planning is more abstract, with general policies and choices that will have impact only years in the future. For those businesses and neighborhood organizations that realize what is at stake and can see beyond the colored maps to what will one day be "on the ground," these choices promise significant long-run influence.

In some communities with open political processes, planning controversies can accommodate just about anyone who chooses to join in. For them, the conclusion by Sayre and Kaufman [1965, 514–

515] about politics in New York City in general is relevant. "The system functions in such a way that anyone who feels strongly enough about any governmental decision need not feel, or be, entirely helpless to do something about it. . . . For any group can fight City Hall, almost every group does, and many are remarkably effective."

However, the road to city hall is lined with obstacles. Many observers would disagree with the above, not only about New York, but also all other cities and regions where the development stakes are high. Planning choices may be fought over, but only when those who are not in the inner circle learn about them in time to intervene and put forth whatever resources it takes to be heard. The number of such choices that a major city or county makes in one year is enormous, and the system would grind to a halt if each one were subject to sustained conflict. Serious participation has as a prerequisite some level of knowledge of the issue—not only of its substance but also of how it is to be handled. Developers and financiers specialize in order to concentrate their resources, and other stakeholder groups have learned that they must also. As a result, a shopping center approval or road relocation choice may take place very quietly, because the stakeholders' attention happens to be elsewhere. In such circumstances, insiders have a strong incentive to withhold information that others need. Further discussion of this issue follows in chapter 8.

At this point, the foundation is laid for examination of the planning process itself. The planning profession, the realities of local politics, and the language of state law combine to channel this stream of decisions between high banks. Yet, the stream is wide enough, with islands and eddies, to allow some unpredictability in its flow. The next chapter surveys the typical courses it can follow.

QUESTIONS FOR DISCUSSION

1. What biases exist in the participation network due to the uneven distribution of power resources and incentives to participate? Who is most and least favored?
2. To what extent do the interests of the profit-making participants differ from those of the nonprofit and citizen participants? To what extent do they coincide? On what issues?

3. What are the major hindrances to citizen participation in planning? What groups of citizens are most disadvantaged by these?
4. How feasible is a formal system of neighborhood representation in public decisions? What are the advantages and weaknesses?
5. What are the relative advantages and disadvantages in the *direct political action* and the *community economic development* strategies of neighborhood organizations?
6. How well are the representatives of government able to balance the special interests of the other participants? To what extent does government bring its own special interests into the decisions?

5 | HOW PLANNING IS DONE

5.1 FROM POLITICS TO PLANNING

The numerous participants who appeared in the two preceding chapters hold great potential for political conflicts. But how can a democratic community which cannot satisfy all interests plan its future without being deadlocked by them? Clearly, planning requires close cooperation by many of its participants, and certain procedures are essential to structure it.

When a planning decision has many participants, its journey from conception to approval and implementation is apt to be complex and lengthy. (See section 8.4 for further exploration of this point.) Further, a project that is finally "on the ground" rarely looks just like it was originally designed to be. Politics, understood particularly as the struggle for power, injects into planning a high degree of uncertainty both as to its outcome and the paths it follows. Even though the results may be largely as conceived at the beginning, as in Detroit's accommodation of General Motors, the track on which the case progresses is not as straight as the initiators hope. Much more often, the intricacy and unpredictability of decisions and events frustrate the original design, as the New Jersey suburbs have done with their state Supreme Court's dictum for expanding housing opportunities.

How well planners (those working for government and for private developers and consultants) operate within the political realities varies with the style of planning that they adopt. Five major planning traditions have contended for dominance on the American scene: synoptic, incremental, transactive, advocacy, and radical [Hudson 1979]. The *synoptic* tradition developed early in the profession's history and still appears to dominate much of it. It stresses a rational approach to urban futures, with decisions made after setting of objectives, identification of alternatives, evaluation of each alternative by means of sophisticated analytical tools, and selection of those alternatives shown to be most efficient for attaining the goals. It is also comprehensive in its approach, taking in the broad range of needs of the community for perhaps 10 to 20 years to come and integrating each choice into a holistic design. This tradition is least compatible with politics as defined here, for in its advocates' view, the pressures and bargains of elected officials and interest groups distort the rational choice process if not bypass it entirely.

The *incremental* and *transactive* traditions, while not identical, are alike in that they come to terms with the political realities. They recognize the difficulties of planning for complex communities far into the future, and so are open to continual adjustment as new information and conditions appear. In doing so, there is continual bargaining among influential persons who not only have conflicting demands but also define the problems and goals differently. While those who plan within these traditions risk losing sight of long-term ends, they may also revise their goals in response to a volatile environment. The transactive tradition is particularly sensitive to demands from an array of citizen groups.

Advocacy and *radical* traditions take politics seriously, but do not automatically endorse whatever plan may emerge from the process. Advocacy planners take the interests of the disadvantaged groups in society as their own, and intervene in planning to advance them. In essence, they exert political pressures on behalf of plans that benefit their chosen clients. Radical planners may or may not be advocates for the poor, but they offer a dramatically different vision of what the city ought to be as an alternative to what currently prevails. Le Corbusier and Howard (see section 2.6), each in his own way, represent this approach. They believe "politics" is dominated usually by contemporary business and citizen groups who are a hindrance to achieving their goals. Radical planners thus seek a different style of politics that would support their efforts.

Although professional planners may prefer the synoptic tradition, most of the other participants appear to practice the incremental/transactive style, and their preference typically dominates. As a New Jersey judge wrote in a 1948 land use decision, municipal planning is "the accommodation, through unity in construction, of the variant interests seeking expresion in the local physical life to the interest of the community as a social unit." [Cited by Haar 1977, 64] Of the "variant interests," we have seen much. To achieve "unity in construction," by which he means coherent planning choices that can be put into effect, is the challenge to the process which this chapter outlines.

Recall the three-point planning cycle outlined in chapter 1. The stages were: goal setting, choice making, and implementation, with a feedback path returning to the first point. Although this explicit sequence is rarely followed, logic dictates that some choice of goals (even though implicit) must inform specific choices, and nothing can happen if the action stage is omitted. A planning process in which each happens publicly and thoughtfully has the best chance of being both democratic and effective.

The processes on which this chapter focuses are generally those for making *comprehensive* plans. They call for a grasp of "big pictures" that incorporate the separate efforts of planners in housing, transportation, and other specialized fields, as well as the efforts to zone land and redevelop land currently in use. Those specialized areas of planning are the focus of chapter 6. This discussion concentrates on the local, rather than the state or national, processes since they supply what comprehensiveness and coherence the plans come to have.

5.2   THE GOAL-SETTING STAGE

Just what is a planning goal? It is different from the values discussed in chapter 2, but is based on them. Simply put, a goal stands midway in specificity between a general value and a particular choice. For example, a city may value highly a beautiful environment with trees, bodies of water, and public open space. A goal that is consistent with this value might be to increase the land area devoted to such uses by ten percent in the following five years. Then, a choice to accomplish that goal would be to purchase Smith's Woods on the edge of town for a park. A goal often indicates the direction and magnitude of change that is desired, but does not give the details of where and how that change takes place.

In many communities, goals are not sharply distinguished from values, though they can be inferred from them. They may rest in the expectations that the public has of its local government—what policies it should pursue, including those on land use. Williams' comparative study [1963] of four Michigan cities produced a typology in which these expectations differed significantly. One contrast appeared between the city that was expected to promote economic growth, and that in which residents demanded protection and enhancement of the residential environment. Whether these were stated in law was less important than the fact that an understood goal for the former was to recruit new businesses and industries whenever possible and maintain the health of the central office and shopping district. The latter would orient its land use planning toward keeping incompatible activities away from residential areas.

The very nature of the city or county's existing land uses, availability of open space, and social and economic status tend to prescribe goals. Affluent suburbs, whose residents draw their income from a nearby city, need only aim to preserve the status quo. But distressed Detroit faces much necessary rebuilding of its economic and physical resources. Where a city has extensive open land within its limits, as in San Diego, more options are available to it than to San Francisco, which can only alter existing developed land.

The larger and more diverse the city or metropolitan area, the more goals have to be set and pursued to satisfy its many constituencies. Chicago's Comprehensive Plan of 1966 set six general "strategic objectives": a healthy environment for family life, expanded opportunities for the disadvantaged, economic development and expanded job opportunities, high levels of accessibility in moving people and goods, the proper allocation of land for all necessary uses, and unified public-private efforts in city development [City of Chicago Department of Development and Planning 1966]. These goals or objectives provide a transition from the functional, moral, and social planning values to the choices that are ultimately printed on a zoning map or poured on the ground in concrete.

For the goals to be usable, they need to be given more definition than those vague statements. For example, the Plan of Chicago further developed its goals for residential quality by stating, "The supply of public housing for low-income families and the elderly would continue to be expanded through purchase and rehabilitation of existing structures, leasing units in private buildings, and construction on scattered sites" [City of Chicago Department of Development and Planning 1966, 35]. The more specific the goals (without naming actual sites or acquisition projects), the easier it becomes to evaluate the progress made toward them. In fact, the Chicago Housing Authority, which was charged to carry out that residential goal, fell far short of it, in the judgment of the plaintiffs in *Gautreaux v. Chicago Housing Authority* (1969), and their aggressive attorney, Alex Polikoff [Babcock & Siemon 1985, ch. 9]. Little was controversial about the goal itself; it was rooted in accepted concepts of justice and current interpretations of the federal and state constitutions. Yet, it touched sensitive nerves, because everyone knew that existing residents would oppose attempts to place such dwellings in most vacant sites around the city.

In many cases, a community planning process must go beyond the general popular goals and set objectives that can directly guide specific choices. In a changing housing market, for example, it is of little help to set "maintain and enhance residential quality" as a planning goal. The participants should ask: "residences for whom? what kind, single- or multi-family? at what price levels?" A community with 95 percent of its housing stock in single-family homes must consider whether to allow duplexes, town houses, and rental units to extend "residential quality" to those who cannot afford or do not need a $100,000 home on a half-acre lot.

The customary means for integrating all of these goals is the *comprehensive plan.* Such plans are normally adopted at a single point in time, with the intention to control future development. However, they need to be continually updated by a comprehensive planning process that responds to new conditions and opportunities as they arise, and by a political process that can implement the plans with specific ordinances, capital investments, and other actions. Table 5.1 is a sample table of contents, displaying the typical elements of such a plan: community goals, the current situation, forecasts of the future, detailed program components, and the means of its implementation.

This plan is ordinarily given tangible form in a map. Figure 5.2 is a simple, comprehensive guide plan map for a hypothetical city. Notice that it includes general anticipated land uses, future highways, and areas of special concern such as flood plains. It differs

---

TABLE 5.1

SAMPLE TABLE OF CONTENTS OF TYPICAL MUNICIPAL COMPREHENSIVE PLAN

I   Planning goals and objectives: statements on the nature and characteristics of the community that are sought.

II. Analysis and forecasts of community conditions; data and general statements on:
   A. Land uses and condition of structures, particularly in areas subject to change.
   B. Economic base: employment, trade, land values, tax base, revenue sources.
   C. Demography: social characteristics, growth/decline rate, population distribution, social needs.
   D. Physical environment and natural resources: topography, hydrology, vegetation, soils, minerals.
   E. Circulation systems: streets and highways, traffic levels, mass transit, airports, rail service, water transportation.
   F. Infrastructures: water and sewage facilities, parks, schools, public safety, energy supply.

III. Elements of the plan
   A. General land use: location and density of each type.
   B. Housing preservation and renewal.
   C. Transportation facilities and services.
   D. Public utilities and sanitation.
   E. Environmental protection and pollution control.
   F. Economic development.
   G. Social services (including education, health, and provision for special needs).
   H. Parks and recreation.
   I. Aesthetics and historic preservation.
   J. Special plans for subareas and neighborhoods embodying any or all of above in greater detail.

IV. Means of plan implementation
   A. Zoning and development ordinances.
   B. Official map indicating planned land uses and zones.
   C. Incentives and programs for securing the desired development and cooperation of private sector.
   D. Capital programs for public investment.
   E. Cooperation with other units of government—federal, state, county, school and special district.
   F. Political processes and institutions for plan adoption, review, and revision, including public information programs and means of citizen participation.

---

from the official zoning map (to be discussed in section 5.4) in that it has less regulatory detail and tends to be forward looking in its estimates of land requirements. Such maps are also prepared for smaller parts of a city, such as a downtown or a rehabilitation project area. If these are carefully done, they can in fact serve as guides to maintain consistency in the more detailed choices.

FIGURE 5.2: Sketch Plan—Future Land Use

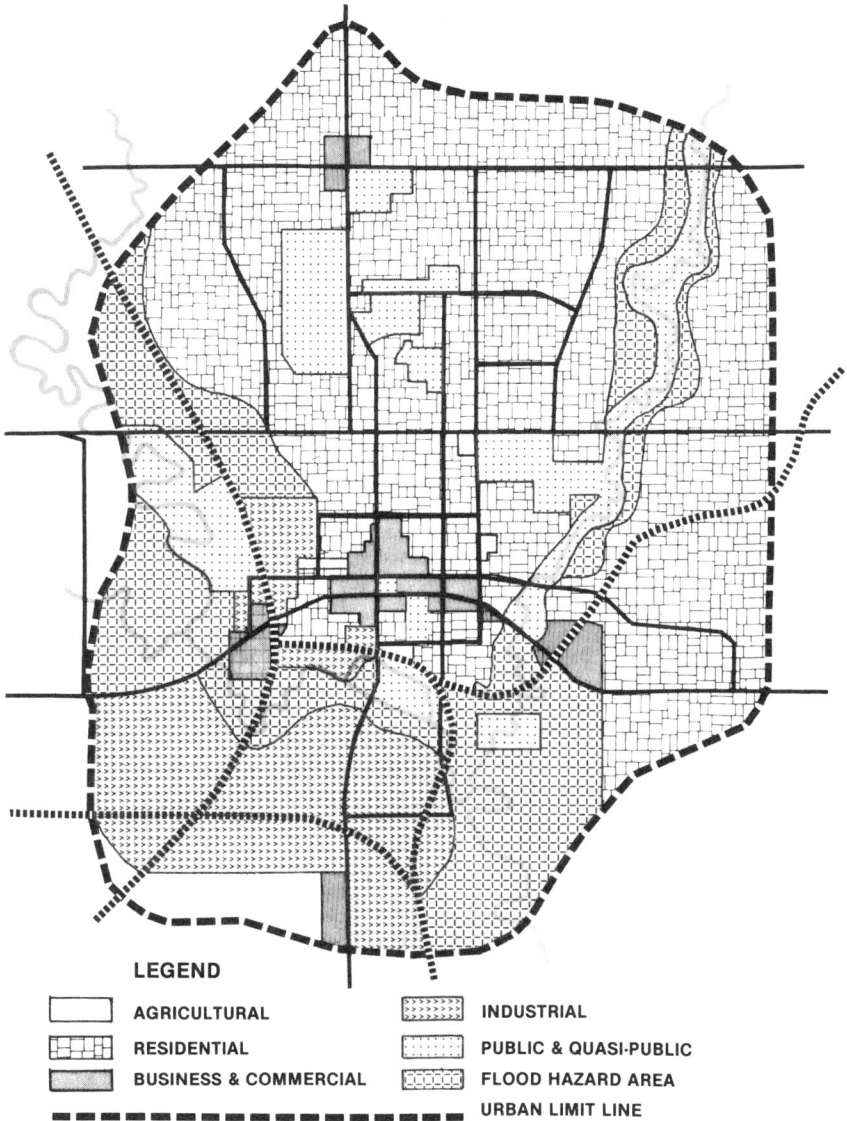

LEGEND

☐ AGRICULTURAL   ▦ INDUSTRIAL

▦ RESIDENTIAL   ▦ PUBLIC & QUASI-PUBLIC

▦ BUSINESS & COMMERCIAL   ▦ FLOOD HAZARD AREA

▬ ▬ ▬ URBAN LIMIT LINE

Several procedures can be used to examine and evaluate planning goals. Many planning departments conduct regular research on the city, county, or region, and others hire private firms or academic specialists to collect data. Without accurate and comprehensive information, planning may be based on myths and misimpressions. A minimum planning data base includes: (a) demographic information on current population, (b) a detailed map of its current land uses, (c) an inventory of the use and condition of all structures, (d) transportation data such as traffic counts, trip origins and destinations, and mass transit use, (e) characteristics of the natural environment, (f) economic data such as income, employment, retail sales, and property values, and (g) the extent and quality of such public services and facilities as waste management, drainage, parks, schools, streets, and care for those with special needs. It should be sensitive to nontraditional information needs, perhaps the demand for and supply of child day-care services, agricultural production, or the location of such hazards as toxic materials producers and gasoline pipelines.

Armed with such information, planners can consider adding or altering goals. For example, Shoreview, Minnesota, in which the author serves as planning commissioner, learned from the research necessary for a revised guide plan that it had within its limits fewer jobs per capita than most of the surrounding cities. This led to a conscious choice to increase the portion of its open land designated for employment-producing uses.

The research should also identify trends and reasons for them. Clear national and regional changes in the economy and personal life-styles can be forecast with reasonable confidence. Where confidence levels are lower, as with forecasts of energy costs, one can still identify a range of possibilities for preparing contingency plans. Efforts to increase employment opportunities should be sensitive to what types of occupations are expanding. High-technology and service enterprises are growing everywhere, but planners must know what their land and support requirements are and be prepared to meet them. In this effort, governmental planners are handicapped in that firms do not release information freely about their needs and intentions [R. Warren & Rosentraub 1986, 46–47].

Data also show that the average age of the population in most communities is increasing and household sizes declining. Planning goals must thus incorporate the facilities and services needed by single parents, persons living alone, and the active and invalid elderly. These trends are further highlighted in section 9.2.

One common method of research is the resident survey. Designed to give citizens a sense of participation in the planning process as well as to elicit their views, surveys can be useful if properly designed and administered. Such a survey was a major factor in the adoption of a growth-pacing program in Petaluma, California. Once the political process had declared growth pressure a serious issue, the city sent out more than 10,000 questionnaires in an effort to define the acceptable limits of expansion. The 24 percent of the residents who responded strongly favored stringent controls, and the city then proceeded to design the implementing measures [Rosenbaum 1978].

On the other hand, a survey that is very broad and general is likely to be of little value. The city of Los Angeles sent out half a million questionnaires in the late 1960s to learn citizens' preferences for the shape of its future growth and for improvements they would like to see. The response was respectable, and a summary report was published in 1969 that integrated parts of all the alternative concepts listed in the survey. But from the view of many observers, it made no long-term difference in that city's built environment. Perhaps the survey could have been better designed to elicit more useful perceptions. But the very size and diversity of Los Angeles can frustrate even the best efforts to learn citizen preferences. Survey designers must guard against bias in responses. Generally, those who have little education, low income, and marginal literacy respond at a very low rate to mailed questionnaires. Their preferences have to be obtained in person, if at all.

Comprehensive goal setting has other difficulties, as necessary as it is. Many citizens and active politicians oppose such planning on principle, believing that it confers too much power on government in general and on nonresponsible planners and other bureaucrats in particular. To them, a truly democratic process is sensitive to public wishes as expressed over the short range and does not commit the authorities to long-range programs which the average person does not understand. Many communities have such a pluralistic or fragmented decision making process that participants cannot make long-term commitments, and would not if they could. For them the future is too unpredictable to foreclose any options [Rider 1982].

Of equal seriousness is the problem of securing widespread popular participation in the goal-setting process. Altshuler [1965, 306–309] found in his case studies in Minneapolis and Saint Paul that the public showed no serious interest in land use goal statements. They were too general to attract any controversy or to indicate to potentially concerned citizens what was to happen on a specific site. The only persons in the private sector with whom the planners could carry on any dialogue were a few individuals in business or civic organizations who were unable to commit their groups to support in any case.

Altshuler [1965, 321] also found that elected officials are reluctant to support goal statements that have not been tested in the laboratories of political debate.

> American politicians typically depend on public discussion to inform them of the interests and values affected by any proposal. If planners cannot spur adequate discussion of their goal statements, politicians cannot, and know they cannot, make informed choices among them. . . . Very few proposals emerge as law from American legislative processes until and unless the vast majority of articulate groups interested in them favors some version of them.

This is why many goal statements are so general. It also explains why, when a city's planning goals do in fact undergo change, as from a single- to multi-family housing emphasis, it happens piecemeal, through decisions on specific parcels and projects, rather than at a single headline-attracting council session. Thus, no clear line separates this stage of the cycle from the next, for a series of small zoning changes may register a *de facto* goal change that is formally recognized in a plan only years afterward when it is politically less difficult.

5.3 MAKING THE SPECIFIC CHOICES

The choice to do a particular thing—to initiate a neighborhood redevelopment project, to construct a highway, or approve a developer's proposal for a high-rise condominium—is what links goals and values with what actually appears on the ground. To refer back to Chicago's housing goal statements above, one has to move from the intent to construct dwellings for low-income persons on scattered sites to the selection of those sites and the types of homes to be built there. This in turn calls for determining that their surroundings also serve that use, such as the proximity of schools and play areas to family housing.

Major planning decisions can require a complex arrangement of interdependent choices, particularly those in Types 3 and 4. In Type 3 were those choices by governments to build their own facilities, such as highways, office buildings, parks, and transit systems. Type 4 referred to joint public-private enterprises with a government agency sharing the role of developer with one or more corporations. Certain kinds of detailed decisions occur over and over in each category:

(1) Design of the overall project—what each part and the whole are to look like and how the parts relate to one another.

(2) Selection of public facilities, whether they are the centerpiece of the project or are accessories to it (e.g., sewers that serve a major shopping mall).

(3) Approval of structures and facilities (such as a hotel, factory, or apartment building) that are to be privately owned, for which government may act as a regulator or financier.

(4) Means of access to the project for persons and goods and storage of vehicles.

(5) Fit of the project to its physical environment: its impact on air and water quality, noise, visual beauty, and protection of sensitive ecosystems.

(6) Management of the project's social impacts—its relationship to crime, personal health, employment and housing opportunities and similar concerns.

The genesis of the Bay Area Rapid Transit system, surveyed in chapter 1, illustrates well Type 3 planning choices. A long design process, necessary to provide the voters with an initial information base, led up to the 1962 referendum on the construction bonds. Afterward, BART planners had to select the specific routes, stations, and equipment, and make all of the technical choices related to construction. At the same time, planners and public officials for each city through which the lines passed work to "fit" them into their land use and traffic patterns. Each station was a potential site for commercial and office development, which affected zoning of the area.

Conflict during the planning was rather muted, and the transit professionals had much leeway to make those choices themselves. But hindsight suggests that some additional questions should have been asked, perhaps challenging the ridership estimates (which proved to be unrealistically high), and the choice of fixed-rail technology. Indeed, the latter was the point of a lawsuit, which charged that it was obsolete and the planners had refused to consider more modern ones. However, all such qualms were drowned in the tide of popular approval of what appeared to be an essential investment [Whitt 1982, ch. 2; P. Hall 1980, ch. 5].

More intense conflict has surrounded a major Type 4 planning endeavor: to rebuild New York City's Times Square and its sleazy Forty-second Street environs. Clearly, its renewal could not be accomplished solely by the city or state. For three decades, city planners and private developers have drawn up ambitious programs to transform, what is from their perspective, an underdeveloped area of Manhattan. The most recent design, announced in 1980 by Mayor Koch and the president of New York State's Urban Development Corporation, would place on the corners of the square four office buildings, a major hotel, and a wholesale merchandise mart. The next step was to choose the developers of each portion, who in turn would produce the detailed designs. Several entrepreneurs competed for the opportunity, including the biggest of them all, Texas-based Trammel Crow.

By 1984, repeated deadlocks over what was to be built at Times Square and who was to build them were tentatively ironed out by the mayor and the developers' agents. Some legal challenges concerning land condemnation and the fate of low-income residents to be displaced by the rebuilding were settled in 1986, but more were pending. Debate continued over how much of the increased land acquisition cost was to be charged to the developers. Construction was delayed at least until late 1988, but reduced demand for office space and doubts on the part of key investors and tenants left some uncertainty at that time. The pieces of this complex project are so interdependent that a weakness at one point can affect all others [Gottlieb 1984; Meislin 1987].

Very few planning endeavors are as intricate as Times Square, with its 13 intensely used acres and its enormous potential for financial profits for some and political glory for others. The governmental choice makers were many: New York City's planning commission, city council, and mayor; the state Urban Development Corporation, which has major financial involvement and thus power over design choices; and the Times Square Development Corporation, which makes the day-to-day decisions on the project and has three representatives of the state and two from the city. Although several developers sought to take part in it, they also sought the best financial arrangements for themselves, and knew how to bargain tenaciously for them. No one was in a position to dictate any outcome, and there is no assurance that any future bargain will be carried out just as intended [Gottlieb 1984].

Type 5 comprehensive planning choices are ideally made in advance of any specific development proposals. But often, the reverse is true and the planning choices must react to the likelihood of major changes. The residents of Sanibel Island, Florida found this to be true in the mid-1970s. That island off the state's west coast first experienced urban development in the late 1960s. Since it was unincorporated, the Lee County Commission controlled its land use, but tolerantly allowed almost anything a developer wanted to build. The island's residents, alarmed at the prospect of as many as 35,000 new homes, as permitted by the county's zoning, began to seek a comprehensive plan that restricted growth to a much lower ceiling [Babcock & Siemon 1985, ch. 6].

Only incorporation as a city would provide the kind of control that the Sanibelites wanted, and in November, 1974, a referendum approved that action. The new city council immediately ordered work to begin on a comprehensive plan. The goal was clear: to limit growth to a level which would preserve the island's fragile beaches and woodlands and prevent the excessive urbanization from which many had fled. A specific growth limit had to be chosen, and after analysis of several alternatives, the planning commission reduced to 6,000 the number of housing units to be allowed in the area for which the county had previously permitted 35,000. The plan, adopted by the city in July, 1976, divided the island into several eco-zones and designated the uses and maximum densities of each according to its development tolerance and accessibility. The eastern end, which was already partially built up, was permitted more intense development than the western portion. The current availability of public services was also a factor in these choices [Babcock & Siemon 1985, ch. 6].

Although most residents supported the plan choices, some who owned land and expected to profit from its development protested. While work was still proceeding on the plan, they filed several lawsuits, charging that the density reduction violated their vested rights to use their land as they saw fit, especially since the county had previously been very permissive. Court rulings ultimately upheld the city on this point. Other disputes centered on the density of permitted commercial (as opposed to residential) development and its impact on traffic congestion. On that point, the city had to compromise with certain developers [Babcock & Siemon 1985, ch. 6].

In Sanibel's case, there were relatively few governmental decision makers, and they were generally agreed on the goals and methods. Yet they had to make specific choices on how much growth to permit, where it should take place, and how rapidly. Such "more or less" choices are at least as difficult to deal with as the "yes or no" choices, and call for criteria that give a rationale for "how much less" that can be defended in court if necessary. Sanibel has one unique situation that helped set such criteria: it is connected to the mainland by one causeway with a limited vehicle capacity. The planners sought to permit no more residents than could be evacuated over that causeway in the 12 hours following a hurricane warning. But other judgments, as on the development capacity of beachfront lands, were more subjective [Babcock & Siemon 1985, ch. 6].

The cases of BART, Times Square, and Sanibel Island illustrate several political facts of life in the move from goals to workable choices. First, those who make the specific choices may face different circumstances or constraints than the ones (possibly the same individuals) who set the goals. The demand for office space in midtown Manhattan could well be different in 1990 than it was 10 or 20 years earlier when the redevelopment aims were taking shape. The publicists for BART sought to build support with the promise that it would serve transit-disadvantaged persons. However, the problems of locating routes that would yield sufficient revenue dictated a priority of serving the suburban riders (which was, admittedly, another goal).

When the choice making requires voluntary cooperation of independent governments or private participants, the bargaining necessary to secure it can lead to unforeseen choices. San Mateo County was to have had a major segment of the BART system, feeding into San Francisco from the south and from the city's international airport. But the network was truncated from the start due to that county's withdrawal. Numerous delays in the Times Square project resulted from disputes with development teams, as builders and investors weighed with caution the enormous financial commitments they would have to make.

It was also difficult to perceive just what choices were optimal to achieving the stated goals. Sanibel had to justify the levels of density it selected to protect its delicate ecosystem of mangroves, waterfowl, and freshwater wetlands, both to environmentalists and developers, not to mention judges with little expertise in ecology. Whether BART was to build a traditional fixed-rail system (as it did) or risk a more innovative monorail or other form of technology was not, apparently, disputed by its planners but was the subject of later debate.

Finally, planning choices are pressured by the legal system. Sanibel defended its plan well in the courts, and needed to make only small modifications. The Times Square redevelopment program had also, by late 1986, survived legal challenges, but a new suit was filed in 1987. A judge, following precedents or setting new ones, can require sweeping changes in a plan. If not reversed upon appeal to higher courts, those changes must be made if the project is to proceed. Those decisions become part of case law, and future developers and planners pay close attention to them as indicators of how a judge would rule in litigation over their projects.

These cases also illustrate three general methods of decision making. First, there is the choice by *fiat:* a relatively unopposed proceeding by governmental leaders or specialists (who may include some in the private sector). They can operate away from public scrutiny, with participation limited to their own circle and the goals they have set. The design of the BART system, once voter approval was given, illustrates this.

Second, choices can be made by *elite negotiation:* private bargaining among a select circle who can deny entry to anyone else. There may be conflict among the parties, and bargains may be hard to strike, but they keep the scope of conflict limited and predictable. The General Motors executives and Detroit officials bargained quietly over the Poletown site, and by the time the residents became aware of the outcome, it was irreversible. Planning for renewal of Times Square began in this manner, although the elites could not reach agreement readily.

Finally, choices emerge from *open negotiation,* a less predictable and potentially chaotic process in which no party clearly dominates and the contestants can change. Such resources as votes, campaign contributions, community organizing and media campaigns can frustrate elite ambitions and cause plans to take a very different shape from those envisioned in the goal statements. Referendums offer one forum for open negotiation, in which the voters may veto a council action, as in San Diego. Where open-membership neighborhood groups are active, as in the South Bronx, there is also potential for this. The maneuvering in Sanibel over the county plans, at first, and then over incorporation and the subsequent city plan, was less formalized, and open to public input at each point. The developers and landowners may have preferred an elite negotiation procedure, but the political climate in that growth-sensitive community prevented secret deals. Where a city desires an open negotiation process, it may have to take the initiative to set it up. This can take the form of public planners meeting with residents of a neighborhood to be affected by a choice. Rohe and Gates [1985] reported, in a study of six cities that had programs to do this on a continuing basis, that such a planning method appeared to be more responsive to local values and resulted in more local improvements, an increase in popular participation, and a more supportive constituency for the plans, than a "conventional" process would have produced.

In other situations, developers are called upon to negotiate directly with citizens in an impacted area (with the city predisposed to ratify a joint agreement), or negotiation may involve all three parties at once. Every developmental and regulatory standard can be open to negotiation and there are regular procedures for its conduct [Rivkin 1986]. The purpose is to settle potential disputes at an early stage or to avoid an oncoming deadlock or lawsuit.

Where an agreement is reached, the political benefits in public support for its implementation are invaluable. Long Beach, California, went through a cooperative process in the late 1970s in planning for its last undeveloped area, which was located in its southeast section. The negotiations involved a network of citizen organizations and the Bixby Ranch Company, the largest landowner in that neighborhood. The resulting plan was widely accepted and met the standards of the California Coastal Commission for shoreline protection [Wrenn & Case 1984]. Those who guide this process must take care that it is inclusive enough to give voice to all who will be affected by it.

5.4 IMPLEMENTING THE GOALS AND CHOICES

The culminating stage in the planning cycle brings the previous two to fruition (or it may fail to). Because many urban plans over the years have not shaped the built environment in the intended manner, those who plan have to pay close attention to the legal and design tools by which land use can actually be controlled and guided.

The oldest of these tools is *zoning,* the origins of which were discussed in section 2.6. Legally, it is rooted in the traditional police power of local government to protect the public health, welfare, and safety. Over the years, however, zoning has been elaborated into a multipurpose device to achieve various social, economic, esthetic, and environmental purposes.

The typical zoning policy consists of a *zoning ordinance* and an *official map.* The ordinance defines the land use zones that shall exist—typically residential, commercial, and industrial. But more zones may be created by a community for special purposes, such as agriculture, open space, parks, and public facilities. The ordinance further subdivides the zones: R-1 for single-family residences, R-2 for two-household homes, and R-3 for multifamily dwellings, for example. A large city may have many residential subzones alone to provide for buildings of different sizes, heights, and densities.

Further, the zoning ordinance states the permitted uses in each zone. A business zone (B-1, for example) located next to a residential area may be limited to convenience grocery stores and similar enterprises that serve a small area. Another business zone (perhaps B-2) would permit a moderate-sized shopping center with supermarkets, banks, and the like. Other zones are designed for large regional shopping malls or specialized business areas, such as those along highways that have service stations, motels, and restaurants. Businesses that are regarded as nuisances, such as adult entertainment centers and scrap yards, may be further segregated into unique zones. It is common to allow particular establishments, those serving liquor for example, to exist in several zones, but only by *special use permit,* provided by explicit permission and often with limiting conditions attached, such as hours of operation.

These zones may be *cumulative* or *exclusive* relative to one another. If cumulative, all of the uses permitted in a "lower" or more restrictive zone are also allowed in a "higher" one. That is, single-

FIGURE 5.3: Zoning Map, Saint Paul

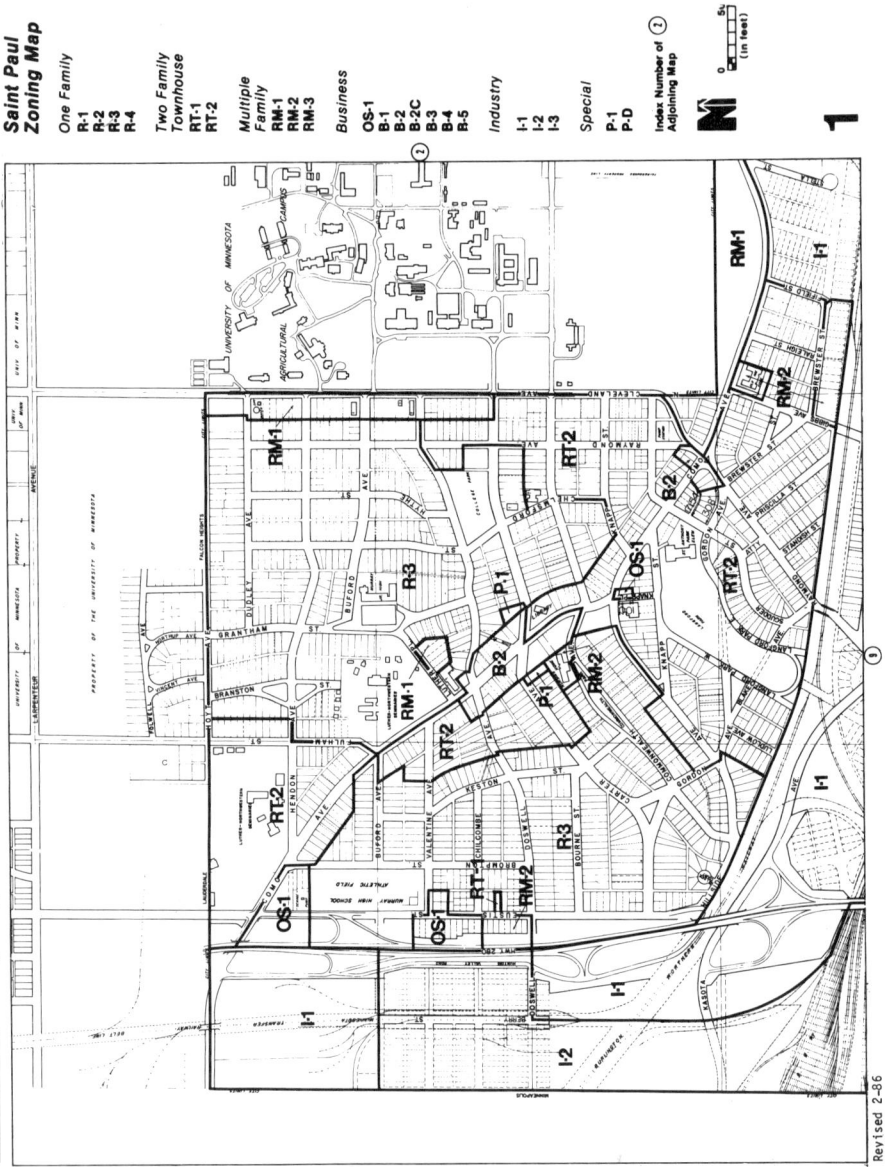

Saint Paul
Zoning Map

One Family
R-1
R-2
R-3
R-4

Two Family
Townhouse
RT-1
RT-2

Multiple
Family
RM-1
RM-2
RM-3

Business
OS-1
B-1
B-2
B-2C
B-3
B-4
B-5

Industry
I-1
I-2
I-3

Special
P-1
P-D

Index Number of
Adjoining Map

Revised 2-86

FIGURE 5.4: Zoning Map, Saint Paul

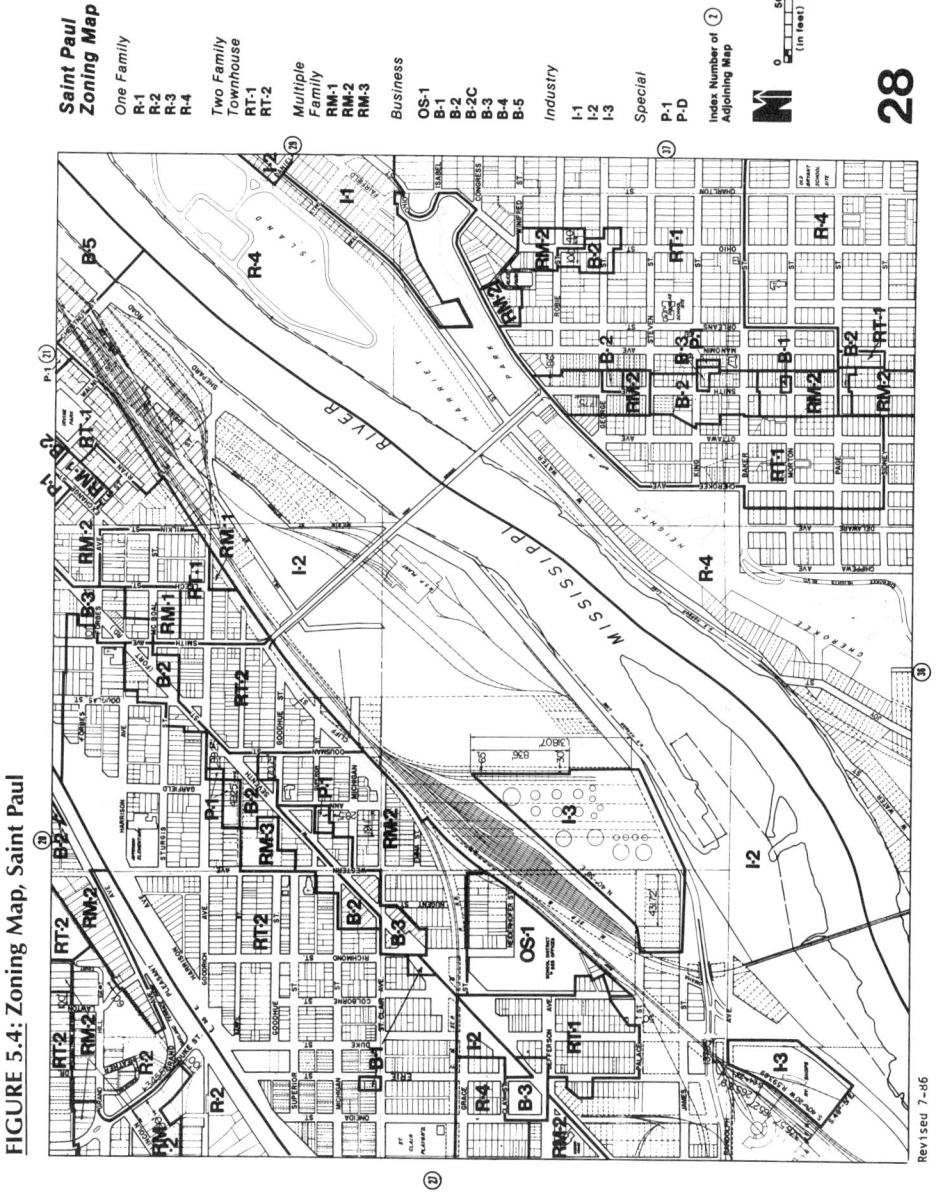

Saint Paul
Zoning Map

One Family
R-1
R-2
R-3
R-4

Two Family
Townhouse
RT-1
RT-2

Multiple
Family
RM-1
RM-2
RM-3

Business
OS-1
B-1
B-2
B-2C
B-3
B-4
B-5

Industry
I-1
I-2
I-3

Special
P-1
P-D

Index Number of
Adjoining Map

0   500
(in feet)

28

Revised 7-86

family homes would be permitted in a multifamily residential zone, although the reverse is not. But if the zones are exclusive, only those uses specified for the zone are permitted. The latter obviously achieves greater separation of land uses.

The *official map* portrays the city or county with each parcel of land designated in a zone. It must be precise enough to leave no doubt as to how the ordinance will apply. This is illustrated in parts of Saint Paul's zoning map in Figures 5.3 and 5.4. The first portrays one of its more attractive residential areas, surrounded by industrial areas and the University of Minnesota. The zones represent efforts to preserve residential quality and local-service businesses while providing dwellings for a variety of income groups. Figure 5.4 covers two parts of the city bisected by the Mississippi River, a major industrial and recreational corridor. Most of the residences are old, yet some neighborhoods are well maintained, and the challenge is to prevent blight from spreading from the business- and industry-concentration areas.

The intricate zoning patterns on both maps signal much potential political conflict, as well. Each zoned parcel represents an implementation decision that could have been opposed. Where such diverse land uses exist close to one another, the likelihood of conflict is further heightened. The neighborhoods on the maps are organized in the Saint Paul district system described in section 4.4, and have active councils that pay close attention to zoning issues. While only the city council has power to rezone, the councils' recommendations and pressures carry weight with the legislators, who are elected from wards, rather than the city at large.

The actual effects of zoning vary with the type of community. When older cities first adopted land use restrictions, planners had to accept what was already there, and they had a real effect only when a change in use was proposed. For example, if a neighborhood were zoned as residential but had an old factory in its midst, that factory would be designated as a nonconforming use. In that status, it could continue to exist, but if it were destroyed by fire, it could not be rebuilt, and nothing but a residence could replace it. Existing dwellings are thereby protected, and the ordinance may provide an incentive to owners to keep them in good repair and rehabilitate those which have deteriorated.

Expanding communities have the greatest need for controls. But they may also find it hardest to foresee their need for the various categories of uses, and this opens the door to political controversies.

At a certain time, it may seem most reasonable to designate a parcel of land near a freeway for multifamily dwellings. But if a large shopping center is subsequently located nearby, that parcel may become more valuable if also developed for commercial uses. If, in the meantime, other residences were built adjacent to that parcel on the assumption that it would be residential, a change to commercial zoning would be disruptive to them. Those who value the freedom of landowners and developers to adapt quickly to market changes and their own entrepreneurial impulses tend to oppose rigid controls (unless zoning protects an investment they have already made).

Zoning is almost universal. Of the larger cities, only Houston lacks it. However, even that city found it necessary in 1982 to impose controls on drainage, parking, and building setbacks from the streets. It does this, though, without specifying land uses in the detail common to zoning ordinances [Reinhold 1984]. In addition, many property deeds there include restrictive covenants which limit the uses to which the owner may put the land, and since they are legally enforceable, they provide some of the controls that zoning does.

Critics of rigorous land use controls argue that zones are too inflexible, for they inscribe into law the preferences of politicians in one time period to bind those living later. And it in fact does this, though its defenders argue that it provides necessary predictability and consistency. Other opponents assert that zoning is a negative way of implementing planning, for it fails to supply the quality of development that a city may seek. It cannot compel a developer to build homes for low-income households, for example. In an economically depressed area, little or no building may take place even though much land is zoned for job-creating uses.

Various policy tools have been devised over the years to add positive guidance to the simple zoning controls. *Subdivision regulations* govern the development of land that will be divided into smaller residential or commercial lots. These controls presume that a large-scale development must be guided by some unifying concepts that ensure the harmony of all of its parts. A typical residential subdivision must meet standards on lot sizes, grading of land, size and location of houses, streets, utilities, and drainage. A proposal must be sufficiently detailed to display all of these features so they can be individually approved. The developer normally bears the costs of all improvements and adds them to the price of the lot.

These subdivision regulations reflect the community's policy choices on how it will reproduce itself. A generally affluent community will require larger (and thus more expensive) lots and homes, and other amenities that will attract new residents who are like the existing ones. A diverse city is likely to select more permissive regulations, with housing opportunities for the less well-to-do. Often, the combination of zoning and subdivision regulations constitute *exclusionary zoning,* a means of denying residential choices to classes of people simply because they cannot afford what is permitted. The Mount Laurel decisions in New Jersey and similar administrative policies in other states were designed to counteract that practice.

Zoning programs can be further refined with special *overlay districts,* additional controls imposed on areas that have unique qualities. Often used in historic neighborhoods, there may be restrictions in signs, lighting, building materials and design that are not required elsewhere in the same zone. It can also be applied to an area with sensitive wetlands interspersed with land more suitable for building so as to restrict development to the latter sites. This method is useful where distinctive policy goals have been set for the given area [Shirvani 1985, 173–74].

A more flexible type of large-area control is the *planned unit development* (PUD). Figure 5.5 portrays a relatively simple design with only four use areas; they are often much more complex. In this concept, a developer proposes a total plan for 10, 100, or more acres which may include several types of housing, shops, offices, and/or public uses. The emphasis is on achieving a harmonious whole that benefits the community, but does not necessarily conform to the detail of every ordinance. For example, there may be, on one part of the site, a higher density residential area than normally permitted, but in return the developer leaves another portion in open space. This tool permits relaxing of some development standards (e.g., one that prohibits mixed land uses) in order to gain a generally more desirable project. Specific decisions are reached through bargaining between the prospective developer and local officials, who have the legal latitude to weigh the unique features of each site and proposal.

Another way to impose controls but avoid the rigidity and excessive detail of traditional zoning classes is *performance zoning.* Rather than specify uses, it sets standards for density, traffic, noise, visual impact, and other environmental effects and allows any use that meets them [Branch 1985, 130–131]. These performance re-

FIGURE 5.5: Planned-unit Development

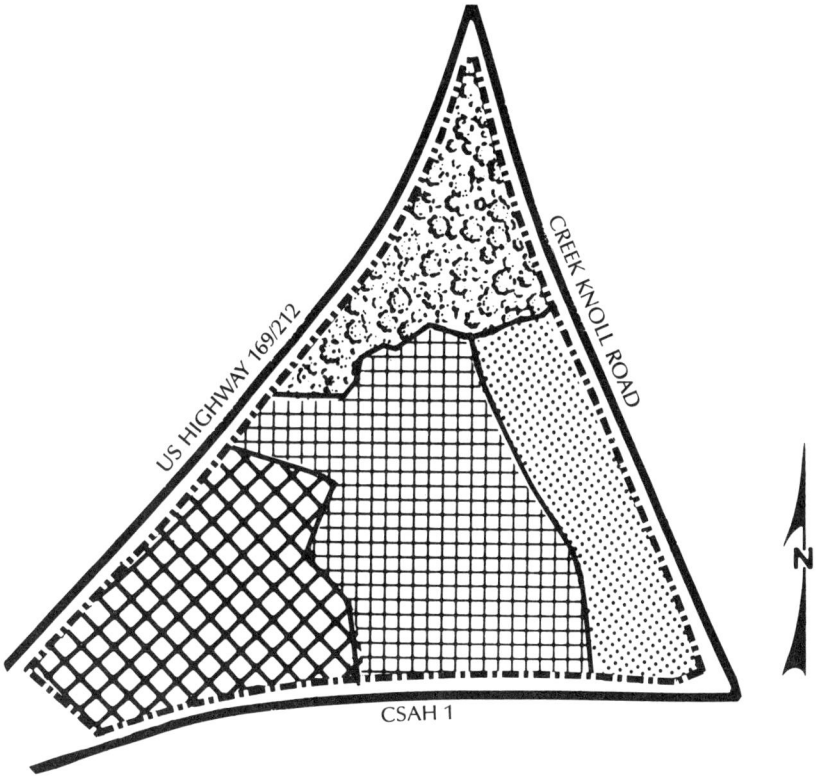

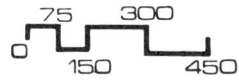

KEY

Single-Family

Park

Office

Industrial

SCALE

75   300

0

150   450

SUMMARY

LAND USE	UNITS	ACRES	DENSITY
Open Space	N/A	3.9	N/A
Residential	26	5.0	5.2 D.U./Acre
Office	60,000 sq. ft.	9.0	N/A
Industrial	60,000 sq. ft.	8.2	N/A

strictions are stricter in residential and environmentally sensitive areas, and more tolerant where industry and high-traffic commercial uses are to locate. It was first instituted in Bucks County, Pennsylvania, in 1973 and has since been adopted by 26 of its 54 local governments. It controls housing development not by lot sizes and setbacks but by limits on density, ground coverage, and open space requirements. Clustering of buildings is encouraged to protect wetlands and minimize utility costs. Its advantages include flexibility to adapt to local conditions and ease of administration [Frank 1982].

Largo, Florida, a city of over 60,000, adopted a performance zoning system in 1983. Instead of a complicated code specifying lot sizes, height limits, and building setbacks, it incorporates such standards as the percentage of the lot which a building may cover. This enabled Largo to replace 20 separate zoning districts with 11 performance-standard areas. Evaluations to date suggest that this method has been especially appropriate for a community that is growing so rapidly that traditional zones would be too confining; yet it still does not adequately address the pressing problems of traffic congestion, flooding, and strip commercial development [Easley 1984].

Incentive zoning offers flexibility of another kind to the local government and developer. It permits the latter to exceed a general zoning standard, such as building size, in exchange for providing a public benefit—perhaps additional open space. The ordinances specify the boundaries to such agreements, but within them there is freedom to bargain. Cities as large as New York and as small as Bellevue, Washington, use this technique. As with planned-unit developments, however, the burden is on local government negotiators to obtain public benefits that are proportional to what the developer obtains [Shirvani 1985, 168–71].

Some communities obtain *public easements* to protect environmentally sensitive areas from adverse development. The southern part of the St. Croix National Wild and Scenic Riverway in Minnesota and Wisconsin borders the Minneapolis-Saint Paul metropolitan area and thus comes under strong urbanization pressures. In order to protect the shorelines and scenic bluffs, the states and local governments have purchased development rights from selected property owners. The easements are the areas so acquired, and permit most residential uses but bar cutting of trees and other specified intrusions on the landscape. To acquire these easements is much less expensive than a complete purchase, but can be as effective as zoning for this purpose.

A final tool that allows flexibility in land use control is the *transfer of development rights*. It permits a landowner who has several properties in the city to build more intensively on one of them—perhaps a taller building than would be allowed in its zone—in exchange for protecting a building of historic importance on another site. It may also be used to delay or prevent development of farmland on the urban fringe [Branch 1985, 127–128]. It permits the same net level of development on all the sites in the agreement, but allows for shifts between sites. As with the planned unit development, careful negotiation is central to the process, and the government representatives must be sensitive to the public interests in order to strike the best bargain possible.

What makes zoning a source of political conflict is its applications to very specific locations. Since it often amounts to saying "no" to a landowner's intentions, politics springs from attempts to change it to a "yes." While the U. S. Supreme Court upheld the basic concept of zoning in 1926, facets of the practice are still being litigated. Decisions of the high court in 1987 held that an owner is due compensation when a land use regulation restricts full use of the property, but left it to the state courts to determine when such a "taking" occurs and how much the payment is to be [*First English Evangelical Lutheran Church v. County of Los Angeles*]. Zoning conflicts provide much work for state judges due to the great variety of situations that could be litigated.

A zoning map is also vulnerable to political pressure because it can be altered at one small point without annulling the plan as a whole. An owner may press to have a quarter-acre site changed from a residential to a commercial zone so he can open a video rental shop in a private home. Such "spot zoning" often takes place on a scale as small as this and a person could make a plausible argument for any one such action. But when a city or county grants many of these, each for a "good reason," it gradually repudiates the plan that was designed to separate residential from commercial uses.

An owner who seeks such a zoning change normally applies first to the city or county planning department if there is one, or directly to the legislative body if in a small community. Many states' laws require a public hearing to be held by the planning commission or city council (or county board), of which owners of adjoining property are notified and notice published in the newspaper. If the change is recommended by the planning commission, the legislative body takes final action; a two-thirds required majority is common. In the cities and counties with a board of zoning appeals, applicants began the process there. One who loses an appeal in these forums may also appeal to the courts. This potentially complex process allows zoning changes to be considered in several different arenas, and perhaps from diverse viewpoints. Both proponents and opponents can be heard more than once, and each opportunity increases the political conflict that may result.

Zoning administration has long been a source of political corruption. All local officials who own land in the city or county have a potential conflict of interest. Family and partisan ties and the flow of campaign contributions can easily bias decisions. Many states and local governments attempt to prevent this with conflict of interest statutes, open meeting requirements and the use of impartial hearing examiners, but creative persons have found many ways to evade them.

Communities that choose to regulate their population growth have adopted special control tools that have spurred vigorous political conflict. Residents of Boca Raton, Florida, an affluent town north of Miami, sought to rein in the explosive growth in multifamily homes by imposing an absolute cap of 40,000 dwelling units. This was adopted in 1972 by a popular vote amending the city's charter. However, two of the largest landowners (and hopeful developers) sued the city, and the state court ruled that the limit violated due process of law and the right to travel from one city to another [Rosenbaum 1978, 47–49].

Efforts to limit the *rate* of growth have met more success. In 1972, the City Council of Petaluma, California, responded to strong resident demands, as expressed in the survey noted earlier in this chapter, and ruled that no more than 500 residential building permits would be issued per year. A Residential Development Evaluation Board allocated those permits to builders on the basis of each application's merit. It has sought to provide a balanced housing stock of single and multiple dwellings for a variety of income levels. That staged growth process was challenged in federal court by the construction industry, and a district judge ruled it an unconstitutional restriction on the right to travel and live where one wishes. But an appeals court reversed his judgment, and a 1976 refusal by the U. S. Supreme Court to hear the case left Petaluma's ordinance intact [Rosenbaum 1978, 50–52].

More comprehensive growth management plans have been adopted by several counties and metropolitan areas. The San Diego plan, at issue in the case in chapter 1, is relatively modest, reserving some areas for later urbanization and requiring new developments to bear the full costs of their public services. Sacramento County, California, adopted a more ambitious program in 1973 to protect prime agricultural land and control the cost of providing urban services to newly built-up areas. Basically, it restricted residential uses to land that already had sewers and roads or could be supplied with them in the near future. This required denial of applications to develop lands that were not contiguous to the existing urbanized area. Over the years, the county has generally maintained the urban service boundary line. However, the inevitable pressures from landowners and developers appear to have eroded public support for key portions of the plan [Johnston et al. 1984].

As population pressures have increased in many metropolitan suburbs and in freestanding communities across the country, rigid growth limitations have not proved feasible, either legally or practically. Efforts in the Austin, Texas, region to apply growth restrictions "have crumbled under the weight of economic growth and pressures for development" [Butler & Myers 1984, 447]. These pressures threaten to overwhelm a city or county's capacity to provide sewers, water, streets, schools, and other necessary services at the rate of the population's growth. That capacity, in turn, is limited by the funds that can be raised from the real estate tax levy, bond issues, and state government aid. Austin's planners and lawmakers found it advantageous to negotiate agreements over specific sites with developers. As a result, building continued with only such restraints as the marketplace imposed, but the city has secured a more orderly process for guiding development [Butler & Myers 1984, 457–458].

A final requirement for the implementation process is communication with the public. This is, of course, necessary at all stages to encourage informed participation. But once choices and implementation strategies have been adopted, affected citizens must be informed so they can make their own plans accordingly. If, for example, a sparsely settled, urban fringe neighborhood is rezoned to permit industrial or commercial uses, its residents must choose the futures they will have there. Presumably they were already notified by means of the public hearings (widely required for rezonings), but they need to understand all of the implications clearly. Some cities and counties use the news media extensively, place planning exhibits in public areas, and call neighborhood meetings to this end. Where resident cooperation is especially crucial, as with area rehabilitation efforts, they need to learn just what is expected of them and what enablements they can receive. Where such communication does not take place, future distrust and political conflict are more likely.

Planners and political leaders must also be skillful in making their case to the public. They must know what information to provide to the news media and how to package it. Catanese [1984, 118] pointed out that the main danger is that complex planning issues can be trivialized or oversimplified by the media, leading to public misunderstanding. If one aspect of a comprehensive plan or development program is headlined to the exclusion of the remainder, any resulting political conflict can be mistargeted.

5.5 EVALUATION AND FEEDBACK: THE CYCLE CLOSED

The history of a planning choice never really comes to an end. A project in a Type 1 or 2 decision on private development may be built and the matter closed, but the experiences with it accumulate and may affect similar choices in the future. A housing development or shopping center that is judged to succeed or fail shapes the planners' frame of mind toward the next application. A major public or public-private effort (Types 3 and 4) may or may not meet expectations, but in neither case will the physical or political environment be the same afterward.

Type 5 choices on comprehensive plans are often hard to evaluate in the short run, since their effects "on the ground" may not be apparent until years later. Yet, to the extent that decisions in the first four types depend on the plan, they collectively stand as evidence for judging it. Many long-range plans for renewal of a downtown area or a deteriorated residential neighborhood have had little effect: some due to lack of diligent implementation and others because the plan itself was unrealistic, too costly, or politically unacceptable. The desperate condition of the South Bronx is a reminder that plans cannot by themselves muster the resources or the political will to succeed.

What criteria can best enable one to evaluate the choices and their implementation? Most center on the twin features of benefits and costs, particularly those which can be defined precisely enough to be quantified. Thus, one can cite improved traffic flows, housing units constructed, and jobs created as benefits and compare them with the dollars and other costs spent to obtain them. When carefully done, they are invaluable to intelligent choice making.

But these calculations and forecasts can mislead, also. Often, sponsors of major redevelopment projects promise a long list of benefits—as many as are necessary to obtain the financing and legal approvals. If there is serious opposition, that list may be inflated. Thus, judgments over benefit-cost ratios become weapons in battles.

Many less tangible factors have to enter the calculations. What benefit is there to preservation of an ocean view, or what cost is imposed on most citizens when it is blocked by a high-rise building that benefits others? It is also necessary to identify *for whom* these are benefits and costs to learn their social and geographic distribution. Ultimately, these are issues of distributive justice which lack precise, agreed-upon standards.

The Bay Area Rapid Transit system has been intensively evaluated by the U.S. Departments of Transportation and Housing and Urban Development, drawing on work of researchers in many fields. Their work illustrates some of the dilemmas one encounters in serious evaluation. A large project of this nature has many effects, more and less favorable, and one must choose which ones to cite as most salient. Different evaluators, who vary in their interests and expectations, can appraise the results differently. Also, the time frame chosen and the amount of experience with the project affects evaluation.

The process of planning the BART system apparently made major errors in assumptions and forecasts. Peter Hall reported that "the decision making process was highly constrained by a perception of what the decision was about, and that this narrowness of vision was shared by businessmen, media people, and voters alike" [P. Hall 1980, 126]. The planning orthodoxy of the 1960s held that fixed-route rapid transit was the only efficient way to relieve congestion, for it had the inherent advantages of lower cost and higher speed to draw commuters out of their cars. The benefits thereby generated would spread widely throughout the region, even to those who never needed to ride it. On this article of faith the BART network was founded, and while on the way to spending $1.6 billion in construction alone, its first segment began service in 1972.

Melvin Webber [1976] summed up the results of the evaluations of the first four years of BART's operation. First, ridership was well below expectations: 131,000 per weekday instead of the 258,000 forecast. Whether the expectations or the performance were more at fault is open to judgment. Second, the system had no noticeable effect on highway congestion, contrary to the promise that it would draw many commuters out of their cars. Third, there was no certainty that BART, in itself, promoted office development in downtown San Francisco and Oakland. That development had occurred, but Webber suggests that it would have done so anyway. A fourth finding was that the system failed to deter suburban sprawl; indeed it may have accelerated it by failing to attract major investors to cluster around its stations. Fifth, the distribution of services and costs strongly favored high income households located in the regions near stations. But more than half of the costs of BART are paid from property and sales taxes, quite regressive in their impact on the lower income payers. A final criticism is that travel by BART is not nearly as cost efficient as buses.

After asking what went wrong with the planners' bright hopes, Webber concurs with Hall that the wrong design trade-offs were made. The system features that were selected, such as its long-haul design and widely spaced stations, are less attractive to the bulk of prospective riders than a more flexible and accessible mode of service would be. The ultimate mistake was the wrong technology, too costly for the numbers of persons whom it would actually serve. Perhaps a network of express buslines using exclusive freeway lanes would have served more people at much lower cost.

Would a different sort of evaluation emerge after 15 years of operation? Again, the choice of evidence preselects the conclusion. This kind of heavy-rail transit technology is no longer chosen for new systems in the United States; Washington, Baltimore, Atlanta, and Miami, along with BART, are probably the last of this type. No other area which began planning after 1976 has copied BART. On the other hand, those who use BART trains find them fast and enjoyable, and they give the region a favorable image of technological achievement. Not all observers would be as critical as Webber, certainly not the downtown investors who have provided workplaces for those commuters. By 1985, BART's daily ridership had increased to 220,000, still short of the forecast number, but suggestive of increasing demand. When a system is in place, however, evaluations must also focus on how to make the best of it. Federal and state funds were financing some service improvements and new rolling stock, designed to increase rider capacity. The BART board, still entirely committed to its transit concepts, had proposed some 100 miles of extensions. But transportation planners in the region also expressed growing concern for suburban traffic congestion in the major travel corridors. The Bay Area has several public transit systems, and they were uncertain how to coordinate them to provide the kind of service that would make additional freeway building unnecessary. BART is a vital part of that system, but it cannot be the sole answer that optimists of a decade earlier anticipated.

Many channels can transmit the feedback into the policy process once again. When a major downtown development falls short of expectations, investors and city officials avoid a repetition of it. They must reassess the market for that kind of space, and conclude either that downtown renewal is not economically feasible, or if officials want it anyway, they must subsidize it more generously.

Popular reactions to planning outcomes can also compel changes. If a neighborhood's wishes were ignored in a redevelopment project, it can spawn a new organization that does exert influence at city hall. The fortunes of referendums and candidates for local office have at times depended on whether particular plans met citizen expectations. San Francisco's politics has been roiled by the proliferation of high-rise office buildings. This has not only increased traffic congestion but also put strong upward pressure on housing costs in the region. Opponents of this "Manhattanization" of their city induced the Board of Supervisors to adopt a 139-page downtown plan that sets strict standards for future development. One unique feature of that plan requires developers to contribute one dollar per square foot for child care facilities for employees [Porter 1986]. Citizen participation is particularly vigorous in that city and is sensitive to planning outcomes, but that potential exists everywhere.

The planning cycle described in this chapter has been described in a very simplified form, revolving in turn from goal setting to choice making to implementation, and back to the starting point by means of evaluation. In fact, if this wheel analogy is appropriate, one might actually observe several wheels turning at once, each influencing, but not controlling, the speed of the others. These wheels stand for the segments of the planning process: one for housing, another for transportation, a third for economic development, and so on. A large city or county planning department has specialists in each of these areas, and smaller communities can hire such expertise from the outside. The purpose of the next two chapters is to illustrate how those distinct planning segments operate, to learn whether they are harmonized and, if so, how it is done.

QUESTIONS FOR DISCUSSION

1. What advantages can a community gain from having an up-to-date comprehensive plan?
2. What factors shape the goals a community sets for itself? How much freedom has it to change them?
3. What factors help to determine whether a given planning choice is made by fiat, elite negotiation, or open negotiation?
4. What problems surround the practice of zoning?
5. How can zoning ordinances and incentives best serve the goals and needs of a community?
6. Why is the effort to evaluate the outcomes of planning choices so subjective? How does this lead to political conflict?

6 | FUNCTIONAL PLANNING

6.1 FROM GENERALISTS TO SPECIALISTS

From the comprehensive "planning in general" activity of the last chapter we move to the more specialized forms which contribute to it. That such specialists are needed is obvious: the technology alone in housing, transportation, and environmental protection demands persons with the expertise to diagnose problems, identify and assess potential solutions, and oversee their implementation.

Each specialty comprises a cluster of planners in the public and private fields. One finds housing expertise, for example, in municipal planning and redevelopment departments, regional, state, and federal agencies, private consulting firms, large banks, and on the staffs of major real estate developers. Often, these experts pool their skills, as in New York City's Battery Park City development. However, because of their employers, their aims and interests may differ widely. A developer generally seeks to build dwellings that will be profitable, while a city housing planner wants to provide homes for those who cannot buy or pay market-rate rents. Thus, each of these clusters may contain a microcosm of the conflict and cooperation found in the political system as a whole.

Planners in such clusters also tend to view their subject narrowly, perhaps to concentrate on mass transit rather than on transportation in general. Those who chose the technology and the routes for the BART system appeared to focus on very limited standards and criteria. But planners of the urban freeways in the 1950s and 1960s gave little thought to the provision of mass transit, let alone the impact of their roads on the people who lived near them. Such tunnel vision tends to exclude from the process relevant data from other specialties, and the resulting plans for a transportation system may conflict with those that a city prepares for a neighborhood's preservation.

Such specialists may also seek to keep the scope of conflict narrow. Since they see their expertise as unique, they may resist influences from "outsiders" whose contributions may be necessary but who lack the professional credentials. Those who designed the major high-rise public housing projects of the 1950s followed accepted architectural standards, but ignored the realities of living in them which residents of existing projects could have told them about. The failure of the Pruitt-Igoe project in St. Louis testifies to this [Meehan 1979, 67–74]. Generalist planners and political decision makers must guard against buying the products of this tunnel vision without question. The conflict which the specialists seek to avoid may be highly necessary to a process which aims to learn all viewpoints and anticipate future problems in implementation.

This chapter focuses on the major specialties in urban planning: housing, transportation, environmental management (a complex which includes protection of natural features, waste management, pollution control, and parks and open space) and the social and cultural amenities. There is also an overview of the urban design process, which is intended to integrate these various planning streams into a coherent whole.

6.2 HOUSING: THE POLITICS OF HOME

The home is the prime symbol of one's privacy and sovereignty over a segment of space. Yet, when defined as *housing*, it also stands as a major area of responsibility of governments at the local, state, and national levels. This tension, between the public and the private character of personal living space, creates a unique form of politics. To conduct this politics requires the planning process to take into consideration the social, economic, and cultural roots of housing issues. Too often, professional housing specialists have seen this as an essentially technical problem to be solved by technical means.

Sternlieb [1986, 164] points to another source of conflict, between the nonaffluent and affluent, the "shelter society" and the "post-shelter society." In the first group are those whose primary needs are adequate physical housing and would lack them in the absence of governmental action. The latter group, however, regards the dwelling unit as a symbol of prestige and accomplishment and above all as means of capital accumulation. These persons' main fear is not the loss of a home as such, but the loss of property values. Not only are these groups inherent rivals for public policy attention, but they come into direct conflict when it is proposed to place homes for low-income families in an established middle- or upperclass residential neighborhood.

The responsibilities of government, typically spelled out in state laws, encompass both of these societies. California, for example, has as a "priority of the highest order" the "attainment of decent housing and a suitable living environment for every family." To achieve this requires "the cooperative participation of government and the private sector in an effort to expand housing opportunities and accommodate the housing needs of all economic levels" [California Planning Law, cited by Gallion & Eisner 1985, 316]. City and county plans elaborate on these responsibilities, as in the Comprehensive Plan of Chicago cited in section 5.2. Federal law, embodied in the Housing Act of 1937 and its successors, reinforces these mandates and aims at expanding the resources needed to carry them out.

Two basic housing policy goals stand out consistently. First, communities seek to establish and protect desirable residential conditions through land use regulation and the provision of necessary services such as water, sewage disposal, drainage, crime control and pollution abatement. Here, it is assumed that private parties will provide the homes for themselves or others on their own initiative, and government need only concern itself with the conditions in which they exist. While this goal is central for the post-shelter society, such living amenities are important also to lower income households who have found and want to retain dwellings that meet their needs.

Second, where the community's housing supply is inadequate, action is needed to expand it. The shelter society consists of "market-disadvantaged households"—those who cannot afford homes priced at conventional market levels, who are excluded from what they could afford by class discrimination, and who cannot live in available dwellings due to physical or mental handicap. Programs in this area supply financial aid to persons in those categories along with, or instead of, providing the dwellings themselves.

As a subset of the second goal, government is also to protect the existing housing stock and if necessary bring about its rehabilitation. Individual dwellings and whole neighborhoods decline and deteriorate for various reasons, which can culminate in the loss of homes to the market. To reverse this decline would also be of most benefit to shelter society households, although in some neighborhoods it benefits more affluent persons who want to live in the rehabilitated area.

A complex mix of policies has been devised over the years since the reformers of the late nineteenth century began to attack the slum problem. Some of them, such as income supplements that enable low-income households to rent decent homes, are on the edge of the realm of urban planning as defined in the first chapter. Others, ranging from public housing projects to regulation of lot sizes, are clearly land use related. This section will focus on efforts in the latter group and on the political cooperation and conflict which attend them.

The first general policy goal mentioned above, to *establish and protect residential amenities,* can be carried out by a wide variety of programs. The zoning laws and building and subdivision regulations discussed in section 5.4 are the most obvious. In residential areas, a prime goal is to exclude, as much as possible, land uses deemed incompatible with the quality of existing homes. For a neighborhood of expensive single-family homes, townhouses costing a mere $100,000 could be "incompatible." More modest areas would simply be zoned to keep out stores and gas stations.

These post-shelter-oriented aims can become controversial where a community of high-cost homes on large lots is required to zone for more modest-cost dwellings, as in New Jersey (recall the case in chapter 1). There, the change of policy would call for smaller lot sizes to accommodate less expensive homes, or zoning for multiple family dwellings. Whether the residential amenities can be adequately preserved thereby, and for whom, then enters the arena of political conflict. Similarly, an inner-city neighborhood undergoing major change in its social composition toward either higher- or lower-income residents will take part in debate over how to serve properly its new populations. Among other choices, it will have to decide whether to permit large older homes to be divided into several residential units to house smaller households at a lower cost.

The second policy goal, to *expand the housing supply for market-disadvantaged households* (and upgrade its quality), demands much more investment of financial and political resources than the first one. Since the late 1930s, much of the support for expanding housing opportunity has come from the federal government, albeit in response to demands from urban planners, elected officials, and housing-related interest groups. The forms of aid have varied: loans and grants to local housing agencies, mortgages at below-market interest rates for eligible households, subsidies for construction of privately owned rental housing, and rental vouchers to lower income persons to spur new home construction [Sternlieb 1986, 34–40].

Despite the flow of federal funds through these diverse channels, local planning systems have remained in the center of decision making. Federal programs always permitted them the option of taking part or not. But almost always the lure of the funds and pressures from expected beneficiaries overcame what reluctance a few local officials had to subjecting themselves to the federal rules that accompanied the dollars.

Having received the money, local planners inherited the hard choices of how to spend it. If new homes are to be built, where? For what income levels and household types? Should home ownership be subsidized? Should the established residential patterns in the city, particularly those of race and ethnicity, be reinforced or changed by public action? What should be done for the chronically homeless?

The public housing project was the most common answer to this problem in the 1940s and 1950s. Local housing authorities, arms of the city governments, used the federal aid to construct dwellings for the poor, and continued to manage them as landlord. Vast tracts were built, and although most of them still provide shelter today, their quality of life varies widely. In general, the high-rise family dwellings are the least desirable; the Cabrini-Green and Robert Taylor projects in Chicago are widely known symbols of the ills of the black urban poor. But many other housing projects, with lower and better maintained buildings, have been relative successes. Long waiting lists of persons seeking to move into them testify to that.

Political imperatives had much to do with the outcomes of

these housing programs. First, such projects were typically located in the less desirable areas of the community. If a pattern of racial segregation already existed, public housing projects were placed in minority neighborhoods or other areas undesirable to white persons. Meyerson and Banfield [1957] document how this occurred on a large scale in Chicago in the 1940s and 1950s. Viewed from 1988, the high concentrations of very poor people created thereby have become highly isolated from the educational and employment opportunities found elsewhere in the region, and this has tended to lock them in the cycle of poverty.

Second, political pressures to keep costs low led to construction of substandard buildings with minimal living amenities. In St. Louis, for example, the typical apartment was too small for the families needing them, and design quality in the massive Pruitt-Igoe project was so meager as to make it repulsive to all but the most desperate tenants [Meehan 1979, ch. 3].

With these positive and negative experiences in mind, Congress reshaped federal housing programs, moving away from big, publicly owned projects to a range of approaches. The Housing Acts of 1968 and 1974 gave incentives for private construction of homes for low-income households to rent or buy, and subsidized the rents of needy families who occupied existing dwellings or moved into new ones built expressly for that purpose. From 1968 to 1985, the federal government alone spent more than $100 billion in housing assistance, and state and local units added to that sum. Yet, because the price of housing rose so sharply during that period, the need is far from being met, even though many projects were quite successful in their own contexts.

In the 1980s, with the Reagan administration's cutbacks of housing aid, state and local governments and private housing interests have been thrown back on their own resources. From this imperative have come many public-private cooperative efforts which, while they have not supplied full solutions, have attacked housing distress in their communities. One example is the mutual housing association, a nonprofit cooperative that constructs and maintains dwellings and is owned and managed by the projects' residents. The Mutual Housing Association of Baltimore has sponsored the Alameda Place project, financed by a package of grants and loans from federal, state, and city governments and corporate contributions. Such associations can thrive with competent management, reliable financing sources, and education of the residents to participate effectively [Schwartz 1986].

A more controversial source of housing funds has been devised by New York, Boston, San Francisco, and Santa Monica, California. In different ways, each city requires the developers of commercial real estate to contribute a proportion of their investment to housing programs. From 1981 to 1985, agreements had been made in San Francisco to subsidize 3,793 residential units, most of them for low- and moderate-income occupants [Keating 1986]. In New York City, about $1 billion will be allocated from the revenue of the Battery Park City commercial project to fund rebuilding of low- and moderate-cost homes throughout the city, including the South Bronx [Schmalz 1987]. This linkage is feasible only in cities with strong commercial markets, in which developers think it worth while to pay the added costs. But it will not be of help to Detroit or similarly depressed places.

The need for new dwellings depends in part on the supply of serviceable older homes. However, the third policy mentioned above, *to protect and rehabilitate the existing housing stock,* requires more forceful plans. In older cities and some inner-ring suburbs, lack of upkeep and modernization threatens many homes that are still structurally sound. This problem may occur in scattered dwellings in a neighborhood, but is most obvious in an area with large-scale deterioration. Landlords and owner occupants alike perceive that building values are declining, and if they do not sell out, they simply cease maintaining their structures. Thus government must seek the cooperation of the private sector—owners of the dwellings, builders, and financiers—to counteract this deterioration.

Many causes of the decline in housing supply and quality are beyond the immediate control of the local planning participants. For example, when a steel mill that is a city's major employer closes due to obsolescence or foreign competition, the surrounding residential areas are likely to suffer as well. But a community can also obtain outside help in combating blight: federal aid, private foundation grants, and investments from many sources have had major impacts on some cities.

One approach widely used by local governments is code enforcement. In this process, the city conducts regular inspections of homes in order to keep them in adequate repair and in conformance with health and safety standards. When it finds a leaking roof or unsafe electric wiring, it orders the owner of the building to make repairs within a certain period of time. If the home or building is worth the repair, in the owner's judgment, it will be done. But often, if the city keeps up the pressure, abandonment of the dwelling results, and if it is not "rescued" quickly, vandals or fire will render it unfit for habitation.

New York City acts of necessity as landlord of last resort, for it has taken over more than 10,000 residential buildings after the owners failed to pay real estate taxes. Approximately 120,000 tenants live in them, most at the low end of the income scale. Although many of the buildings are still structurally sound, they cost $150 million in 1983 just to maintain. However, a realistic cost estimate to restore only the 6,000 vacant structures to full liveability is $2.4 billion. Further, there is no assurance that the buildings would attract buyers even after that [Wald 1983]. The competing pressures for public funds in a large city clearly preclude anything close to such an expenditure; yet the city would seriously suffer if those homes were completely lost to its people.

Community development agencies, drawing on federal and state as well as local funds, provide grants and loans to lower income homeowners to upgrade their properties. Some cities have turned the old residences they obtained through foreclosures and tax forfeit over to selected households for a token sum on the condition that they spend the money needed to improve the house up to city standards. Minneapolis, for example, has transfered ownership of 238 homes to such persons since 1974. This urban homesteading effort has been popular but on too small a scale to have major impact. The current needs and continued pace of deterioration exceed these efforts.

One of the largest of the public-private partnerships is supported by the Neighborhood Reinvestment Corporation, which pools government funds with contributions and private loans. It then transfers these resources to locally run nonprofit Neighborhood Housing Services chapters in more than 100 cities. These in turn have financed home repairs, energy efficiency improvements, and upgrading of public facilities in areas which private lenders refused to serve.

Another major nongovernmental source of housing aid is LISC—the Local Initiatives Support Corporation, founded in 1980 with support from the Ford Foundation and six business corporations. By 1987, its lending activity had benefited more than 400 community development groups and produced 10,000 new homes. It played a role in the South Bronx (recall the case in chapter 1) by enabling the Banana-Kelly Community Improvement Association to restore an 85-apartment block. While it aids all forms of inner-city renewal, and so deserves mention with those forms of development financing to be described in chapter 7, housing has been its major emphasis. LISC's goal has been described as "uniting today's scattershot efforts to help troubled neighborhoods, drawing in hundreds of banks, corporations, and local and state governments that still sit on the sidelines" and to realize the self-help potential of community-based organizations [Peirce 1987].

Voluntary organizations with business, neighborhood or religious orientations have also entered the field. Habitat for Humanity, which has drawn publicity due to former President Carter's participation, is an international ecumenical Christian group with many local affiliates that buys and renovates homes for low-income families. Many neighborhood organizations, as those in the South Bronx previously mentioned, have secured dwellings for renovation and resale, usually aided by a blend of public funds, foundation grants, and bank loans.

The political nature of housing stems from the interplay between the groups who would enjoy better or less expensive homes as a result of a public effort and those who would benefit from providing those homes. When their aims coincide and someone can profit (financially or politically) from meeting a need, a program can be born. Yet, as the program matures, it must actually deliver those benefits to all participants in order to survive. The danger is that, as with public housing, the residents may suffer while construction interests prosper. Alternatively, the homes may be built and meet some needs well, but if no one else receives a benefit, the program may be terminated.

A further political dilemma concerns the identity of those persons who do invest in marginal or deteriorated neighborhoods. Many cities have observed middle- and upper-income households buying older but restorable structures, evicting their tenants (usually of lower incomes), rehabilitating the building, and if they do not live there themselves, selling or renting to others. The former residents cannot afford the higher prices or rents and so are forced elsewhere into a tight housing market. This process, called *gentrification,* is controversial in its distribution of costs to those who can least afford them and benefits to the already well-off. Yet, the city does gain an improved housing stock, at least in the area that is "gentrified." Many of the programs already discussed aim instead at *incumbent upgrading,* in which current residents are able to retain their dwellings after improvement.

Serious efforts at providing homes for low-income households are expensive, no matter how it is done. Thus they have to compete for funds with many government policies, including other benefits, such as education and health, to the same persons. It is also necessary to trade off between quality of homes and their quantity. Planners and policy makers must gain skill at doing the most possible with frustratingly limited resources.

6.3 TRANSPORTATION: THE POLITICS OF MOBILITY

The most distinctive feature of urban areas—their high concentration of people and activities—also poses one of their most serious policy problems. Concentration can easily become congestion, which when excessive frustrates the very purposes for which people come to cities. Planners have long followed the example of Daniel Burnham's 1909 Plan of Chicago which held as a prime goal maximum mobility for people and goods. The 1966 Chicago Plan asserted, "Increasing freedom of movement and choice of travel mode through the transportation system is essential in order to expand human opportunities and strengthen the economy" [City of Chicago Department of Development and Planning 1966, 67].

The urban transportation system resembles housing in that it is basically dominated by private market choice. Altschuler [1979, 19] reported that governments at all levels control only about ten percent of the spending on mobility in urban areas. Thus they have major difficulties in "steering" the system, and must be sensitive to the diverse demands of the transportation market. Basically, governments' investment consists of fixed facilities: streets and highways, parking garages, rail transit networks, airports, and harbors. On the other hand, most of the vehicles used are private: cars, trucks, airplanes, rail cars, and ships. With few exceptions, then, the public sector provides the infrastructures of which the private sector makes use.

Transportation planning is at least as complex as housing, due to the many modes of travel and their varied impacts on other land uses. It calls for balancing the demands for highways and mass transit, for reconciling the presence of major freeways with the areas through which they pass, controlling the environment of airports, and providing for those who cannot use or afford the transportation currently for sale to them. These choices present the planners with a bundle of political conflicts.

"Maximum mobility" entails several subsidiary goals, not all of them easily reconcilable. These include: (a) the lowest feasible travel time consumption, noise levels, environmental pollution, and public and private costs in using the system, (b) maximum safety and energy efficiency, (c) travel opportunities for the disadvantaged, and (d) the most beneficial impacts on land use as defined by the comprehensive plans of the community. For example, it is convenient to have a major airport close to the city center, as in San Diego and Boston. But the noise, pollution, and congestion it causes reduce this advantage, and harm some residents of the city while others primarily experience the benefits.

Urban mobility planning can be divided into several functional areas, each with a unique set of problems. First and often most visible is the *vehicle movement* sector, focused on means to maximize accessibility for private cars, trucks and mass transit vehicles to all parts of the region. The point of departure for such planning is the presence or expectation of congestion: too many vehicles in too small a space over a given period of time. This has been endemic in central business districts for centuries, and many programs, from one-way streets to bypass freeways, have aimed at reducing traffic tie-ups.

Congestion is a moving target, however, for it can appear on the very freeways designed to combat it. Recently, some metropolitan suburbs have begun to experience "gridlock" due to their rapid growth as commercial and industrial centers. Commuting trips are less oriented to the central cities and more inter-suburban in direction. This places heavy vehicle loads on roads and intersections never designed for them [Cervero 1986]. The freeways intended to speed suburbanites to downtown jobs serve equally well to carry traffic to destinations in the opposite direction. Suburban Long

Island, New York, is estimated to need $5 billion in road investments to prepare for the expected vehicle load by 2000 [May 1986].

Suburban planners and developers are increasingly working together on traffic management schemes. Many communities now require developers to contribute to road and transit improvements. The latter find this to their own advantage, since congestion reduces the value of their investments. However, it has proven risky to foresee traffic loads in suburbs very far in advance because of their often erratic pace of development and the unpredictability of commuter routes [Cervero 1986].

The typical traffic plan for a city or region designates routes as freeways, expressways, major and minor arterials, collector streets, and local streets, depending on the type of travel they are to serve. They are to be spaced as appropriate to serve anticipated demand, and their width, movement controls, and speed limits are then set accordingly. It often happens, though, that the location of a new shopping center, for example, causes congestion on the arterial roads serving it and patrons respond by using local residential streets to reach it. It is difficult for planners to keep current with such developments and even harder to make timely improvements.

A second sector of urban mobility planning is *vehicle storage.* Cars and trucks take up space at the end of their trips, and when they are parked at a workplace or shopping center in great numbers, they present problems of their own. Curbside parking, the simplest of all arrangements, often hinders vehicle movement, and has been banned in many business districts. Off-street parking in high-use areas is expensive, and the cost must be borne either by the user or by someone who benefits from the user's presence. Some parking ramps are owned by local governments, but most are private property. Clearly, no new commercial or industrial development will succeed today, in central city or suburb, without free or moderate-cost parking for employees and customers.

The third sector interacts with the first two: provision of mobility by means of *shared-ride facilities.* This focuses on moving people as distinguished from vehicles. If there are more persons traveling in a given vehicle, there is less traffic congestion and reduced demand for parking. Thus a major task of planners is to make these facilities as usable as possible.

The most obvious form of shared-ride facility is mass transit, whether on fixed rails or on rubber-tired buses. Medium-sized and larger cities provide some form of mass transit, usually owned and operated by the local government or a special transit authority. The very largest ones have not only buses but also rapid rail transit, ranging from New York's extensive subway-elevated system to San Diego's "Tijuana Trolley." The networks built in the past two decades in San Francisco, Miami, Baltimore, Atlanta and Washington have required extensive planning of routes and stations to reach the optimal number of riders and have the most positive effects on vehicle traffic and adjacent land uses. Since the federal government began in the 1960s to pay much of the capital cost of these networks, plans proliferated on urban drawing boards around the country to take advantage of it. Very little federal money is now available in the late 1980s, and transit plans have become proportionally modest.

Planners have learned, however, that the enormous investments required for rapid transit systems make them impractical for most metropolises. Designed to carry large volumes of traffic on fixed routes, they best serve narrow, high-density travel corridors. New York, Chicago, Boston, and a few other places have these. But as suburban areas continue to grow, those corridors tend to dissolve and new ones do not develop. A smaller and smaller proportion of total trips are appropriate for a fixed-route system. The low ridership of the new system in Miami is evidence for this. In 1975, the Minnesota legislature rejected plans for a billion-dollar subway system for the Minneapolis-Saint Paul area, perceiving that its highly diffused travel patterns would not benefit sufficiently from it to justify the investment.

The past decade has seen planners turn to other options for personal mobility, particularly in the suburbs where the new congestion problems are appearing. The large bus is the mainstay of most transit systems and federal funds flowed in abundance for new purchases in the past two decades. Relative to rail transit, the bus has the advantages of lower fixed costs and flexibility in altering routes to fit travel patterns. However, it is still too big for many purposes, and a bus with a capacity of 40 need not be used on a route with a normal ridership of 10 or 15. Thus, many alternatives have appeared, often under private rather than public enterprise. A company may run a fleet of small buses or vans to cover a suburban community more frequently and thoroughly than large vehicles can. Employers across the country make vans available to their personnel to share rides to work. Thus government's role can shift from being a provider of service to that of facilitator or subsidizer of service by other providers.

Other transportation issues enter the planning process more sporadically. For example, a major airport not only generates significant traffic that has to be managed, but also presents a major locational choice to begin with, and a continuing challenge to control land uses in its vicinity. Since international airports are now located mostly in urban fringe areas, the governmental map on which they are placed may be fragmented into several municipalities or counties. Even when a special authority operates the airport, control of nearby development usually rests with those smaller jurisdictions. Since an airport is not a good neighbor to residential areas, political conflicts easily arise over noise, air pollution, and ground traffic management.

Some communities also pay special attention to human-powered transportation. Designated bikeways provide incentives to nonmotorized travel for short distances and even for work trips in some cases. A city may encourage pedestrian travel in downtown areas by providing walkways above the street or underground tunnels linked with parking and transit facilities. Malls on streets that are closed to vehicles further encourage the use of feet on shopping trips.

A typical city faces a serious challenge in integrating all of its transportation plans and policies with each other in a manner that is consistent with its overall land use plans. On a small scale, Appleyard's [1981] "livable streets" concept represents one approach. Ideally, the street as a carrier of traffic has to be planned and managed so as to protect the residential, social, and esthetic environment of the persons for whom it is a significant part of their lives. A neighborhood cannot survive as a desirable place to live when its streets become barriers to human interaction and hazards to life and peace.

The transportation/land use nexus on the large scale recently provided intense political conflict in New York City's Westway proposal. In 1973, a section of the city's deteriorating elevated West Side Highway collapsed. A proposal to rebuild it, along with development projects on newly filled land along the Hudson River, surfaced shortly afterward. In subsequent years, federal and local political leaders bickered over the relative merits of a highway, mass transit expansion, and the landfill, and no action was taken. The transportation questions were so interwoven with the land use and environmental impacts that the contestants could find no common ground for resolution [Roberts 1984]. In 1985, Governor Cuomo and Mayor Koch admitted defeat of the Westway and yielded to a proposal to trade in the $1.72 billion of federal funds that had been committed to the project for mass transit aid instead. Such a road would have shaped all future development of the waterfront and adjacent areas, and alternatives to it will have equally great but less predictable consequences.

Political systems, as they encounter demands for transportation choices, behave in characteristic patterns, according to Altshuler [1979, 11]. Generally, they

> seek to accommodate new demands as they emerge by means, insofar as possible, that leave previous settlements (programs and administrative arrangements) undisturbed, that involve the least possible disruption for private enterprises, and that involve the least possible inconvenience and annoyance for individuals who have built their life-styles around the expectation of system stability.

Policies aim to protect the status quo until they prove to be clearly unworkable, and any adjustments typically add to, rather than replace, existing arrangements.

All transportation programs, whether of government or a private enterprise, must face the economic and political realities of competition. Altschuler [1979, 85–94] asserted, "The ideal innovation is one that consumers will buy voluntarily in the marketplace at a price high enough to cover its cost." Further, its costs should be diffused among many users. If it becomes necessary to restrain some form of travel behavior, such as closing a street to traffic, it is best achieved if it solves a widely recognized problem, and carries little or no cost in money or travel time. Hardest of all to implement, he further states, are those innovations "that entail substantial costs or interference with established patterns of behavior, imposed in such a manner that the blame will fall clearly and inescapably upon the public officials who adopt the innovation." A major restriction on parking space or a surtax on parking fees intended to reduce downtown congestion would probably be in this last category.

Evidence of the "minimalist" strategies mentioned by Altschuler as more preferable comes from Hartford, Connecticut. To combat its congestion without building new roads or rail systems, it "has put together a more comprehensive package of measures to limit the number of vehicles on city streets than most [cities], and it has received an unusual degree of support from the private sector in devising and carrying them out." This includes everything from computerized traffic lights to vanpools sponsored by the banks and insurance companies that are the city's major employers [Armstrong 1985]. Voluntary strategies are politically popular, but if they are to have the desired effect, they must be sensitively managed.

Three political arenas produce all of the substantive public decisions on urban transportation [Lupo et al. 1971, 189–190]. First, the state legislature and governor establish and maintain policies on the highway network and the extent of funding for mass transit. Few states have comprehensive policies for this, and choices are subject to intense competition between highway interests, cities with mass transit dependence, and the constituents of both.

Second, metropolitan planning agencies in some states have given coherence to transportation choices. Efforts of regional transportation study agencies in the 1960s provided the first opportunities for this. The Metropolitan Council of the Minneapolis-Saint Paul region has a close relationship with the state Department of Transportation and has policy and fiscal control over the metropolitan commissions responsible for transit and airports. Since most metropolitan agencies have only advisory powers, they must supplement their advantage of a comprehensive view with politically effective persuasion on the final decision makers.

The city and county governments make up the third policy-making arena. Lupo and associates [1971, 190] concluded,

> Any comprehensiveness in transportation planning that has occurred has been largely due to the intensive concern of the government of the central city and its allied interest groups, the city's professional capability to identify its own interests and translate them into programs, and its influence in the metropolitan, state, and national decision making bodies.

Even so, these local units are handicapped by the diffusion of governing power in their metropolitan areas and the limited funds which they have to implement their plans. However, the example of Hartford, above, suggests what can be done.

6.4   PLANNING FOR THE NATURAL ENVIRONMENT: THE POLITICS OF TREES

This group of planning activities comprises parks and open space, protection of sensitive natural features, management of wastes, and defense against natural disasters. These have little in common on the surface, but they all affect the natural environments of urban communities. They are often treated as unrelated in policy making and administration, too: those who work in flood control may have no official contact with others who oversee waste disposal or regional park development.

Two broad objectives stand out in such planning. The first springs from the set of esthetic values introduced in section 2.2. The nineteenth century planners' belief that trees, grass, and ponds ennobled the city's inhabitants and supplied fresh air for them to breathe may be regarded today as quaint; yet modern city plans do demand the presence of green spaces amid the concrete and asphalt.

A second objective is more recent: a sensitivity to the city's "metabolism." An urban settlement may be likened to a human body, in that it takes in means of life support and disposes of unneeded products. In practical terms, this points to the supply of clean air and water and the safe removal of wastes [Wolman 1965]. In a broader view, this also includes such management of the lands and waters as to minimize dangers of natural disasters and loss of valuable natural resources. Although these are separate processes, they have an underlying unity in that the segments of the environment are interdependent and so require coordinated planning. Like housing and transportation, they entail conflicting human values and interests and so are just as susceptible to political conflict.

To begin with, parks have had several missions in city plans, from "islands of nature" amid the works of man to locations for physical activity and recreation. Rose gardens and basketball courts may have little in common, but are often planted together. In this part of the chapter the former mission of parks comes under attention, a legacy of those who planned Central Park in New York, Golden Gate Park in San Francisco, and many other inner-city and fringe-area green spaces. Today, those parks are jealously guarded by planners and the public alike as a humane relief from the congestion of the surrounding areas. More recently, many metropolitan areas expanded their acreage of regional parks—Oakland, Phoenix, and Denver are examples. In the 1960s and 1970s, federal funds were supplied to cities and counties to acquire even more open space. Such parks are politically advantaged, ordinarily, in lacking serious opposition. Acquisition of new parkland may arouse dissent from adjacent landowners, fearing congestion and noise, but the likely beneficiaries are far more numerous.

Akin to park management is the second focal point, the protection of sensitive natural features. On the physical margins of many cities are bodies of water and their shores, marshes, steep slopes, woodlands, and ground water recharge areas. Besides their scenic and esthetic values, they provide habitat for wildlife, purify surface waters, reduce wind velocities, replace carbon dioxide in the air with oxygen, and replenish underground aquifers. Ian McHarg [1971, 57] asserts that in them, "nature performs work for man." He has scaled each of these areas for their unsuitability for urban development and thus their need for special protection from the advancing wave of growth.

To establish that protection requires the legal capacity to deny the owners of marshland, forest, or shore the permission to alter their land, depriving them of expected profits or amenities. A community may well have to compensate the owner for that preservation if it does not buy the land outright. For example, the scenic wooded mountains between California's Pacific coastline and the south end of San Francisco Bay are highly desirable for residential development. In order to prevent that, the voters in 1972 created the Mid-Peninsula Regional Open Space District to establish a greenbelt for public use in those hills. By 1984, it had acquired about 18,000 acres, using funds from property taxes, federal and state grants, and gifts. It has a plan for future acquisitions of the highest priority land [Simmons 1984]. But what the residents of that area, which includes Silicon Valley, could afford may be out of the reach of less affluent communities.

A third problem area of concern to specialized planner groups is waste management. "Waste," conceived broadly, is any product of a human activity that is perceived as having no further use and must be removed from public view. It is the end product of the urban metabolism cycle described by Wolman. This includes sewage and garbage, chemicals produced by industrial plants and motor vehicles, radioactive materials, dust and soot. These contaminate the waters, air, and land, and enter the biosphere to the ultimate harm of humans.

Public policy responses to such waste are highly fragmented, but they fall into two broad categories: first, to dispose of or otherwise manage such wastes after they appear; and second, to plan for such uses of land and facilities that reduce their volume. The first is by far the largest, but the latter offers planners much room for innovation. Further, these policies are a complex mix of federal, state, and local statutes, and enforced by an equally intricate web of administrative agencies. Urban master plans often encompass these waste issues, but they are difficult to reconcile with one another.

All urban areas use landfills to dispose of garbage, sewage sludge, and often toxic chemicals. For some, these are hardly more than "dumps," close to inhabited areas, which allow harmful products to drain into ground or surface waters. Although planners recognize the need to use other management means, they also perceive the higher cost of the alternatives, whether resource recovery schemes, burning, or other forms of treatment. These wastes are land use problems, for they must be located somewhere, and any unwanted use like this encounters strong political opposition. In the past, they have often been placed near the communities and social groups that have the least power to resist them. The most workable alternative for settling siting conflicts include negotiations leading to compensation for those living near the chosen locations [Popper 1987; Seley 1983, ch. 10].

Air- and water-borne wastes are less often thought of as a local planning problem, in that they leave the metropolitan region—dispersed to "someplace else." Federal and state laws, however, place the burden on local communities to deal with some of these at their points of origin. A city must process its sewage before it passes into a body of water (although many are doing it inadequately). The federal Clean Air Act of 1969 requires cities to control the levels of six major pollutants produced by industries and motor vehicles. Major cities have pinpointed high levels of ozone and carbon monoxide in certain congested locations, and must limit traffic there to comply with the regulations. Los Angeles and Denver, which lead the nation in such pollutants, have planned, but with only marginal effect, to make reductions. New traffic routes, reduced use of cars, and more efficient traffic controls are often necessary to make important reductions in pollution—which links this policy area with the previous category of transportation.

There is much variation between communities in implementing these federal and state mandates. The federal Safe Drinking Water

Act of 1975 requires local units to maintain certain standards of purity. However, a study of seven communities in eastern Massachusetts showed widely different degrees of diligence in complying with that act. In general, towns with a more "cosmopolitan" leadership (that is, more oriented to the world outside one's community) took more vigorous action to protect their groundwater from hazardous wastes [Powell 1985]. Many factors affect such responses: political interest groups supporting and opposing strong conservation measures, funds available to clean up dumps or construct treatment facilities, and the residents' perceptions of the seriousness of the problem.

Planners must also foresee natural disasters that are caused or intensified by certain uses of the land. Floods, landslides, and earthquakes are the most common of these. California has been persistently plagued with all three, but they can occur almost anywhere. Communities that allow construction on flood plains or unstable slopes, inadequately channel storm water, or set too lenient building standards in earthquake-prone areas fail to show this foresight. However, even when the dangers are perceived, there are political barriers to effective responses. The city of Los Angeles did not pass an ordinance for reducing earthquake hazards in existing buildings until 1981, even after several tremors had dramatized the dangers of life. A number of political factors had to come together to spur action, including a state law, media publicity, and fears of legal liability for the resulting death and destruction [Olson 1985].

A major tool for environmental management in planning is the *environmental impact statement* (EIS). First required of federal agencies by the National Environmental Protection Act of 1969, it has since been extended by most states' laws to cover their own departments and local governments. Basically, an EIS must be prepared for major development projects, describing the purpose of the action and its expected consequences for its environment over the short- and long-term. If a project, such as an electric power plant or an airport, is defined as having serious detrimental effects on the proposed site that cannot be avoided or compensated for, planners have the data necessary to justify moving, altering, or rejecting it. The statement may be prepared by the local government or agency, or by the private initiator of the project. Ideally, it will be objective, but the many uncertainties in even the best-designed proposal leave room for political judgments and pressures to creep in. Furthermore, to study a really complex project can consume years and thus delay or prevent its realization [Branch 1985, 144–152].

6.5 PLANNING FOR THE HUMAN SPIRIT: THE POLITICS OF CULTURE

Land use choices often have cultural meanings beyond the tangible structures they produce. A city's identity is rooted not only in its citizens' homes, means of mobility, and physical environment, but also in its history, the places where its citizens can gather for edification and entertainment, and in the symbols that give meaning to their lives. Planners and politicians can easily overlook their place in the urban environment and unwittingly degrade them.

Our society requires tangible evidence of years and cultures gone by. Perhaps this demand is strongest in periods of rapid change in life styles and in the built environment. Preservation of historic structures and sites has gained markedly in the priorities of urban planners since Congress passed the Historic Preservation Act of 1966. Collins [1980, 89] defined historic preservation as "the act of retaining the tangible elements of our national heritage." It encompasses not just buildings and their sites, but also whole areas that are unique and valuable symbols of human experience and accomplishment. Great age or beauty is not necessary; railroad stations and waterworks have qualified where they are significant to local history.

Kevin Lynch [1972, 57] provided an eloquent rationale for this.

> The contrast of old and new, the accumulated concentration of the most significant elements of the various periods gone by, even if they are only fragmentary reminders of them, will in time produce a landscape whose depth no one period can equal. . . . The esthetic aim is to heighten contrast and complexity, to make visible the process of change. The achievement of the aim requires creative and skillful demolition, just as much as skillful new design.

The 1966 Historic Preservation Act put the subject on localities' agendas, although the major effects awaited another decade. That act set up the National Register of Historic Places and mandated that federal agencies consider the effects on such places of projects which they finance. Tax reform acts of 1976, 1978, and

1981 provided tangible incentives for private investors and owners of such historic property to rehabilitate it. The response was so great that by 1984 the building industry was spending more money on renovation than on new construction. Even though the 1986 tax reform reduced the investment tax credit from 25 to 20 percent, it remains an attractive magnet for funds because many other real estate investment incentives were eliminated.

Local government planners have much to do with this wave of historic preservation, although most of it has been financed by profit-seeking investors, individual property owners, and national and local foundations. Often, cities create overlay districts with specific boundaries within which restrictions apply to preservation and alteration of structures. The financial incentives mentioned above are also available there. Williamsburg, Virginia, has one of the best known of these.

Savannah, Georgia, illustrates the public-private partnership that often emerges to support historic preservation. That city, founded in 1733, has about 1,100 buildings listed on the national register; by 1984 fewer than 100 remained to be restored. The private Historic Savannah Foundation and the Savannah Landmark Rehabilitation Project have spearheaded this effort. But the city is also unique in having 20 public squares, laid out in its original eighteenth century plan, each with some kind of fountain, monument, or gazebo. The city government supplemented this restoration program by refurbishing those public spaces and developed an esplanade along the riverfront with shops and restaurants. It also established an architectural review board to ensure that new construction is compatible with its surroundings [Anderson 1984].

Two kinds of conflicts typically fuel the politics of historic preservation. First, most historic structures are privately owned, and the wishes and financial interests of the owner may not coincide with the community's definition of its "best use." In 1986, the trustees of the Church of St. Paul and St. Andrew in New York sued to have its status as an official historic landmark revoked. They wanted to tear down the 89-year-old church, which is expensive for the congregation to maintain, and replace it with a smaller edifice and a condominium building, but cannot do so without city approval [Berger 1986]. However, the highest state court denied this appeal.

A second problem appears when, in the process of restoration, a structure's use is changed. One of the historic buildings renovated in Savannah was acquired by the Savannah College of Art and Design and turned into a 60-student dormitory. The city zoning code does not permit that use on the site, and efforts to alter the code ignited conflict between residents of the neighborhood and defenders of the college [Scardino 1985]. Often, historic buildings and districts are in transitional areas of the city, in which land uses are changing, and economic pressures may frustrate the preservationist goals.

When a community and its leaders are sensitive to history, they are also likely to pay attention to its overall "social esthetics." This term points to the quality of its public spaces and sights, and their effects on people's meeting, thinking, learning, recreating, and generally identifying with their places. The early City Beautiful enthusiasts perceived this significance for cities that were the products of the Industrial Revolution. Modern planners can be no less sensitive, but they act against a backdrop of cities of the Information Revolution. Standardized architecture, computers that know people only as numbers, and the disconnectedness of a highly mobile society dehumanize. The challenge is to link people in renewed and innovative ways.

Downtown public spaces have come in for recent scrutiny, since so many areas around new high-rises are shunned except by those who have to walk across them. Rather, asserts Project for Public Spaces, a nonprofit corporation of scholars and designers, they can be planned to be attractive and interesting, where people can spontaneously meet one another. Gardens, fountains, and sculptures add a dimension beyond the mundane [Davies 1985].

Indoor public space, either privately or government owned, further adds to an area's vitality. New inner-city shopping malls can offer esthetic and social experiences; San Diego's Horton Plaza and community theater complex is likened by imaginative observers to a Renaissance Italian hill town. Saint Paul's Town Square not only houses three floors of shops and restaurants but also an indoor public park on the top level. The dramatic interior space of the new State of Illinois Building in Chicago and the restored Old Post Office in Washington, D. C. illustrate this potential on the large scale.

Community cultural centers—art galleries, theaters, and museums—command attention for their economic as well as esthetic values. Such large-investment projects are typically partnership ventures in which the local government provides incentives to giving by foundations, community organizations, and wealthy patrons. But cities have also encouraged small-scale arts efforts. Saint Paul aided conversion of old downtown buildings into artists' lofts and helped finance renovation of the theater that housed the popular public radio program, "A Prairie Home Companion."

Planning efforts must also account for sports facilities, from the neighborhood playgrounds that provide inner-city youths with outlets for physical energy to the massive stadiums for major league sport-industries. Key criteria for these, as with the cultural centers, include the accessibility to the users and compatibility with the surrounding land uses. But to compare the value of a domed stadium seating 50,000 with 100 local basketball courts or 10 swimming pools is an act of political, not technical, judgment.

Political conflicts over social-esthetic issues can become as heated as other kinds. To place a sports stadium or museum in a central-city location may draw neighborhood opposition to the disruption it creates. Further, since the benefits of arts promotion are not tangible or measurable in dollars, they may lose out in competition with programs to improve housing or transportation. And, a powerful council member may simply not like the new abstract sculpture in front of city hall!

6.6 BLENDING THE STREAMS: THE POLITICS OF URBAN DESIGN

Specialized planning can easily become fragmented and competitive planning. We have already seen in chapter 3 that many governmental units and agencies share in planning for a single urban area, and they have different constituencies and purposes. Further, we have seen in this chapter that an array of specialists dominate planning for housing, transportation, open space, recreation, and other fields, who may or may not communicate with other specialists. Beyond this, each cluster of planning decisions has its surrounding cloud of interest groups, focusing its attention of low-income housing, airport noise, arts facilities, or scenic-area conservation. What can be done to harmonize what is so naturally separate?

Integration begins when those who take part in the planning process take a holistic view of a city that transcends all of its distinct parts and interests. This view should not be an ironclad vision that leaves no room for adjustment or bargaining. But it should have enough form that it can guide a choice of whether to rehabilitate an old apartment building on the edge of a downtown area for the benefit of low-income elderly persons or to allow it to be demolished to make way for an office building. It should enable suburban planners to decide between competing developers' proposals for a shopping center and an apartment complex on a parcel of land next to a new freeway.

An approach to such integration is expressed in the concept of *urban design*. According to Barnett [1982, 12] it is "the process of giving physical design direction to urban growth, conservation, and change." Ideally, it integrates all elements of land use planning in one coherent vision: overall land use objectives, environmental conservation, zoning, historic preservation, open space, transportation facilities, building designs, and the publicly provided infrastructures. So conceived, it would overcome the fragmentation that the many specialists discussed in this chapter would foster. The urban design process is applicable to every kind of choice: urban expansion, renewal, redevelopment, preservation, and land use regulation.

The most dramatic display of urban design skills has been the creation of new towns. These are settlements built according to a single plan that accounts for all of its elements: housing, transportation, commercial centers, parks, utilities, and schools. These differ from the common residential subdivisions in their greater degree of self-containment. Some towns have been entirely free standing, from the 1733 plan of Savannah to the atomic energy city of Oak Ridge, Tennessee. Many more have been designed as appendages to an existing metropolis: Pullman, near Chicago (see section 2.6), Columbia, Maryland, and Woodlands, Texas. A few have appeared recently as "new towns in town"—major central-city redevelopment projects.

New towns draw their inspiration from mankind's age-old hope of "beginning again." Upon seeing old cities plagued by extensive decay or new suburbs with seemingly random development patterns, one is tempted to dream of "doing it right next time." That dream synthesizes many values: closeness to nature, energy efficiency, ease of pedestrian travel, mix of social and income groups in the residential areas, or nonpolluting industry. It can be likened to a fabric into which varied strands of material are woven—hopefully producing a pleasing and legible whole.

In practical terms, new towns require many planning choices, including: (a) what residences? how many? for whom? where? (b) what commercial and employment facilities shall there be? where? (c) what traffic circulation patterns are necessary to give adequate access to these without congestion? (d) what land shall be left open for recreation? conservation? future use? (e) what cultural facilities shall be provided? where? (f) what "character" shall the city have to distinguish it from other new communities and give it an identity that residents will value? All these must fit on a map with their predicted interrelationships.

Most American new towns have been planned by private enterprise. While they were oriented to serve commercial interests, their designs varied widely from each other's and some were also innovative for their times. The design had to sell, basically, whether to prospective residents or to investors in the commercial facilities, who had other attractive choices as well.

However, the U. S. government has also built or encouraged new towns. In the 1930s, the Resettlement Administration built three "greenbelt" towns on the outskirts of Milwaukee, Cincinnati, and Washington D. C. on the garden city model. These principles were also applied to a lesser extent in Oak Ridge and Norris, Tennessee, built by the Atomic Energy Commission and Tennessee Valley Authority, respectively. Some imaginative design work went into them, but they failed to serve as effective models for further urban development due to popular opposition to the federal government's role as developer and landlord [Corden 1977].

The federal government's policy shifted to one of financial encouragement of new towns with Title VII of the 1970 Housing and Urban Development Act. It created a New Community Development Corporation within the Department of Housing and Urban Development to provide loan guarantees to private and governmental developers of new towns as well as loans for interest payments on the debts incurred. It also furnished grants for public facilities, demonstration projects, and overall planning. In 1975, the program was suspended after aiding 15 projects [Corden 1977, 131–150].

In many ways, that program was a failure. It had four general goals: to achieve a social balance among the residents of the towns, to enable those residents to gain some degree of economic self-sufficiency, to encourage decentralization of urban populations, and to stimulate development of the surrounding region. They proved to be somewhat contradictory, and private developers found that to stress any one of them was to increase the financial risk they incurred [Corden 1977, 146–149].

One of the 15 has been a marked success, however: The Woodlands, Texas, just north of Houston. Begun in 1974 on a 25,000-acre parcel, it had 19,000 people and 280 businesses as of 1984. It is basically a middle-to-upper class community, but 12 percent live in low-to-moderate income housing. Louv [1985, 101] described it as

> a paradise of lakes, streams, and forests of ancient magnolias. It has its own equestrian center, offering 2500 acres of wooded trails. . . . Two helipads are located in the Village of Grogan's Mill, for those who want to skip the traffic. . . . Among other amenities, The Woodlands boasts an athletic center with a fifty-meter Olympic-sized swimming pool, racquetball courts, and one of the largest golf complexes (eighty-one holes) in the nation. This is a town that bugged itself, with its own two-way interactive cable television network and computerized central command post.

Aside from the federal loan guarantees, its design was entirely the work of a subsidiary of the Mitchell Energy and Development Corporation.

Local governmental planners show little interest today in such new town efforts. Practical economics dictates that the high costs of such developments can be borne only by persons at the upper end of the income ladder. They do not, contrary to earlier hopes, offer any realistic opportunities to relieve the blight of older cities— which must be dealt with where it is. There, typical redevelopment efforts are painfully slow, a house or block at a time. Also, the political system cannot easily process the "grand plans" that new towns require; it always seeks to break down urban development choices into small, specific units and consider the separate implications of each.

The Meadowlands area of northeastern New Jersey is a politically intricate endeavor at urban design. Not far away from Manhattan, it was long bypassed by urban development since its swampy land was used largely as a garbage dump. However, the 1970s saw a boom begin with warehouses and office buildings placed there, drawn by land costs half as great as in New York City. Since the Meadowlands' 32 square miles are divided among 14 municipalities, no one government is able to plan for the whole. In 1969 the Hackensack Meadowlands Development Commission was created to remedy this. Granted broad design powers, the commission can override some of the cities' planning authority. It has prepared a master plan for the area that covers housing, industrial uses, environmental cleanup and restoration, and transportation arteries, and has enjoyed some success in controlling initial development. The commission has not lacked for political problems, though. On one hand, the municipalities did not relish the loss of planning powers over such a large area. And on the other hand, it has not secured enough residential construction to house the people employed there, and workers must commute long distances from homes they can afford [Lueck 1987].

The Meadowlands design effort points to an important area of concern not yet discussed: the relationship of urban planning to economic health and development. This issue has often been in the near background of the issues just covered, particularly that of transportation. Economic values exercise a powerful influence over all of the participants in the planning process, governmental and private. They also contribute to a certain coherence in planning choices, though they contain obvious biases as well. The next chapter attends directly to these economic issues and the means of making land use decisions within that framework.

QUESTIONS FOR DISCUSSION

1. How can the efforts of the functional planning specialists best be coordinated with one another and integrated into comprehensive plans?
2. What are the political implications of thinking of "homes" rather than "housing"?
3. What are the major barriers to adequate housing for low income households?
4. What factors shape the public-private division of responsibilities for urban transportation facilities?
5. How does waste become the subject of political conflict?
6. How can an apparently innocuous subject like preservation of historic structures arouse political controversy?
7. What political skills and power are required to plan holistically for a major new community?

7 | THE POLITICAL ECONOMY OF URBAN PLANNING

7.1 THE POLITICS AND ECONOMICS OF URBAN LAND

Land is worth money and can be used to make more money. Whatever else it means to the city and its people, its current and prospective dollar values dominate the political choices made about it. In studying the politics of planning, we must remember that the marketplace for urban land and those who do business in it give that politics its unique shape.

Economic development and employment generation appeared on the list of goals of urban planning in section 1.5. The total urban system, taking in both public and private enterprise, seeks three basic economic goals, according to Wilbur Thompson [1965, 1]. First, it aims for *affluence,* measured in a high and rising level of income, goods, and services available to its people. The second goal is *equity*—the fair distribution of earned income and of government's taxes, services, and transfer payments. Third, it pursues *stability* of economic activity, in terms of income and efficient use of resources. Since the Depression of the 1930s, local authorities, like the national government, have been expected by the public to take a greater role in pursuing these economic ends. For localities, the major upsurge in this responsibility has come in the past ten years. The land planning system has necessarily responded to this, as demonstrated by the Poletown case in chapter 1.

Recent works on urban politics have directed attention anew to cities as economic enterprises. In the most often cited of these, Paul Peterson [1981, 4] asserts, "The place of the city within the larger political economy of the nation fundamentally affects the policy choices that cities make. In making these decisions, cities select those policies which are in the interests of the city, taken as a whole." Those holistic interests are the economic goals that cities pursue, particularly "a competitive edge in the production and distribution of desired commodities relative to other localities" [Peterson 1981, 22]. This edge supplies the prosperity that fuels the government's ability to provide public services and amenities that win political support from a satisfied citizenry.

To achieve this condition, a city's economy must make efficient use of the three major factors of production: land, labor, and capital. Of these, local governments have major control only over their land, and by the zoning and development decisions already surveyed in this book, they determine the economic uses to which it is put. They also provide the public services—transportation, utilities, and social amenities—that help to fix the market value of each piece of land. Finally, by the complex of choices cities make for a larger area— such as renewal of a deteriorated industrial district—they set the limits and possibilities for the use of any one parcel within that area.

Thus, a central purpose of urban planning, whether by government or private enterprise, is to seek the "highest and best" (in a holistic sense) economic return from land. This return may consist of a profit for a specific developer or landowner on one site, or the creation of a maximum number of jobs on another. For land that is defined as best occupied by homes, the return is in residential amenities that can attract the needed labor force. This search for economic benefit can clash with the esthetic, social, and moral values discussed in chapter 2, and political conflict often springs from such dissonance. Often, though, those values are redefined and applied within an economic mindset. For example, the quest for better housing for lower income persons may be linked with industrial growth, in the view that higher paid workers can better afford homes. Or a city council might argue that it cannot spend more on parks until its tax base is strengthened by commercial and industrial growth.

This quest for maximum economic benefit from a city's land raises a major question: do the local planners really make the choices themselves? Or do they simply discern what the regional, national, and international markets and investors demand and respond accordingly? Peterson and some other scholars answer this second question in the affirmative, arguing that planners have only the option of accommodating the investors (and on their terms) or not doing so (and thereby condemning their communities to decline). If Detroit had not accommodated General Motors with the support for the new plant, it was widely believed those Cadillacs would instead be emerging from an assembly line in another state.

In this perspective, urban development is

> the product of technological changes of global scope, financial decisions by heads of multinational corporations, and political outcomes resulting from decisions made in Washington or the state capitals. The fate of the exterior city hinges on a technological and demographic upheaval which is beyond its control

[Savitch 1979, 2]. In such a situation, the city's leaders must act like the executives of a corporation in a highly competitive struggle for "market share." They win if they can perceive what the customers demand and supply it [Peterson 1981, 22–24]. The competitors in this case are other communities with the same aims, who might give just a bit more to lure a prospective employer. When General Motors announced in 1986 that it would build a factory for its new Saturn car "somewhere," governors and mayors fell over each other in promising incentives if GM would build it "here." Spring Hill, Tennessee, won that contest with apparently little effort.

But other observers assert that the economic system has enough "slack" to permit a range of political choices and thus reward enterprising politicians and planners. That myth of economists, perfect competition, exists nowhere, because neither business entrepreneurs nor public officials fully understand the market. Investment is not always mobile; many types of enterprises cannot move to find the optimal conditions. Further, those conditions that government can affect—taxes and development incentives—are only minor factors in the locational choices of many industries. Thus, where economic choices are not rigidly logical or consistent, political pressures and arguments can incline them in one way or another. This widens the opportunity for officials and planners to serve public interests in contrast to the more privatistic business aims.

7.2 THE ENGINES OF THE URBAN ECONOMY

Before concluding whether the "economic determinism" or the "political opportunities" interpreters are right, we must recognize that urban areas differ widely in their roles in the national and global economy. These roles shape the demand for uses of their land, and thus their opportunities for development. The National Research Council's Committee on National Urban Policy recently reported, [Hanson 1983, 38–39],

> The new urban system is characterized by the growing dominance in corporate and producer services of a relatively small number of national and regional 'command and control' centers. In these centers, strategic economic and political decisions are made that affect both these cities and the rest of the urban system. . . . The remaining urban areas are more specialized in their economic functions, which tend to be subordinate to the decisions made in the command and control centers.

The report identifies New York, Chicago, Los Angeles, and San Francisco as the major national, diversified command and control centers, followed by the 136 next largest metropolitan areas classified as diversified service centers, specialized service centers, consumer-oriented centers, and production centers [Hanson 1983, 41–44]. These centers have close relationships with one another: a decision in New York to build or close a factory or office can reverberate from Miami to Anchorage and alter the choices which local planners must make. Decisions made in Seoul, Stuttgart, and Sao Paulo can also have those effects.

Why are these distinctions important for land use? The report asserted that the diversified command and control centers have the best prospects for future economic development. Any urban area needs a steady infusion of capital to develop its land and maintain its existing structures, and those centers have the complex of resources that attract a varied group of investors [Hanson 1983, 55–56]. Although it is an older urban area, Boston is currently booming due to its broad base in education, finance, publishing, and high technology, enabling its governments to invest in housing and necessary infrastructures. Detroit, by contrast, lacks such a base and is less successful in diversifying beyond the heavy manufacturing that is its declining mainstay.

Urban areas will increasingly find their prosperity in the presence of the management functions of the economy, by definition concentrated in the command and control centers. These centers alone said Hanson [1983, 57–58],

> offer easy access to the entire array of services that the modern corporate complex needs to perform its management functions. They also provide advantages in transportation, communications, and cultural resources. While some traditional headquarters activities, such as records centers, can and will be relocated in the suburbs or in subordinate centers, management functions are becoming more heavily concentrated in the major national, regional, and functional centers.

It is also important to look inside metropolitan areas to see how these economic functions affect the distribution of land uses. Two classic models of land use provide alternative portraits of this process. According to the *concentric zone* model, growth spreads outward from the original city center and forms, in turn, rings of more or less equal width. As the structures in one ring age and deteriorate and the area becomes less desirable, new growth occurs farther from the center. The older zones are then occupied by the poorer residents and the least desirable (from an environmental perspective) industry. While no city displays this pattern perfectly, Chicago has often been used to illustrate this model [Park et al. 1967]. Many scholars thought of this as a natural process; slums were to them an unavoidable feature of urban landscapes.

The *sector* model was devised after observations that growth in many regions failed even to approximate the concentric zone pattern. In this view, urban expansion depends not primarily on distance from a central business district, but on lines of transportation and natural land features [Hoyt 1939]. Growth in the century from 1850 to 1950 occurred most intensively in railroad corridors and along rivers and shorelines. Since then, freeways and airports have attracted commercial and industrial development. These corridors or areas are thus the sectors that draw the bulk of major investments, and the development of the remainder of the metropolitan area is oriented to them. Although this model does not account for all of the geography of growth, it is more useful than the first. This model also has the advantage of flexibility: it implies that decline of inner-city districts is not inevitable, and growth can be channeled by means of deliberate choices.

For planners' purposes, we can distinguish four kinds of "sectors" in terms of their potential for near-future development. First, there are the *growth centers* that will draw the major commercial activity and the related building that serves the management and retailing enterprises. Historically, these have been the downtowns of central cities, but one must now add the "outer cities—the major shopping centers, office parks, and multiuse complexes found along the freeways of every metropolis. Land costs there are high, but the market perceives equally high advantages in these locations.

A second sector type is the *inner transition zone*. This is typically near the downtown and comprises the smaller business and industrial buildings that may be abandoned or underused; yet they stand in potentially desirable locations. Some of the land is vacant or occupied by parking lots. There may also be homes of lower income persons—rooming houses, cheap hotels, and older single-family dwellings. This zone has potential for major future development or for further deterioration, depending on the choices of investors and governments. Some cities have rehabilitated the older housing or placed new homes there, while others take advantage of lower land values to expand public institutions. Poletown and the South Bronx, highlighted in chapter 1, exemplify this zone.

The third sector, the relatively *stable, established areas,* has lower change potential. Much of it is taken up by homes, neighborhood shops, schools, and churches. Its main challenge (as seen by its residents, at least) is to maintain its quality and keep out the kind of development that would threaten its residents' sense of security. When a part of it is disrupted, as with a freeway routing, then it becomes more of a transition zone with the varied potentials for change.

Finally, there is the *outer transition zone*—land with low-density uses on the edge of the developed area that is ripe for expansion. Land values are relatively low; yet it may have good access to transportation facilities. The challenge is to control this change from rural to urban land uses in an orderly manner to avoid environmental damage and traffic problems. The suburban New Jersey housing conflict and San Diego's growth moratorium, also briefed in chapter 1, concern this type of area.

Three major factors determine economic development in the region as a whole (compared with other urban areas) and in each of the four zones. First, *accessibility* is crucial. Basically, this depends upon ease of transportation (a function of the mode of travel, its distance, and its cost) to and from sites important to the investor. Why do so many lawyers, managers, public relations people, and financiers want to locate "downtown" even though they can communicate electronically anywhere in the world? They seek face-to-face contact, they want to sit down together over lunch, and they want to be seen in prestigious central locations. Only Manhattan can be Manhattan—Newark won't do. Thus, BART's central function has been to nourish this feature of San Francisco's commercial center. In a different manner, proximity to freeways and airports for personal and freight transportation is as vital as the railroad siding was a century ago (and still is to some industries).

A second central factor is *land availability* and its cost relative to need. This affects virtually every kind of commercial site choice and impinges upon residential location as well. The growth centers offer such land and it is in demand even at its high cost. The lower cost and greater availability of land in transition zones has not usually overcome its less desirable features. However, government has had a major role in making land available to the kinds of development it seeks at a lower cost than the market would charge. Thus, General Motors' selection of Poletown hinged on public action to supply this factor.

Third, availability of a variety of *living amenities* influences economic growth choices between and within metropolises. These comprise the traditional parks, schools, museums, and environmental beauty, but can extend to boat marinas, sports stadiums, and trendy historic districts. Boston's wharfs and waterfront warehouses have been transformed in the past decade into condominiums with their own boat docks, chic professional offices, and food markets selling gelati, croissants, and organic meats. The upscale investor, on whose choices turn much urban growth or decline, would not choose Boston solely because of its Quincy Market, but is encouraged by the image of a city that provides such attractions.

While there are many other factors fueling the urban economy, such as climate and the presence of a skilled labor force, these three are heavily affected by the quality of a metropolitan area's planning process. A good airport, coherent freeway system, and efficient mass transit are at the core of a site's accessibility. Land supply and cost are affected by zoning, and cities have financial tools to modify the market when it will attract development. Whatever amenities are sought, planner action influences their location and supply to a greater or lesser extent. Thus, planning is putting a hand on the faucet that can increase or decrease the volume of urban development. It can obtain some kinds directly, when it subsidizes an office building, and exert indirect influence by locating a rapid transit route or sewer line in a certain corridor.

That these economic development choices are political—marked by cooperation and conflict—is also obvious. That is, those entrepreneurs who wish to use urban locations to make money will apply what political influence they have to secure necessary aid and approval. General Motors executives used their insider status to apply heavy pressure on Detroit's Mayor Coleman Young and the city council. Smaller communities across the nation have spent much to renew their central business districts after major merchants emigrated to fringe-area shopping malls. In many such instances, the cooperation has been more evident than conflict.

But in other cases, conflict has split communities over programs for economic development. Opponents sponsor alternative values such as protection of a sensitive environment, an historic structure, or the homes of lower income households in attempts to block an office building or shopping center. In other cases, there is simply opposition to the level of subsidy required to bring in a new employer. Three later sections, which outline specific economic development strategies, develop this political perspective further. But first it is necessary to examine the sources of capital upon which communities depend for their investments.

7.3 WHERE THE DOLLARS COME FROM

Capital for urban development has several sources. They differ not only in the mechanics of raising it and the amounts they produce, but also in the political choices they entail. One dollar is not the same as another; each comes with certain obligations and limits imposed by political decision makers as well as financiers. The flow of funds is extremely complex, with many branches and technical details. This survey is necessarily simplified, but provides a view that planners must take into consideration.

The first category of funds is public tax revenue. In local governments, much of this comes from real estate levies, although its proportion of total local government income is declining. These dollars are used for many purposes—to patch streets, pay salaries, and plant trees. Some small-scale capital investment is financed by current revenues; in Type 3 planning choices, governments undertake these projects on their own.

A further use of local tax revenue is to repay loans used to finance more significant development projects that will have a life span of several decades. This borrowing procedure is described below; it is sufficient here to mention that when these loans are backed by the total tax revenue of the city, county, or district, a portion of that revenue must be earmarked each year for their repayment. Where the debt load has become heavy due to ambitious borrowing, this repayment load rises proportionately.

Several other means of development financing are built into the revenue systems of some communities. One is *tax increment financing,* a program that diverts part of the taxes that would normally be paid on a new project into subsidizing the construction of that project. In 18 states, a city may use it as an incentive for industrial and commercial development. Typically, it will contract with a developer to pay some of the costs of a project, such as land acquisition and clearance, utilities, and parking facilities. It then recoups that sum over a period of years from the "tax increment." It has also been used for housing construction, including dwellings at the upper end of the income scale.

Such financing reduces the amount of tax revenue available for general purposes, and the city's policy makers have to weigh the need for the project against other expenditure demands, clearly a political choice. If it is a depressed community, with many social needs, that lost revenue could be painful. On the other hand, it can be argued that without such subsidies, no development at all would occur, and the tax base would decline even further. Such predictions as to the long-range success of tax-increment projects are risky at best, and often allow those with the best political resources to prevail.

In other situations, a city or county may draw in or retain an employer with promise of a *tax abatement.* This is a simple forgiveness of part or all of the normal tax levy for a certain number of years. New York City's Industrial and Commercial Incentive Board has granted abatements since 1977 to encourage new construction and remodeling; at least $245 million was provided during its first five years [Goodwin 1983]. The arguments in favor of this are that it also attracts investment that would not come otherwise, and allows the industry a defined period in which to develop its full profitability before it has to pay taxes. The political arguments on this scheme are similar to those on tax-increment financing.

A further form of revenue used by local authorities is the *improvement assessment*. A project such as street paving, storm or sanitary sewer, or water supply, improves property values in its immediate neighborhood. Thus, the owners of the benefiting properties are charged part or all of its cost. Such assessment choices can be highly political due to lack of agreement on the need for the project, who shall be included in its boundaries, and the proportion of the costs to be assessed. In new subdivisions, the developer pays these assessments in advance and then passes on the costs to buyers.

A newer form of local revenue has grown rapidly in importance: *development fees* or *exactions*. In high-growth areas, especially in the South and West, cities and counties charge commercial and residential builders not only for the cost of the streets and sewers on the project, but also for fire and police stations, parks, schools, and road and drainage improvements in the surrounding area. The rationale is that new developments impose costs on the community as a whole and should share that burden. Fulton County, Georgia (in the Atlanta metropolitan area), required in 1984 that developers of a $350 million office park contribute $4 million to rebuild bridges, widen roads, and reconstruct a freeway interchange to handle the resulting traffic increase [Schmidt 1985].

These exactions have been particularly controversial in California, where hard-pressed cities and school districts have used these fees to pay for schools, libraries, and roads nowhere near the development that was assessed. The courts have generally upheld these exactions, but in 1987 the U. S. Supreme Court ruled that the improvements paid for must be directly linked with the project. Otherwise the exaction is a taking of private property contrary to the Fifth Amendment [*Nollan v. California Coastal Commission*].

The issue of locally obligated debt is more complex yet. Cities, counties, school boards, and special districts can borrow by selling either *general obligation* or *revenue* bonds. The former are guaranteed by the full revenue base of the jurisdiction, and so entail a relatively low risk for the lender. These bonds are ordinarily used to finance projects that will not produce revenue—schools, roads, sewers, and parks, for example. Most states require that such borrowing be approved by the voters in a referendum, a safeguard against a community piling up excess debt as well as an opportunity for the public to judge the project itself. In 1984, local governments owed approximately $118 billion in general-obligation debt [Aronson & Hilley 1986, ch. 9].

Revenue bonds have grown in significance, and now comprise a local debt of about $200 billion. These are used to finance projects expected to produce income sufficient to repay the bonds—such as public utilities and sports stadiums. There is more risk to lenders, since they are not guaranteed, and a lack of revenue could cause a borrower to default on them. As a result, they carry a higher interest rate than general obligation bonds.

These bonds are especially significant for urban development since the proceeds can be turned over by the governmental borrower to private developers as *industrial revenue bonds.* That is, the city may offer the money to a corporation if it will build a new plant there; the latter repays the bond on an agreed schedule. They have been widely used in all states, and cities find themselves competing against one another in offering the best incentives (which may also include the others described above).

A special feature of both kinds of local bonds (state governments use them also) is that interest paid to the lenders is free from federal income taxation. They are also free of state taxation when held by residents of the state in which they are issued. This permits such units to borrow at a lower rate of interest than corporations can; in 1984 the average municipal bond sold at an interest rate about 2.5 percentage points lower than the typical high-grade corporate bond [Aronson & Hilley 1986, ch. 9]. An industrial revenue bond thus constitutes an indirect subsidy to a corporation, financed by the loss in federal and state income tax revenue.

The 1986 Tax Reform Act sharply restricted their future availability and tax exemptions. Tax-exempt status is now limited to bonds used for public purposes, such as schools and highways. Aid to public-private partnerships is also restricted: no more than ten percent of a tax-exempt bond can be provided to a private developer. As a result, local governments are financing these commercial improvements with taxable bonds, and some are even making agreements to share in the profits from the projects [Moore 1988].

Federal and state aid in several forms have been a major source of funding for urban development since the 1940s. Section 2.6 recounted the origin of the federal housing and urban renewal programs, which enabled many cities to take the initiative for the first time in their own economic and structural development. When the results of these fell short of expectations, a succession of other programs followed. By the late 1980s, two major forms of federal assistance remained.

First, the Community Development Block Grant provides cities and counties with funds for housing and economic development projects, public facility improvements, and other amenities designed to benefit low- and moderate-income persons and combat blight. In 1984, it provided $3.9 billion to 735 cities, according to a complex formula of apportionment. Since then, it has been cut back in response to federal budget pressures.

Washington also provides a series of tax credits for selected forms of urban development. For example, renovators of buildings over 30 years old qualify for direct reduction in their tax liability of certain percentages of their costs. The size of the credit depends on the age of the structure and its historic designation. In many cities, factories, warehouses, waterfronts, and railroad stations have been given a new economic life because of these incentives. An estimated $440 million in revenue was foregone in 1986 in the historic preservation tax credits, and another $410 million for rehabilitation of nonhistoric structures.

Some state governments have also been active in urban development financing. Often, these efforts supplement federal aid programs. For example, the state of Minnesota provided over $6 million in 1984 to enable cities to offer below-market loans to new or expanding businesses or to undertake improvements that would support commercial development. Another development aid, permitted in 23 states, is the establishment of local enterprise zones. Basically, they provide tax reductions over a period of time to businesses that locate or expand in an area designated as economically distressed. Some states also loan money and give other kinds of assistance to would-be occupants. In 1984, about 400 communities had one or more such zones. While a number of them could boast of successes, their general impact is limited unless substantial resources are brought in to overcome the disincentives of such distressed neighborhoods. Congress debated the wisdom of federally established enterprise zones, but did no more.

All of these governmental sources of urban development funding are dwarfed by the size of the private financial sector. In 1983, the vast array of institutions engaged in real estate finance, from home mortgages to equity in office buildings, had $531 billion in investable funds [Downs 1985, 323]. Figure 7.1 portrays the flow of funds through the system, from the primary investors to the developers, builders, and owners. These investments take two basic forms: mortgages, which constitute a loan to the owner secured by the real property, and equity, a share in the ownership of the property and thus in its ongoing profits or losses.

The origin of much of this investment is the savings depository. Of these, mortgage originators provide loans directly to real estate projects, nonoriginators transfer funds to other institutions which do provide mortgages, and equity syndicators arrange the shares of ownership. Secondary market transformers buy mortgages from their orginators and alter them into other kinds of loans (e.g., transforming short-term debt into long-term). Such governmental agencies as the Federal National Mortgage Association (Fannie Mae), established by Congress to facilitate the credit flow, play a major role here. They also repackage mortgages into securities which are then sold to investors; the currently popular "Ginnie Maes" originate with the Government National Mortgage Association. Mortgage bankers are also major marketers of loans to the final users [Downs 1985, 63–66].

This immense system of real estate finance has undergone much change in the 1980s, and will continue to do so under the phase-in of the 1986 Tax Reform Act. First, the markets have been partly deregulated, removing many of the restraints on financial institutions, ending ceilings on interest rates, and permitting many new kinds of mortgages and other instruments. Second, housing lost some of its previous advantages in credit markets and investors shifted priorities to commercial and industrial construction. Third, interest rates rose for a number of reasons, and investors concerned about future prospects for inflation demanded higher levels of return. Fourth, such technological innovations as electronic funds

FIGURE 7.1: Structure of Real Estate Financial Markets[a]

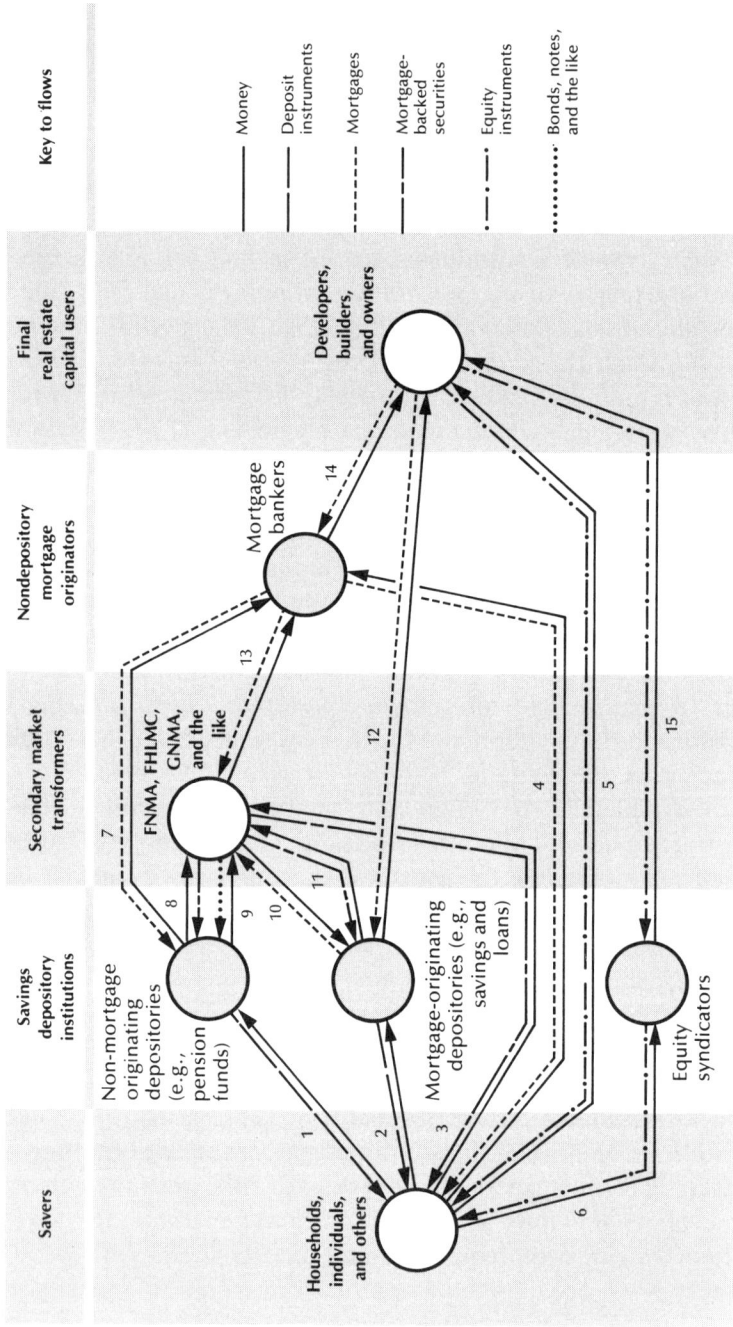

Key to flows

——— Money

— — Deposit instruments

‐ ‐ ‐ Mortgages

— ‐ — Mortgage-backed securities

— · — Equity instruments

· · · · · Bonds, notes, and the like

Savers | Savings depository institutions | Secondary market transformers | Nondepository mortgage originators | Final real estate capital users

Non-mortgage originating depositories (e.g., pension funds)

FNMA, FHLMC, GNMA, and the like

Mortgage bankers

Developers, builders, and owners

Mortgage-originating depositories (e.g., savings and loans)

Households, individuals, and others

Equity syndicators

[a]Flows are numbered for convenient reference in the text. See pages 168–175 for a full discussion of this diagram.

transfer has speeded the process of raising funds and thus the pace of decision making [Downs 1985, 1–2]. Many observers in 1988 foresaw fewer dollars going into commercial structures, but the investment markets have been so volatile that no prediction should pass without challenge.

Governments have only modest power to control this financial complex. Local and state governments have practically none; indeed, their ability to borrow money hinges on its cost in the New York bond markets and their own credit ratings as set by Moody's or Standard and Poor. Communities have been forced to postpone projects when the interest rate asked on Wall Street exceeded their budget. The federal government has tools for controlling the money and credit supply, but the entire system resembles a huge oil tanker that takes much time and distance to speed up, slow down, or turn. Even so, changes in the federal tax code can marginally affect investment choices between residences, office buildings, shopping centers, and factories. Debates over such changes become political contests between advocates for builders, hopeful homeowners, city planners, bankers, and many other interests. There is little that the urban political process, within its own boundaries, can do about this except capitalize on the financing that is available and direct it locationally through its zoning, capital improvements, and partnership enterprises.

These changeable flows of real estate capital can frustrate even well-designed city and county plans. The changes of the 1980s in the financial system have spurred widespread construction of office buildings and hotels, even though vacancy rates in existing buildings are higher than average in many areas. Some urban fringe areas are subjected to major development before their planners have established adequate guides and controls. At the same time, the housing market is neglected, except for residences for the wealthy. Nearly all of the dollars that enter the real estate market are in search of profit (or "tax losses"), and the capital that would meet the majority's need for homes falls well short of needs. This is a political issue of the highest order, but is very difficult for policy makers to address even at the national level in the present market-oriented economy.

7.4 THE POLITICS OF INDUSTRIAL DEVELOPMENT

The steel mill closes, the automobile plant moves to Tennessee, and the computer chip factory opens in the suburbs—these events portray the massive industrial change which the United States is experiencing. These events also change the ways in which people earn their living, often for the worse. A former steel worker who earned $20 an hour now drives a truck at $6 or fries hamburgers at $3.50. Detroit's Poletown project was one response to this problem. The ups and down of southeast Michigan's dominant industry—automobiles—and its impact on the area's economy, has been well-documented by Jones and Bachelor [1986, chs. 1–4].

These changes are also evident in the built environment. An abandoned multi-block factory is a blight on an inner-city neighborhood, while a new facility of equal size pours heavy traffic onto two-lane suburban roads. Manufacturing enterprises demand a great deal of land, not only near a railroad in many cases, but more importantly, within easy reach of an interstate highway. Central city sites of this size are few—recall Detroit's land clearance efforts on behalf of General Motors. Suburban and small-town sites are abundant, but they are in communities that often have little experience with planning for such large enterprises and inadequate facilities to serve them.

Planners face three major challenges, depending on their location: to draw into their area and retain the sources of their economic livelihood, to fit the new enterprises most compatibly into their surroundings, and to secure the most constructive redevelopment of derelict industrial land.

In meeting the first challenge, the political and economic leaders must first appraise their community's potential and not attempt the impossible. A national or regional command and control center—Chicago, Denver, or Atlanta—can lure a much wider variety of enterprises than would be interested in Detroit. Climate, access to suppliers and markets, available labor force, local taxes and operating costs, and the preferences of executives for attractive places to live confer more advantages on some areas than others. Orlando is a tourist magnet; Boston has a strong educational market, and major West Coast cities are on the front line of the booming Pacific Rim trade network. Planners must build on these strengths, though they need not be limited to those features. Smaller cities that lack distinct economic identities but market themselves effectively may also be able to secure development appropriate to their scale. Some investors seek the lower costs and less congested environments of nonmetropolitan New Hampshire, South Carolina, or Oregon.

Urban areas are in a competitive market for these enterprises. Tampa as well as Orlando seeks tourists, New Haven is likewise an educational center, and Portland vies with Seattle for the Asia trade. Generally, an investor seeking a location surveys several prospects, and if none stands out with a clear inherent advantage, the nod will go to the city that gives the highest "bid." That bid can consist of the preferential financing described above—industrial revenue bonds, tax abatements, and the rest—along with aid in securing a site, educational programs for employees, or simply personal attention to executives.

A similar process is necessary to retain an employer who reveals interest in moving, whether a General Motors or the much more numerous small enterprises. In an example of the latter, Chicago recently provided a grant/loan package to enable Guernsey Dell, a manufacturer of ice cream flavorings, to build a new plant in what used to be the stockyards. The company needed a larger facility and was considering a move to another state. Often, it is less expensive for a city to keep an existing employer from leaving than to attract a new enterprise of the same size [Greenhouse 1986].

Cities and counties use their zoning powers and development of industrial parks to promote their employment base. Zoning, as chapter 5 showed, is primarily a regulatory device, more useful for excluding unwanted uses of land than for inducing the desired ones. However, such restrictions can be important to a developer looking for a high-amenity site for a corporate headquarters or high-technology laboratory. Many communities have special zones that are limited to such development and thus are an open invitation to them. Tight controls prevent excessive noise, smoke, outdoor materials storage, and heavy truck traffic, and require landscaping and attractive architectural features that give the site a campus-like appearance.

The industrial park combines an integrated zoning and development program with government provision of roads, utilities, and other infrastructures that will attract employers. These are common in suburban areas with their expanses of open land, but also appear in large city redevelopments. The former Chicago stockyards, mentioned above, and the Bathgate Industrial Park in the South Bronx are examples of this. On the previously occupied land, the costs of site clearance make it a more expensive proposition than on a "raw" suburban site, but utilities are already in, public transit is available, and prospective employees are likely to live close by.

The difficulties for many cities in securing major economic growth are enormous, however, and ambitious efforts do not necessarily pay off. In 1966, the U. S. Economic Development Administration initiated a program to bring new jobs to Oakland, California, which then suffered from a high unemployment rate. It had several components: new hangars and an air cargo terminal at the Oakland Airport, a marine terminal and industrial park at the Port of Oakland, and a number of loans to enable small businesses to expand. Planning began with high hopes, and the EDA committed $23 million to the program. But by 1969, only $3 million had actually been spent. In the words of two analysts of that effort, "construction has only been partially completed, business loans have died entirely, and the results in terms of minority employment are meager and disappointing" [Pressman & Wildavsky 1979, xviii]. The primary reason for this is that the administration of the program was enormously complex, involving five federal agencies, the city of Oakland (itself bifurcated between its mayor and the bureaucracy), the semi-independent Port of Oakland, and a variety of constituent groups and would-be clients. Joint action on the public works program alone required 70 successive positive decisions before it could be completed. Although that was possible, the organizational friction kept the pace too slow to reach the goal [Pressman & Wildavsky 1979, ch. 5].

Political conflict over industrial development can occur at several levels. Residents in the area may oppose building a factory or office on an open site near them, fearing the traffic or the intrusion on their views. Economic development in a region requires that chemical plants, waste processing facilities, truck freight terminals and similar "bad neighbors" be located somewhere. Such "LULUs" (Locally Unwanted Land Uses) present serious challenges to planners of both the public and private sectors. As Popper described them, LULUs have large negative externalities—noise, danger, ugliness, smells, or pollution. They impose costs on their neighbors (or are believed to) and pose health and safety hazards that could multiply if they were mismanaged [Popper 1987, 2–3].

While some LULUs have defenders, such as those who hope to be employed in them, they typically arouse organized opposition. When politically active, such groups cultivate popular fears (well-founded or not) and have natural political advantages in securing delays and denials from public planning agencies. When the dispute concerns electric power plants, whether nuclear powered or not, extensive federal and state environmental quality regulations and procedures generally work in the opponents' favor [Popper 1987].

On a more general level, when a public incentive is provided to obtain the employer, taxpayers should ask, "How much is really being given away?" and wonder what they get from it. They perceive that benefits will fall to some and not to others. Perhaps they will pay higher taxes as a result (but their levies could decrease if enough new tax base moves in). A further concern arises if the public perceives the subsidies going to a wealthy corporation which could easily finance the new facility from its own treasury. Essentially, the political process has the final word on how much the city or county pays in order to be competitive.

A further dilemma concerns what the community can demand of the employer so aided. In 1980, Chicago provided $1 million from an industrial revenue bond to the Playskool Corporation, a toymaker, for new equipment. The company stated it would add 446 jobs to its 1,150. Instead, the number of workers was cut to 700. In 1984, the Milton Bradley Company acquired Playskool and announced that its Chicago plant would be closed. The city sued, charging a breach of agreement by the company. The case illustrates both the difficulties in forecasting long-term outcomes of economic development programs, and the lack of obligation that firms have to communities which do aid them. The market, with all of its uncertainties, is still sovereign [Belsie 1984].

An important political force for economic growth in both small communities and large metropolitan areas is the local industrial development group (LIDG). It may be a public or semipublic agency, nonprofit corporation, or a branch of the chamber of commerce. Ottensmeyer and associates [1987, 570] report that they

> expend billions of dollars annually either directly or indirectly in
> various promotional and community improvement efforts to enhance

the industrial and commercial vitality and viability of places. In this role, LIDGs frequently serve as conduits for federal and state development policies whereby billions of dollars of public funds and tax expenditures have been funneled to communities and business firms.

Their success levels have differed widely, but where they are effective, they provide a crucial link between local planners, political leaders, and the business community. Their precise influences on local land use policy have not been researched, but could be substantial.

7.5 THE POLITICS OF DOWNTOWNS AND UPTOWNS

The most visible character of a metropolitan area is its downtown—that cluster of major office buildings, retail stores, government edifices, hotels, and cultural and amusement centers. Only some of the newer suburbs lack a distinct center of this type. Its very visibility gives it a political dominance as well, as mayors and city legislators are often judged on how well this focal point of the urban economy flourishes.

Many downtowns, of course, are not flourishing. Their structures dating back a half-century or more, they have lost customers, employees, and consequently investors. This is not true for Boston, Chicago, and San Fancisco and other command and control centers. And many others with fewer resources are spending to seek a resurgence in their traditional business districts. But this does not happen without political conflict over how and where those limited public resources are spent.

Actually, there are five kinds of business districts in metropolitan areas, understood primarily as retail centers but also containing offices and other enterprises. The *traditional downtown* is one, of course. If it is experiencing reasonable prosperity and even growth, it is still likely to have declining retail activity and an increasing concentration of offices. Managerial, financial, legal, and governmental offices must stay in the information stream to be effective, which requires continuous personal contacts with its carriers. "The central city continues to offer a location where channels carrying information of potential relevance to corporate offices are concentrated. This information is produced, stored, and exchanged through a dense inter-organizational network" [Friedland 1983, 65]. What retail activity remains is generally keyed to the needs of the daytime office workers or of the lower income households who live nearby. These offices require few low-skilled employees, and so most of their personnel live in the more affluent central-city neighborhoods or suburbs.

The challenges that downtowns present to planners vary with the circumstances. In some cities, it may be necessary only to regulate the growth that the private market initiates. On the opposite end of the spectrum, it may be difficult even to keep it from deteriorating further as an economic center. Most places are between these poles, and must combine efforts at maintenance and rehabilitation of older structures with attracting new investment and helping it locate in the most advantageous places.

A second type of business district serves the *neighborhoods* of the central city or its suburbs. Here one finds the grocery, hardware, and drug stores and others which serve the ordinary daily needs of the residents. Medical and legal offices, banks, and restaurants occupy other spaces. In past decades, these sprang up at the intersections of streetcar or bus lines, while now they locate where cars have easy access and parking. The economic and physical health of these centers depends on the neighborhoods that surround them— the amount of money their residents have and where they choose to spend it.

The third group consists of the *new downtowns*—the major suburban shopping centers that have drawn so much of the trade out of the first two types.

> Retail trade was pushed out by rising central-city land prices associated with high density use, and pulled out by the homeowner retail dollar receding across the horizon. Suburbanites took their purchasing power out of the central city and the retail sector followed its best customers to the suburbs. . . . Financed by the largest department store and retail chains, the centers draw on a vast freeway-borne market.

[Friedland 1983, 71]. These tend to be largely retail, with adjacent office development connected only with the largest of them. However, vast office complexes that lack close contact with the shopping centers have also risen along some suburban freeways.

These fringe-area downtowns pose complex challenges to planners. First, many are in suburban cities or unincorporated county areas, and no coordination may exist between their plans and those of other affected communities. Planning offices in those communities are less well staffed, and part-time public officials may not be able to examine the proposals in sufficient depth. Second, the centers' reliance on the automobile can pose severe traffic congestion. Mass transit service to these is minimal, and even a short walk from a center to a nearby restaurant may be impossible due to lack of pedestrian access [Cervero 1986]. They may also put demands on water and waste disposal services that are not adequately developed in that community.

A fourth type of commercial center is often smaller than the first and third, but like the suburban complex, owes its existence to the automobile. The *highway service strip* or cluster typically borders major roads on the outskirts of cities and encircling freeway interchanges. Increasingly, they also surround major airports. Common to these are automobile dealers and service facilities, truck terminals, motels, and restaurants. General shopping centers may also be located nearby. Unlike the comprehensive center of the third type, these have grown up spontaneously with no central design. Each new gas station or fast-food stop was added to what was already there, and they in turn attracted more business to the area. Unmanageable traffic flow is the major result from this lack of planning. Yet, service to travelers is a vital source of revenue and jobs to many communities, and they are reluctant to restrain this kind of development.

Fifth, *specialty retail centers* have appeared in many cities in the past decade—typically in the older areas. Visitors to Quincy Market in Boston, Harborplace in Baltimore and Trolley Square in Salt Lake City have seen some of its best-known representatives. Usually, it occupies one or more old buildings (perhaps an erstwhile factory or warehouse) that have been remodeled just enough to provide space for shops, restaurants, and other attractions, but preserve an historic ambiance. Some new construction may expand the original facilities also. The clientele for these is decidedly middle class—there are no discount stores or supermarkets. They supply a moderately affluent younger population with interesting alternatives to the traditional downtowns and the stamped-from-the-same-mold suburban shopping centers. They may also incorporate some professional offices whose tenants prefer their unique ambiance.

These specialized developments are spawned by private developers, as are the others, but often government has been an indispensable partner. Since these are actually redevelopments, the public subsidy has been instrumental in obtaining the sites and structures, assisting with utilities and parking and often in the remodeling. The planning challenge has been to forecast the financial success of an proposed project, and to scale its size both to the anticipated market and to the level of public support available. Since its location is often in a less desirable part of the city, its backers must determine that it will both attract patrons who would never venture into that neighborhood otherwise, and that it will have a positive relationship with its surroundings.

The best publicized political cooperation and conflict has often centered on renewal of the traditional downtowns. It has been of high priority to smaller and medium-sized cities that are losing business to other communities. One effort to aid them is the Centralized Retail Management program (CRM). In late 1985, the U. S. Department of Housing and Urban Development and the Urban Mass Transit Administration joined with the private International Downtown Association to give technical assistance to central business districts in 16 cities. CRM is a strategy wherein downtown property owners, retailers, and city officials plan for marketing, street improvements, parking, security and maintenance. By early 1987, planning was underway in such cities as Oak Park, Illinois, Eugene, Oregon, and Shelby, North Carolina. This approach allows each community to select the features most appropriate to its economic and political conditions [Stokvis 1987].

In some cases, large areas of central business districts have been rebuilt. New Haven, Connecticut, pioneered at this, having begun to obtain federal urban renewal funds as early as 1955. Its Church Street project, initiated in 1957, provided the city with two modern department stores, a hotel, a shopping mall, and several office buildings. It consumed $66 million in urban renewal funds, another $37.5 million of direct public construction costs, and some $64 million in nonpublic construction. But the experience also illustrates the risks entailed: today that downtown is seriously depressed, having lost many of its customers and clients to the suburbs. A further problem was not politically controversial at the time, but has been raised since—the severe displacement of low-income households that it caused and the forced relocation of more than 700 businesses [Fainstein et al. 1983, ch. 2]. Whatever benefits urban renewal projects like New Haven's have provided to cities, the net loss of low-cost (and admittedly, often substandard) housing has placed a hardship on those least able to afford homes at the same time that business interests benefited.

Another city in Connecticut—Hartford—also experienced downtown rebuilding, but for a time the government took a more active role in redevelopment. Led by Nicholas Carbone, a city councilman from 1969 to 1979, it began to acquire partial equity in several projects so as to obtain funds for housing and services in lower income areas. It further required that developers and owners of such projects provide jobs for minority city residents. This policy was dropped before it was fully implemented, since Carbone was defeated in his 1979 try for the office of mayor. The sharp-edged personality traits that enabled him to be effective in the short run accumulated enough opponents to bring his political career to an end [Clavel 1986, ch. 2].

Too much downtown growth may not be a common problem, but San Franciscans have defined it as such. In a 1984 referendum, the voters expressed their opposition to the Manhattan-style proliferation of office towers. A year later, the board of supervisors adopted a 139-page ordinance that imposes a 550-foot height limit on buildings (reduced from 700), an annual cap on the rate of their construction, protection of 251 historically or architecturally significant buildings, and strict design standards on new structures. Developers must further provide usable open space on or off the site and control the wind currents that would ordinarily sweep through the open areas at street level [Porter 1986]. San Francisco has a healthy downtown retail trade as well, nourished by a good public transit system, and politically active residents prize the unique character of their natural and built environment.

The tug of war between sponsors of central city and suburban locations for new retail developments also sparks political disputes. From the mid-1960s through 1974, Sioux City, Iowa, had spent $18 million in public funds to renew its central business district, and had just given the green light to a massive new project launched by a team of businessmen. Suddenly, a developer from Des Moines bought land on the city's edge with the intent of building a regional shopping center there. Unwilling to jeopardize its investment, the city council stalled on the rezoning necessary for the latter. Legal battles and financial bargaining continued until an electoral change in the council tipped the balance toward the suburban center. As two observers concluded, the people of Sioux City didn't really care that much about downtown; "many were ready and willing to accept regional shopping centers and malls as *their* way of life" [Babcock & Siemon 1985, 133]. Such contests between landowners, developers, and related interests have occurred in large and small cities across the country, but defenders of the "old" downtowns have rarely stemmed the rise of the "new."

7.6   HIGH STAKES AND HARD CHOICES

The evidence in this chapter shows that planning for economic development takes place in a tension between many political and economic forces. Government does allocate some valued things in this process, but it rarely does so apart from the influences of the marketplace and those who exert power within it. The number of influentials in a typical choice is far smaller than the sum of the stakeholders in it, however.

Public leaders and planners encounter in that tension between the marketplace and the council chamber some questions with no final answers. Recall the plight of the South Bronx, introduced in chapter 1. It has large areas suitable for industrial and commercial redevelopment, but those prospects are good only with substantial public subsidies for investors. Its planners seek employers and merchants who will employ or cater to the predominantly lower income residents of that area. But should they welcome a high technology facility that will employ mainly better-educated persons who live elsewhere in the region?

One question that hangs over the South Bronx, and every other urban region, is what kind of economic development should planners pursue? What, if anything, should they reject? One area, because of its site and situational factors, is likely to be more suited to heavy industry than anything else, while another could attract nothing more than motels and fast-food establishments. High-technology laboratories and offices are in much demand due to their upscale image and low-pollution nature, but there are not enough of them to go around. If an ·industrial waste processor proposes to locate in the South Bronx, will the community accept its job and tax base as fair compensation for its objectionable presence? A community that desperately needs even low-paying employment can ill afford to be picky.

A second question touches the more directly human factors: whom shall this development benefit? Who shall bear the burdens and disadvantages? This problem of distributive justice plagues all public policy choices, but when the benefits and burdens are "on the ground" they are all the more visible. This distribution can be by population groups—business executives as distinct from the unemployed, for example. Or it can take a geographic form, as when one neighborhood is favored with business district improvements over another. Central-city suburban distribution of benefits has long been a point of contention in such matters as industrial park development.

To illustrate this second issue, downtown renewal projects have been notorious for displacing the poorer residents who live in cheap hotels and rooming houses. This is one cause of the dramatic rise in homeless persons in the past few years. The paradox is obvious: modern structures replace what might have been eyesores and more jobs and tax revenue flow to the city as a whole. Yet those benefits are denied to the very ones who may pay the highest price for them. To be sure, the displaced may find another place to live, but the pressure on low-income housing tends to raise their costs. In Poletown, some of the residents welcomed the General Motors plant, expecting to find a better place to live, while others were much more pessimistic. If the Detroit housing market had been as tight as Boston's or San Francisco's, the distress from that dislocation would have been much more severe.

A further distributional problem lies in the competition between economic development and other uses of limited investment funds. When a city chooses to spend its supply of bonds, grants, loans, and infrastructure improvements on a renewed downtown or an industrial park, it has less to spend on the residential neighborhoods and their living environments. Such "downtown versus uptown" conflicts over the distribution of resources are common in city councils. Simply to subsidize industrial or commercial development rather than housing encounters opposition from advocates for the poor. One lower income neighborhood may have to compete with another for developmental resources that are inadequate to go around.

Other choices face government decision makers on the extent

of their own role in development. What should it pay, if anything, to bring in a McDonald's restaurant with its low-paying "McJobs"? Or should it subsidize a downtown shopping center with stores that cater to upper-income persons? Amid pressures for shelters for the homeless and health care for children, how much can it spend for infrastructure improvements to draw a new employer which might pay for itself in 30 years? So much depends on planners' forecasting abilities and their skills in convincing others that their prediction X is more realistic than prediction Y which is advanced by the chamber of commerce.

These choices leave much room for discretion, and into that room can move some broad ideological viewpoints which offer guidance to decision makers in such quandaries. The "trickle-down" view, held by most planners, public officials, and business leaders, stresses the broad public benefits which downtown renewal, industrial parks, and suburban shopping and office centers provide. They increase employment opportunities for citizens of all income levels, and expand governments' tax bases for schools, social services, and other public goods. Even though a new skyscraper may not directly employ many of the hitherto unemployed, it is likely to generate a flow of business that eventually will reach them. While this can hardly be called an ideology, it does embody a scenario of how the world works and guides future decisions about it.

Advocates of an alternative view of urban political economy reject such a unitary view of progress. They perceive society as divided into classes, with enough barriers between them to prevent many of the benefits for middle- or upper-income residents from trickling down to those at the bottom. As Sawers [1984, 7] draws the contrast,

> The conventional wisdom views the government as a neutral arbiter among competing interest groups. . . . The political economist, however, sees the government not sitting astride the class struggle but playing an active role in it. . . . The government, if it is to protect the prosperity of the economy and the livelihood of its constituents, has no choice but to rationalize or even subsidize the process of capital accumulation.

In this second perspective, urban officials have "a consistent bias towards redevelopment which favors the interests of business firms, elite institutions (hospitals, universities), and middle-class residents." What results is "a deeply rooted system of municipal mercantilism biased against the lower classes" [Fainstein et al. 1983, 251]. Redevelopment policies in the older large cities thus claim urban territory for business and middle class interests. What remains in run-down neighborhoods and cleared areas is simply "reserve land," waiting for future use which may be decades away, depending on market and governmental choices [Marris 1982, 29]. The South Bronx is an obvious example of idle ground, which has not yet been chosen by investors for improvement. But when they do, this view predicts, there may be precious few jobs or homes for the very poorest.

These two views do not differ significantly in their perceptions of the process. In both, the dominant development interests have the bulk of the power in planning choices that are significant to them. They part company primarily in their judgment of who benefits from those choices over the long run, and whether those benefits should be targeted more directly at the disadvantaged. A secondary difference is over how permeable the system is to influence by the poor and minorities; those who hold the trickle-down position claim there is adequate opportunity for them should they choose to use it.

The evidence here indicates that the large corporate interests and the public officials allied with them clearly controlled the major development choices, from Times Square to Poletown to BART. It is not as easy to show who has benefited from them, since some "disadvantaged" persons may indeed have been helped while others were not. But there remain the "hinterlands" of small-scale and neighborhood planning in which the large interests take no real part. In the South Bronx and Southeast Baltimore, popularly initiated programs direct benefits to the residents, although they are by no means extensive enough to meet all the needs. Often, the conflict is not between "corporate interests" and "the people" at all, but between other alignments, as in the San Diego moratorium vote and the New Jersey housing choices.

Recall the "economic determinism" versus "political free will" debate introduced in section 7.1. It has stimulated scholars of urban political economy to produce a wide variety of evidence, most of which leans toward the latter position. Clarence Stone [1987, 4–5] concluded from it,

> Local decision makers do not simply follow the imperatives that emanate from the national political economy; they must also inter-

pret those imperatives, apply them to local conditions, and act on them within the constraints of the political arrangements they build and maintain. . . . Local politics matters, but it is shaped by the political-economy context.

The investors of capital and the public officials who are accountable to the people share the stage of power, but they can reach many different kinds of accommodations, and other actors can join them on that stage to shape the outcomes.

Local political systems thus have varying degrees of freedom to develop their communities as they wish. That freedom depends heavily on their economic goals, though. To attract a Japanese auto plant or retain an American one, it has to conform to strict corporate expectations. But to seek a variety of small enterprises instead, several strategies can work. It also depends on the current dynamics of growth. A city with a healthy economy has more political options than one with a stagnant economy: contrast San Francisco and its housing linkage policy with Detroit's obeisance to General Motors. Political choices can do much in the long run to enlarge that freedom, which puts much responsibility on planners to design programs with high future payoffs.

Ultimately, the plans and outcomes of urban economic development demonstrate who is really in power, who has the final authority to make or unmake decisions. While there may not be an exact correlation between who governs and who benefits from that governance, they are not likely to diverge widely. If money and the ability to direct its flow indeed amounts to political power, then "municipal mercantilism" is a valid concept. But if that resource does not automatically make one powerful, other perspectives open up. To weigh these alternative explanations is the burden of the next chapter.

QUESTIONS FOR DISCUSSION

1. How does the evidence supporting the Peterson "determinist" view of the political economy of urban development compare with the "slack system" position?
2. What political factors influence a city's choice to subsidize a particular industrial or commercial development?

3. What kinds of industries are most and least desired by cities? What locations are best for each kind?
4. What advantages and disadvantages accompany investments in the traditional downtowns as compared with the other kinds of business districts?
5. What evidence would the advocates of the conventional and class-based views of urban political economy use to support their arguments against one another?

8 | THE POWER TO PLAN

8.1 WHAT THE POWERFUL HAVE THAT OTHERS DON'T

Power: what difference does it make to the planning process to have it or lack it? This chapter begins by looking back on the ground already covered and asking some pointed questions about who does planning. Chapter 1 presented a very brief definition of *power:* one person or group securing an action or outcome in a situation that would not otherwise come about. But this concept must be expanded, now that the extensive cast of participants has appeared in chapters 3 and 4 and their myriad activities in the three chapters that followed. To organize all of this evidence demands more discriminating concepts of power.

The goal of this chapter is to portray the structures—the consistent and predictable relationships among persons and institutions—that allocate valued things through the planning process. With this, one might explain why, for example, major developers consistently secure approval for their projects in most cities. Further, with good explanations, one can prescribe with some degree of confidence policies that can realistically guide the growth of a metropolitan area in the next decade. A grasp of the "power map" of an urban area is essential to these ends.

But what then is power—what does one have, really, when one has power? Definitions abound, often devised by a theorist or researcher to name a concept important to that person's purposes. And, like the efforts of the proverbial blind men examining the elephant, all of their insights can be useful. Five views merit discussion here. Although they overlap somewhat, each highlights a dimension important to the planning process.

First, power can exist in one's ability (the "one" can be an individual or a collective) to define a problem and determine whether it is public in character. The reformers in late nineteenth century American cities perceived the wretched conditions in which the poor lived, as did the conservative wealthy, if they cared to look. But was it a problem? and for whom? Those who defined slums as a natural and inevitable fact of city life, not to be tampered with by government, used their power to exclude housing quality from public policy debates. When the reformers won public offices and gained popular attention, they obtained the power to define slums as a genuine public problem, a necessary prerequisite to action on them. Thus, to be able to add issues to, or exclude them from, the public agenda, is an evidence of power [Bachrach & Baratz 1963].

A second way of viewing power is to define it as the ability to act in a future conflict. This potential power exists behind the day-to-day control of money, credit, jobs, land, information, or other valued items. It is like a lake behind a hydroelectric dam: the water is there but not currently being used to generate current. Some scholars deny that this potential is genuine power. But Hunter [1953] concluded from his research in Atlanta that a "law of anticipated reactions" is at work. That is, because a person in the community has a great deal of money, or is a major employer, others will seek to fit their plans and actions to his because they expect he will use his resources to induce them to act in that way. Since planning is inherently a future-focused process, these anticipations are important.

A third kind of power exists in actual conflict situations. There, it is not the possession of "things" but a quality of relationships that confers power. Bachrach and Baratz [1963, 635] state that it exists when "(a) there is a conflict over values or a course of action between A and B; (b) B complies with A's wishes; and (c) he does so because he is fearful that A will deprive him of a value or values which he, B, regards more highly than those which would have been achieved by noncompliance." For example, a city council may be reluctant to subsidize a new plant for a major local industry. But when the company announces that if it does not get it, it will close and move out of state, it poses the prospect of unacceptable deprivation to the city—loss of jobs and tax base. In most such cases, the council yields to this show of power.

A fourth view examines the outcomes of political conflict—to paraphrase Lasswell [1958], "who got what, when, how." Planning distributes home and business locations, means of mobility, access to parks, opportunities for employment, and many other benefits. The "powerful" are defined as those who have maximized their advantages at the expense of the weaker. Employers of office and service workers increasingly select suburban locations, preferably near airports, freeways, and high-amenity residential areas. But the employees themselves often cannot afford to live in those highly desirable areas, and are confined to less desirable central-city neighborhoods and a long trip with no public transportation. Such a distribution reveals who really has the power, according to this perspective, more clearly than any analyses of specific conflicts.

Last, a form of power resides in the control that individuals have over groups and institutions which in themselves exert power (or influence). The president of the major bank in a city, which is the source of many development loans, can determine whether a projected office building does in fact rise on a site. This power is not personal but institutional. In the same way, a mayor or planning director can steer the city council or bureaucracy toward or away from support of a neighborhood renewal program. The group is the intermediary between the person and the action, and the power must first be exerted on it. The one with the most power in the group need not be its formal head; a dominant council member or lobbyist may be able to override a mayor's wishes on key issues.

Combining these five perspectives portrays power as a key element in all stages of the planning and decision making cycles, from the initial identification of a potential issue to its resolution. It has different "faces" in the contexts of different choices. Thus, although the reformers secured the power to place slums on the public agenda, it took decades in most cities to initiate large-scale housing programs to deal with them—an effort of much greater magnitude.

Power also needs some distinctions in terms of what enables a person or group to exert it. The definition from Bachrach and Baratz under the third form above states that B complies to avoid being deprived (by A) of something of value. This needs to be interpreted broadly. For example, power can be exerted through physical force, in which the valued thing can be B's life or property. While this is a central theme of international relations, it scarcely applies to domestic politics. Persons have brandished shotguns to defend their homes against demolition to make way for a new freeway, but these conflicts are typically resolved by legal processes.

Many factors confer power upon one in "normal" political situations. The command of money and credit is crucial in land development, as is the ownership of the site itself. Votes, and the ability to sway them toward a candidate (or toward one outcome of a referendum), are currencies in which all elected and many appointed officials trade. But conflicts are also managed with resources that do not involve "A depriving B," at least not directly or with tangible values. One example of this in choice-making situations is what is often called *influence*. Using it, A still prevails in a conflict, but without the threat of deprivation of something that B values [Bachrach & Baratz 1963, 637]. Perhaps A could be a small group of environmentally concerned citizens who seek to prevent a wildlife-rich swamp from being filled for development. If they succeed, it is not because they can threaten council members with electoral defeat, but because they present information about the value of that wetland to the community, and their argument is accepted as valid. Influence may come from a personal gift of persuasiveness, from the possession of specialized information that others respect, or even from a plea for aid that draws sympathy from decision makers. The range of influence sources is wide and the line between it and power is often blurred.

Another important source of power is legal *authority* vested in an elective or appointive public office. Such a person has been vested with certain powers (note the plural) to act on the public's behalf. While many of these powers are defined in local, state, and federal law, they leave much discretion to each incumbent on how and when to use them. The San Diego referendum on La Jolla Valley did not challenge the city council's right to specify development controls, but rather the widsom of the choice itself. On the other hand, many New Jersey suburbanites rejected the authority of their state courts to "dictate" residential zoning choices of local units contrary to citizen wishes.

Complex programs which involve many separate planning decisions, as Detroit's accommodation of General Motors in Poletown, demonstrates all forms of power at work. What it took to convince Mayor Young to support the effort in the beginning stage was much different from the solution imposed on the Poletown residents at the end of the conflict. One kind of power is used to induce allies to cooperate; another kind works to enable one contestant to prevail in open conflict.

In all five views, power is the ability to accomplish one's purposes against opposition in whatever scenarios of competition and cooperation arise. There is no established formula for it but a intangible blend of resources, skills, knowledge, and contacts that are appropriate to their context. It is a function both of having the necessary resources and the will to apply them toward one's ends. To be *powerless*, therefore, is to be unable to affect a situation through lack of either or both. It makes much difference whether one is powerless only due to the lack of will or because the resources are absent. The uneven distribution of power in society has deep roots, but efforts to secure its realignment are themselves targets for cooperation and conflict.

8.2 WHO HAS THE POWER IN THE COMMUNITY?

The next step in this inquiry is to learn how power can be structured. Only with systematic insight can one answer such questions as "who is powerful *here?*" and "who is likely to prevail in the next planning conflict here?" Fortunately for observers of political power, the same individuals and groups tend to appear time and again in similar actions. This is the basis for a *power structure,* which Bryan Jones [1983, 176] defined as "the regularized exercise of power within a social system. It is distinguished from single exercises of power in that it takes place repeatedly over time. . . . and involves a set of regularly interacting individuals."

We can survey several models of power structures. Each draws upon empirical evidence of decision making in one or more American cities, planning issues included. They differ rather sharply in their overall pictures, due to their research methodology and the cities they surveyed.

The *elitist* model is the oldest, first set forth by Russell and Helen Lynd [1929] in a study of Muncie, Indiana, in the 1920s. They found that the city was effectively run by one family; no important public decisions were made without its participation or acquiescence. Floyd Hunter [1953] sought in various ways to learn who were the top decision makers in Atlanta. Several land use and development issues were included among those on which this power could be displayed. Basically, he found the "powerful" ranked in four layers: on top were the industrial, commercial, and financial owners and the top executives of large enterprises; on the second level were the corporate leaders just below the highest executives and, significantly, the city's government officials. Underneath them on the ladder of influence were the public and private organization personnel who carried out the will of the top two ranks, and the communications specialists who publicized them. Corporate and service professionals, such as ministers, teachers, and social workers occupied the fourth rank [Hunter 1953, 107–8]. He also found a similar structure among Atlanta's black community, which was as a whole subordinated to the white leadership [Hunter 1953, ch. 5].

In its most basic form, elitism consists of several claims: (1) political power in the city is wielded by a single group of persons in the upper socioeconomic class of the citizenry; (2) they use their power to protect or advance their own class interests; (3) they are cohesive in that they agree at least in principle on what key decisions should be made; (4) they are exclusive, preventing entry into their ranks by those with different interests; and (5) they select and/ or dominate the elected officials, who, if they are not part of that elite, do their bidding. Some scholars add the claim that the elite is regional or national in scope, linked with broad corporate and financial powers that have specific interests in many local communities [Domhoff 1978].

Five years after Hunter's study of Atlanta appeared, Robert Dahl put forth a rival model based on his research in New Haven, Connecticut. He examined decision making on three specific issues: urban renewal, education, and political party nominations. His evidence pointed not to a single power elite but to separate influential groups for each issue. Only one person proved to have real influence in all three areas: Mayor Richard Lee. He further argued that power exists not in the reputation for having it (as Hunter conceived it in Atlanta) but in actually using it in observable relationships. He concluded that New Haven's political system was pluralistic in that it had "slack resources" (that is, opportunities for new entrants to gain influence), decisions were dominated by professional politicians with their accountability to the voters, and it contained built-in limitations to the influence of all participants [Dahl 1958, 305].

The central claims of the pluralists are: (1) the resources for power—money, votes, publicity, information—are widely distributed around communities, thus, political power is not the monopoly of a single group; (2) many groups are in position to compete for public decisions, which often represent a wide cross section of the population, such as labor unions, small business owners, and neighborhood organizations; (3) these intergroup conflicts are often mediated by elected public officials, who can act independently of them; (4) policies and power relationships can shift over time as power resources ebb and flow; and (5) ordinary citizens indirectly shape public policy not only through the groups that represent them but also by their votes. Even if only a few have real decision making power, they are (in this model) competitors who make the contests more public and so create greater opportunities for outsiders to become involved. It is alleged to be more democratic a model than elitism for this reason.

A traditional form of power structure that has both elitist and pluralist features is the political party machine that has ruled many cities and counties. Headed by a "boss" or oligarchy, its power base is its ability to command the votes of the masses. These votes, in turn, were "purchased" by a host of favors—jobs, food, public services, and less tangible goods—distributed by the boss and his lieutenants. However, the machine seldom took the initiative in planning issues, allowing these decisions to be made by the business community with which it was usually allied. The Daley machine in Chicago (1955–1979), probably the best researched, had a close relationship with the industrial and downtown corporate interests, assuming that what benefited business usually served its own political purposes as well.

A third perspective is that there is *no* stable power structure that can be counted on to make consistent decisions. Yates [1977, 34] described as "street-fighting pluralism" a situation plagued by "unstructured, multilateral conflict in which many different combatants fight continuously with one another." The many powerholders get in each other's way and often prevent agreement on issues or implementation of agreements that do emerge. This was not based on specific research data, but the many references to New York City in his book suggest that he had in mind large cities in general, struggling with difficult housing, transportation, and social-service dilemmas amid a host of socioeconomic groups competing for benefits.

Another form of "nonstructure" is familiar to observers in many small communities: power is low-keyed and personal; there are few if any organized interest groups, and issues are quietly settled by public officials and the few private citizens who choose to participate. If a controversial choice arises, one or more groups appear to contend over it, but vanish afterward. Elections to executive and legislative posts have little organized competition. If one or a few persons do dominate, it may be more by default than a conscious grasping for power. Wildavsky's portrait of Oberlin, Ohio [1964, ch. 18], comes close to this model; only the activity of one council member gave that community significant leadership. Participants took part largely as individuals speaking only for themselves.

Power structure research, however, has often overlooked another question: the *geographic scale* on which the power is exercised. Most studies confined their scope to a single city, a demanding enough task for serious inquiry. Rarely has any unit larger or smaller been surveyed. Nevertheless, neighborhoods, counties, metropolitan areas, and larger urban regions are also significant arenas for exercise of power and influence.

Neighborhood organizations, surveyed in section 4.5, can serve as power structures within their boundaries. Most subareas of cities have a power vacuum, with no real leadership by individuals or associations. Others have a single source of influence, such as the Southeast Community Organization in Baltimore, which appears to be very pluralistic internally [Cunningham & Kotler 1983, 71–81]. Power in the East Los Angeles neighborhood is divided between two groups, although they have different functions and modes of operation [Ventriss & Pecorella 1984]. Still others, such as Chicago's Uptown, seem to be highly fragmented, though perhaps not to the "street-fighting" degree [E. Warren 1979]. In cities and counties which elect legislators by wards, that representative is often a significant figure in neighborhood politics.

It is difficult to conceive of a power structure that covers an entire metropolitan area, since it lacks a single general-purpose governing authority. Yet it is obvious that counties, special authorities for sanitation, transit, airports, and parks, and state highway departments make critical land use choices for those regions— who exercises influence over them?

The findings of Roscoe Martin and his associates [1965, 323] in the Syracuse, New York, metropolitan area seem typical.

> There tend to be as many decision centers as there are important decision areas, . . . power is fragmented among the institutions, agencies, and individuals which cluster about these areas. . . . There appear to be many kinds of community power, with one kind differing from another in so many fundamental ways as to make virtually impossible a meaningful comparison.

Thus, the usual intracity pluralism is compounded by the fragmentation of authority between governments. It is quite possible that a small elite can control the narrow choices of a drainage district at the same time that the region as a whole lacks cohesive leadership on larger issues.

It is also possible to identify regional leaders and power structures in the "Bos-Wash Megalopolis," the heavily urbanized region between Boston and Wahington, D. C. It has many interrelated land use problems, from transportation and housing to pollution control and recreational space. A cluster of organizations and their leaders have increasingly been communicating among themselves, with their local and state governments and with the relevant federal agencies. While they do not constitute a full power structure (for the same reasons that metropolitan areas do not), they do exert influence on a wide range of public policy choices [Miller 1974].

All of these power structures, whether elitist or pluralist, have vertical as well as horizontal dimensions. That is, they have connections with entities outside their community or region that can either expand or restrict their choices. The local industrial manager who heads the chamber of commerce may really be serving the corporate headquarters in New York. The president of the union local shares convictions with superiors in Detroit. And of course, the rules and finances provided by state and federal government agencies constrain everyone.

In this context, Domhoff [1978, 45] criticized Dahl's pluralist findings on urban renewal in New Haven because he failed to consider state and national influences. If he had, he would have found links with major economic interests and the upper-class network of Yale University graduates and administration. These essentially shaped the plans to which the "pluralist" network gave approval. Dahl had admitted [1958, 115] that "urban redevelopment had been the direct product of a small handful of leaders," although he minimized the role of the federal officials who financed most of it.

Depending on the specific vertical pressures exerted on local decisions, one could view the local community as either a "sandbox" (in which, like castle-building children under adult supervision, local officials are dominated in their major choices by those outside forces) or a "shopping mall," in which local leaders gain resources from the outside to accomplish more than they could otherwise [Wirt 1985, 86–87]. These external influences may thus serve to centralize power at the local level in some instances, but fragment it in others. Most of the evidence in this book supports the "shopping mall" model, although the resources obtained vary widely with the community and project.

8.3 POWER STRUCTURES IN PLANNING CHOICES

If a city or urban area has any power structure at all, it should be evident in major planning choices. One might expect that an elite structure would make those choices more easily and quickly, with less conflict, than a pluralist system. However, once the latter made the decision, it would be better accepted by the public—so it could be assumed. There are too many variables to draw such an easy conclusion, however.

This section will again make use of the types of planning decisions introduced in chapter 1. The display of power can be expected to vary with the scope and nature of the choice, whatever other variables are present. The additional cases presented here portray the complexity one encounters in seeking clear identities of the "powerful." In particular, they illustrate interplays involving more than one government and competing private interests.

First, decisions in Type 1—small in scale and limited in impact—will rarely attract the attention, much less the efforts, of the larger power wielders in the community. Only if one of these appeared to be a link in a chain of more consequential decisions would some larger interest group intervene.

Type 2 choices deal with major private development projects with much broader impact than in Type 1. Here, government also acts as regulator, choosing whether to allow them after due consideration for all of their effects. Who the developer is becomes a crucial issue. A major employer or investor in the city who has long been part of the power structure stands a good chance of winning approval. Assuming that the project is not a heavy polluter or is otherwise perceived by the public's representatives to degrade property values or living amenities, the benefit of the doubt is typically in its favor. If it will provide significant new employment or expand the tax base, opponents are likely to be few and unconvincing.

For example, in 1980 General Motors, which had major plants in Pontiac, Michigan, chose to build a new facility and selected a 500-acre site in semirural Orion Township, just north of that city. Township officials delayed the necessary rezoning, fearing heavy traffic, pollution, and loss of their valued tranquility, but ultimately gave approval. Opponents forced a referendum, which failed, and the plant was finally built. The city of Pontiac was not at all pleased to lose that tax base, yet backed the project since it had no suitable sites within its limits.

> The ability of General Motors to generate overwhelming support for a move *out* of town is important evidence of the ability of a corporation to influence community decision making by indirect means. . . . Making decisions that were contrary to the wishes of GM in Pontiac seems to have been simply out of the question.

[Jones & Bachelor 1986, 177]. Similarities to the Poletown case are obvious.

Government undertakings constitute decisions of Type 3. This process of choosing is legally more public and thus invites more open conflict. Because most such projects benefit (or harm) private interests and purposes, they are often subject to intense pressures. Highways, airports, mass transit systems, and harbors embody particularly high stakes and so furnish excellent examples. In this type, conflict is as likely to arise between units of government as between nongovernmental participants. Alliances form between one or more governments and a cluster of private groups who happen to be on the same side of the issue.

Highway building provides many examples of complex Type 3 conflict and cooperation. One of the more durable power structures in public works policy is the highway coalition, composed of construction, trucking, tourism, and related interests. Born in the 1910s when a significant number of motor vehicles were beginning to clog the streets and roads, the coalition has flourished due both to the demands of motorists for highways and the willingness of legislators to tax them for their construction and maintenance.

In the New York metropolitan area, the 1950s and 1960s witnessed the completion of many new freeways and toll roads. The New York and New Jersey state highway departments, flush with federal funds, had full authority to determine whether and where they were built. Neither local officials nor local private elites in the various suburban communities through which they passed could block them. Only concerted action by all of the suburbs and their allied interests stood a chance of altering the alignments, but this did not come about in those decades. In fact, those communities which were not in the proposed rights-of-way had an incentive to support the highway planners, since they could benefit without being disrupted [Danielson & Doig 1982, 120–122].

As the 1970s proceeded, however, the environmental protection movement gained followers, and among its targets were major highway projects. Increasingly, highway departments found themselves facing a united front of local officials, civic leaders, and neighborhood associations. They were forced to reroute, redesign, or cancel outright their newer efforts. For example, plans for a bridge across Long Island Sound, east of New York City, were torn up by Governor Rockefeller in 1973 after residents and protectionist groups mounted a vigorous campaign against it. This occurred even though many of the governmental and business leaders on both sides of the Sound endorsed the bridge initially [Danielson & Doig 1982, 133–136].

This interplay between political leaders, private interest groups, and government bureaucracies is also visible in Type 3 choices within cities. McCormick Place, Chicago's massive exhibition hall on its south lakefront, was conceived in the early 1950s by Col. Robert McCormick, publisher of the *Chicago Tribune*. Other business interests quickly joined him in hopes of attracting more convention dollars to the city. Its largest meeting hall at the time was the International Amphitheater, on the edge of the odiferous stock-yards. McCormick assembled a coalition that induced the Illinois legislature to establish a special authority to finance and build it. Another coalition came into being to block it for a variety of reasons, buoyed by the Chicago Plan Commisson's objections to the chosen site. The legal and political maneuvering went on for several years, during which time Richard Daley became mayor and gave his support to the hall. The relative influence of the *Tribune* and the mayor remains uncertain, but each found it advantageous to agree on the project from which they both would benefit. The overall process was pluralistic, but not simplistically so [Banfield 1961, ch. 7].

The *public-private partnership* choices of Type 4 are based on a simple logic.

> The map of any urban region can be seen as a series of development opportunities that have various risks and rewards for developers and various costs and benefits for the public sector. The market and public policy are two countervailing forces. Often, these forces are in consonance, and positive growth that is well planned, well received, and remunerative is the result.

[DeSeve 1986, 60]. Thus, an ideal partnership is rooted both in a sound plan and in a realistic grasp of the market. The partners recognize that each has some of the ability (or power) necessary to undertake a project, but not all that is required.

This situation underlines the cooperative aspect of planning rather than the confrontational. This is not to ignore the conflict that often arises, but to stress that the negotiations required to establish that working relationship dominate the political process. Chapter 1 noted several steps in Type 4 bargaining, from justifying the project to its final implementation. The partners may number only two in simple projects, but in more complex ones may include two or more government agencies, business corporations, nonprofit organizations, foundations, universities, and neighborhood associations. On the surface, at least, power may be shared by many competing interests, although if a "street-fighting pluralism" prevails, the effort may never succeed.

In spite of the apparent equality of the partners, one of them may still dominate the decision making. Thus, it is necessary to examine who initiated the project, whose initial terms prevailed, and who gained the most from it in financial or political goods. Reliable evidence for any of these is scant, and any answer must largely depend on inferences. For example, in Pittsburgh's experience with urban renewal between 1943 and the early 1970s, it appeared that

> corporate political strategy was to dominate the origins of urban renewal planning, while political elites—especially Democratic mayors—were highly visible in the execution and implementation. . . . Corporate organizations had already set the parameters—often through corporate-financed redevelopment plans—within which later urban renewal controversies would rage.

[Friedland 1983, 94]. Because the corporations and the politicians had different but complementary goals, both could be satisfied.

Pittsburgh also provides examples of neighborhood renewal by partnerships. Many of the city's residential communities have active citizen organizations that are able to plan for housing improvement and economic development. The city, together with several local foundations and lending institutions, has funded many improvement efforts designed by the neighborhood groups. Since the late 1970s, $76 million in public funds has been matched by private investment approaching $100 million, over 2,600 new homes have been built, and 20,000 older homes rehabilitated. Surveys have shown increased public satisfaction with their neighborhoods [Ahlbrandt 1986]. In this case, the power structure appears to have empowered persons and communities who would have had little otherwise (though their voting potential was always in the political leaders' minds).

Type 5 decisions that entail long-range, comprehensive plan making present the greatest challenge in discerning power arrangements. Because they embody many decisions that could affect diverse constituencies, the cooperative dimension must dominate this process also. But because they are projected well into the future, they are always regarded as tentative. Thus some potentially powerful participants may wait until a choice to implement the plan is made before contesting the issues raised by it.

Controversies over long-range planning erupt most often not over the goals and principles of the plan, nor its overall design, but over specific points. A neighborhood homeowners' organization may notice on the projected land use map a nearby vacant parcel designated for industrial use—and strongly object to the entire plan on that basis. When several groups find specific features with which they disagree, they may join to secure the plan's defeat, even though they separately find nearly all of it acceptable.

It is in this realm that professional planners and citizen planning commission members often enjoy the most influence. To begin to plan may be their choice, and they take the lead in setting forth the goals and standards. They also possess the information about the community on which the plan is based: its natural environment, housing conditions, employment base, and traffic problems. This gives them some credibility when they advocate expansion of moderate-income housing supply, reconstruction of bridges, or addition of park land.

Planners have found, however, that a good plan is only a small beginning, and even the meaning of "good" is fuel for political fires. In the late 1950s, the Planning Department of Saint Paul, Minnesota, prepared a comprehensive land use plan that was regarded as quite cautious and in the mainstream of public preferences. However, it was basically ignored by the political and civic leaders, who could see in it no relevance to the central choices they had to make just then [Altschuler 1965, ch. 2]. No one saw any reason even to try to exert power over it.

In partial contrast, planners in its twin city of Minneapolis were at the same time working on a design for future development of its downtown core. It embodied more specific recommendations, including turning Nicollet Avenue into the car-free shopping mall which it has become. The Downtown Council, an important network of business and real estate interests, came to see the plan as embodying their own objectives. Although that council did not endorse it wholesale, it did select it as a point of departure for continuing discussions. As for the planners,

> they achieved their objective of working within the most relevant framework of power . . . the City Council and mayor would normally ratify proposals for downtown behind which downtown businessmen united so long as they did not require substantial expenditure by the city. The reason was not that central area businessmen possessed great power, but that no other interest groups were likely to challenge them on downtown affairs.

The planners had already used the Downtown Council's consultants in drafting the plan's economic objectives, and thus had coopted it to some extent [Altschuler 1965, 285–286]. To be involved in long-range planning requires close and sustained interest, and only well-organized groups with clear economic stakes are likely to seek power over it.

8.4 PLANNING BY COALITIONS

Several points stand out after review of the evidence so far in this chapter. First, decisions are normally made by a few. Even when mass public opinion exerts influence or the voters make a choice, the situation has previously been framed and defined by those who had been active to that point. This does not, of course, specify which few are involved in any given case nor whom they represent.

Second, the circle of players who are cooperating and contesting with others can expand or contract. Few decision episodes are entirely closed, but in even fewer are "outsiders" likely to be welcomed. Those who want to retain power often find that it depends in part on their determination not to share it with others.

A third point is that who exerts power depends on the kind of decision made. The nature of the project proposed and whom it impacts inherently draws in persons with some kinds of interests rather than others. Types 3 and 4 normally have the most complex patterns of political influence.

An additional point has not yet been clearly demonstrated, but will be in this section: the alignments of power often change as the decision moves through several stages of specific choices. Thus, time is a crucial element of power wielding, creating opportunities for those who realize the right moment to intervene.

The theme of this section is that power in complex planning situations is best understood in a *coalitional* perspective. The evidence cited in this book portrays some intricate patterns that do not fit a simple elitist versus pluralist dichotomy. It is probably impossible, in a medium-sized or large city or metropolitan area, to find a single cohesive elite ruling consistently and without serious challenge. But classic pluralism, with many groups competing equally across a range of important issues, is also uncommon.

Frederick Wirt [1974, 5–6], introducing his research on San Francisco, defined the city as a complex set of transactions—exchanges between persons and groups for material and symbolic goods that each finds of value. These goods can include housing, jobs, the opportunity to develop a parcel of land, or a pleasant mountain view. The boundaries of this exchange extend far beyond the city limits; transactions made in many places, by governmental and private actors, in Washington, New York, and Tokyo, determine who gets what, when, and how. To make these transactions, alliances (or coalitions) are being constantly formed, reformed, and realigned. A study of power must focus on these coalitions.

Coalitional politics interweaves cooperation and conflict. People may join in agreement on one transaction—perhaps a downtown renewal program—but oppose one another on a highway project. Some groups, such as downtown business interests and bankers, are frequent allies, while labor unions and neighborhood associations may seldom make common cause with them. The fragmentation in both private interests and governmental authorities in a large urban area makes these coalitions necessary, since no one participant has the wherewithal to undertake a major development by itself. But this same condition renders these coalitions unstable from one issue to the next. Planning politics (and that of other high-stake urban issues) centers on the task of creating and maintaining agreements among groups and leaders who have good reason to disagree but also stand to gain from cooperation.

Wirt [1974, 47–48] offered a useful typology of community power models based on diverse coalition forms. At one end of a spectrum (from most to least centralized or "elitist") was the *stable dominant group* that consistently decides all issues of importance to it. This approximates Hunter's power structure of Atlanta [1953]. One step over is the *stable dominant constellation (consensual),* composed of two or more clusters of interest that prevail over all rivals in a contest. The interaction of the automobile manufacturers and the United Auto Workers in Detroit suggest this type. The third is the *stable dominant constellation (dissensual),* which resembles the second except that those who are not in the winning group tend to reject the legitimacy of the outcome. This form is rare, since a participant in the coalition is unlikely to be totally excluded from the benefits.

A much looser form is the *occasional coalition:* an alliance that prevails in policy choices more frequently than others, but does not win often enough to dominate the process. At the far end is the *temporary coalition,* lacking the cohesion to exert power on more than one issue. These coalitions may well specialize by issue: one that takes an interest in transportation will probably not have time to address housing problems. The larger the city or region, the more likely this specialization is to occur, judging from the cases of New York and Chicago.

It is important to understand, also, who is *not* involved in whatever coalitions control a community's planning. Certain groups are politically disadvantaged in the typical city: the poor, racial and non-English-speaking minorities, the physically and mentally handicapped, and the transient. However, coalitions can expand to include them if they push hard enough; the election of Mayor Harold Washington in Chicago in 1983 gave the black population a major place in the coalitions governing that city. In other places, the physically handicapped have organized to shape housing and transportation policies in their favor. Hispanics have remained in the disadvantaged class except where, as in San Antonio, they have mobilized their votes to elect a mayor and council members from their ranks.

Planning decisions in Types 2 through 5 are not instantaneous, and often emerge within broader policies. The interplay, according to Stone [1976, 14], is complex to a fault.

> Policies usually result, however, not from a few key decisions but rather from a series of decisions, many of which appear to be unimportant when viewed singly. . . . Decisions at one stage may be negated by the absence of follow-through actions at a subsequent stage. Conversely, proposals rejected at one point may be revived, altered, or even replaced by substitute proposals that still enable objectives to be realized. . . . Cumulative results give shape to policies.

The more time this process takes, the greater opportunity there is for the participating coalitions to shift in composition and influence. E. E. Schattschneider's description [1960, 4] of how conflict can expand as it proceeds through time is relevant here (see section 3.1). Some contestants seek delay to give them time to regroup their forces, secure new allies, or revise their proposals. It also serves to distract public attention from the choices, in many cases. As Stone [1976, 4] observed, "the populace is seldom in a position to observe the full scope of official conduct and to weigh the cumulative results of governmental actions." When private actors, such as a downtown business association or consortium of land developers, are deciding, they can restrict the information flow even more.

In general terms, complex decisions move through five stages, somewhat parallel to the planning cycle described in chapter 1. The first concerns definition of the problems which the decision aims to solve, setting of the goals, and preliminary design of the solution. Usually, this coalition is small, even though the problem may be widely recognized. Recall the discussion of the Bay Area Rapid Transit System in chapter 1: the business-oriented Bay Area Council began working on transportation problems in 1944. A handful of people meeting over lunch can take the first steps toward a multi-billion dollar project, and so set the direction in which it will thereafter move. The few principals give their efforts no publicity, and expand the group only as they see fit.

A second stage opens with formal project planning. If a small business group controlled the first stage, it would probably at this point bring in some government officials. If a public endeavor, more participants are engaged to provide the technical and design expertise. The specific plans for BART were drawn in 1956 by an engineering firm hired by the Bay Area Council and California's Rapid Transit Commission. There is as yet little publicity, but if a group learns of the plans and opposes them, it can open the door to much wider controversy.

The third stage is a turning point in the decision's journey: a time for public review and response. One or more public hearings and sessions of city, county, or state legislative bodies must review the location, design, benefits, and costs of the project. There may be extensive media coverage at this point, and the opportunity is greatest for new groups to enter the coalitions for or against the project as they learn of its impacts. For BART, this was the preparation for the 1962 referendum in which the voters granted the needed approval. Depending on the outcome, the process may advance to stage four or five.

If the supporting coalition is unsuccessful in winning quick approval, a fourth stage of debate and renegotiation begins. The response from political leaders or the public may be negative or uncertain, and the coalition may have to adjust its plans, membership, or both. In Los Angeles, a rapid transit plan similar to San Francisco's was thrice rejected by the voters, in 1968, 1974, and 1976. Only in 1980 did the business-labor-governmental coalition succeed in winning a referendum with a package sweetened by $225 million in federal funds. Even after that, further action was delayed by lawsuits, and ground was not broken for the first route until 1986. Generally, the new coalition that emerges from this stage may have a more diverse membership, with conflicting aims and interests. But many other projects have long languished in this fourth stage for lack of adequate support.

Finally, the stage of implementation and assessment generates social and economic impacts to which the interested coalitions must respond. New conflicts and coalitions may emerge to alter the course of similar decisions still under consideration. In some cities, popular reactions to total-clearance renewal programs halted subsequent efforts and shifted the coalitions' emphasis to neighborhood preservation. On the other hand, a program widely considered to be successful strengthens the sponsoring coalition for further accomplishments.

The type of decision-making process depends on the size and composition of the coalition at each stage. Three methods were mentioned in section 5.3: fiat, elite, negotiation, and open negotiation. In general, fiat is most common in the early stages and where only a handful of professionals control the situation. It most closely fits the classic elitist model. Elite negotiation appears in what Wirt called the stable dominant constellations, where some differences of interest have to be resolved. Open negotiation occurs in the occasional and temporary coalitions, after the scope of conflict has widened and no one group is in control—the most pluralistic of situations. It may be that no successful negotiation can take place in a "street-fighting" pluralism.

8.5 THE ENDS OF POWER: GROWTH

After surveying these coalitions waxing and waning through successive stages of decision making, we need to ask if there is any thread of consistency that unites them and is common to most or all urban areas. One way to frame this inquiry is to search for any *system bias* in the planning process. Stone [1976, 18] pointed out that "a city's governmental machinery may be influenced to operate *consistently* in favor of some interests at the expense of others— even if the other interests are a sizable and active political force."

System bias can be present equally in an elitist and a pluralist structure, for it is imbedded in the factors that cause land use issues to become political to begin with and which draw some to participate and others not to.

A persistent theme in the studies cited in this book, whether dominant or recessive, is *growth:* growth in population, wealth, knowledge, and mastery of natural forces. This ideal is deeply imbedded in Western culture. In the American tradition, growth equals progress, while lack of it is virtually the synonym of stagnation. A further article of faith is that growth benefits everyone, including those who are at the bottom of society at any given time. Rather than redistribute wealth toward them from the higher ranks, American thought (to which the Reagan administration gave strong endorsement) holds that growth will create a larger pool of wealth from which all those who seize their opportunities can benefit.

Growth is likewise a dominant theme in urban planning. Those who have sought to channel that growth in certain directions argue that human intelligence can perceive ways to maximize the benefits from it. Molotch [1976, 310] characterized the city as a "growth machine," the governmental and private power structures of which have an indelible bias toward policies and interests that promote it. He argued that it "provides the key operative motivation toward consensus for members of politically mobilized local elites, however split they might be on other issues, and that a common interest in growth is the overriding commonality among important people in a given locale."

Molotch [1976, 311] further asserted that it is necessary to view each map of a neighborhood, city, or region as "a mosaic of competing land interests capable of strategic coalition and action." On one level of competition, "each unit of a community strives, at the expense of the others, to enhance the land-use potential of the parcels with which it is associated." On a higher level, however, these interests can cooperate when they perceive an opportunity to enhance all of their interests at the same time. Thus, they will support economic growth efforts in a way that causes the city to act as an entrepreneur in the manner described by Peterson [1981, 22]: "cities seek to improve their market position, their attractiveness as a locale for economic activity."

While growth as an ideal has many noneconomic dimensions, it is usually operationalized in material terms: dollars invested, buildings constructed, jobs created, miles of streets paved, acres annexed to the city (for those which are able to do so), and numbers of inhabitants. These efforts require public as well as private resources. Many local influentials demand that their tax dollars be "invested" in what will have larger future payoffs; thus even schools, parks, and art museums are to attract and facilitate the sought-for growth in their own distinctive ways.

It is not a contradiction that proponents of growth occasionally take part in growth-limitation efforts. The moratorium in San Diego, which refers to itself as the "city on the move," did not bring development to a halt. It had only the effect of temporarily channeling commercial and residential growth onto other vacant land, and permits opening the affected area to development after 1995. In general, the suburban growth limitation effort aims either at controlling the pace of growth to permit adequate servicing of it (as in Petaluma, California) or to keep unwanted land uses (and lower income people) away from the more affluent residential areas. Those residents certainly favor growth elsewhere in their metropolitan area and often reap abundant profits from it.

An historical perspective on this growth bias is helpful here. Elkin [1985, 18] has characterized urban politics and planning in the first three decades of this century as "privatist" [using the concept from Warner 1968]. That is, local governance was organized to promote business growth by leaving entrepreneurs free to pursue capital accumulation and by providing the essential services, such as utilities and streets, necessary to this goal. Burnham's Comprehensive Plan of Chicago of 1909 (see section 2.6) should be read from this perspective, even those parts on esthetic improvements. After all, that plan was commissioned and paid for by a business coalition. Likewise, the institution of zoning in New York City in 1916 primarily benefited the dominant partners in its power structure.

Continuing on the historical path, a change began to occur in the 1930s and fully emerged by the 1950s: the replacement of privatist by "pluralist" regimes. As Elkin [1985, 15] defined them, their primary feature was "an inclusive coalition which dominated land use questions, particularly those linked to the economic vitality of the downtown." Its major aims were to improve the declining tax base, improve transportation into the central business district, and make land uses more productive and attractive. To the business partners in those coalitions were added professional planners, members of the growing public bureaucracies in housing, transportation, and other functions, and above all mayors and allied political leaders. This was not a total change in makeup of the coalitions, but an expansion with new members seeking other benefits. The coalition which Dahl [1958] found backing the extensive downtown renewal in New Haven, Connecticut, and which he used as an example of pluralism appears to be of this type.

Mollenkopf [1983, 1–6] offers further insight into these progrowth pluralist coalitions. He argues that they had a national base, built on the increasing flow of funds from Washington to the cities to finance housing, urban renewal, airports, highways, transit, and other functions. Local politicians saw in these funds opportunities to build their own power and standing, and thus took the lead in the rebuilt coalitions. Usually they were Democrats, but had little or no trouble joining forces with Republican business leaders. They were, in effect, *political entrepreneurs* who "reshape politics and create new sources of power by establishing new programs (or 'products')." In the process they also create new supportive constituencies among the beneficiaries of those programs. Essentially, the politicians took the initiative for growth from the business community while serving its interests as well as their own.

To illustrate this national/local progrowth coalition at work, Mollenkopf [1983, ch. 5] draws examples from Boston and San Francisco. Initially, it enjoyed great success both in downtown renewal and investments to enhance land values in the inner city. However, those coalitions gradually weakened due to internal disagreements over policy and the cumulated effects of those changes upon urban neighborhoods. In particular, programs for clearance and renewal in Boston's South End and San Francisco's Western Addition aroused such grass-roots opposition as to alienate some of the constituencies on which the coalition rested.

What coalitions exist now? Certainly growth is no less a priority in 1988 than it was in 1908, and the many interests described throughout this book make up formidable coalitions for commercial and industrial development. They differ in purpose between cities, however: Boston, San Diego, and San Francisco have secured abundant private investment, and the choices there are more in the nature of Type 2, in which government takes little or no initiative. By contrast, declining industrial and agriculture-based cities require growth coalitions that are much more proactive and can mobilize public investment. They must reach beyond their legal boundaries to draw resources from the state capitals, Washington, and corporate boardrooms around the world.

Even with this emphasis on economic growth, however, those coalitions do not lack for political opposition. Since the civil rights movement of the 1960s, a growing number have come to deny that growth in fact benefits the disadvantaged. When the neighborhood and citywide groups of minorities gained enough power to enter the governing coalitions (at least marginally), they called for direct redistribution of benefits in housing, jobs, transportation, and other services. Their impact has varied widely with time and place, but to the limited extent that a local government can redistribute goods, they can show partial successes. Strong neighborhood organizations appear to be most successful in claiming a share of the resources that would normally go to downtown renewal or industrial development. The grass-roots organizations in the South Bronx offer evidence of this, although their share is still woefully small.

8.6 PLANNERS IN THE POWER STRUCTURE

What part is played by the planners in these coalitions—the professionals and the citizens who serve on voluntary boards? Few, indeed, have occupied places in which they exercised obvious power. Yet planning is an exercise of power, and a specialist in it has the resources of information and legal authority that many respect.

There is considerable flexibility in the leading planners' roles. One typology of these was suggested by Anthony Catanese [1984, 59]. The most traditional is the "apolitical-technical" role. Persons in this role stress the formal techniques of synoptic planning and make no overt effort to advocate particular political or social values. Yet this is a political role in a larger sense, for such a technician implicitly adopts and implements the political choices of the dominant coalitions. This occurs, for example, when a planner in an upper-scale suburb drafts a zoning ordinance that makes it impossible for a lower income household to acquire a home there.

Catanese's second role depicts the planner as somewhat more involved in political choices: the "covert-activist." These persons "will usually take on the position and appearance of the apolitical-technical role but become significantly involved behind the scenes with political action and politicians." They want to influence the substantive value choices that surround the planning, but find it best to do so in private meetings with the top policy makers. When they are heeded, it may be due to the officials' or developers' need for their expert support for the projects they are sponsoring. Norman Krumholz, planning director in Cleveland from 1969 to 1978, played this role under three very different mayors. He was a strong advocate for the interests of the poor and minorities, and advocated redistributive planning policies. Yet he operated behind, rather than in front of, the elected officials [Catanese 1984, 49 & 76].

The role most explicitly injected into the power coalitions is the "overt-activist." Planners in this role openly "support politicians, political parties, and causes that they believe are most in keeping with their values" [Catanese 1984, 60]. They seek public visibility, assuming that their professional expertise and standing adds credibility to their causes. Such activity does not, in their view, violate the ethics of the planning guild, but rather advances the progressive values for which the profession has always claimed to stand.

Two variants of this overt-activist role stand out. One is dramatically typified by Robert Moses, for more than 40 years the initiator of tens of billions of dollars in projects in New York State and particularly the New York City metropolitan area. Beginning with state parks in Long Island, he planned and secured funding for parkways and freeways, bridges and tunnels, urban renewal efforts, and finally the 1964 World's Fair. His relationships with elected politicians and lending institutions were so close that no one was able to thwart his plans until Governor Nelson Rockefeller maneuvered him out of his power base in 1968 [Caro 1974]. Moses represents the project-oriented activist, who concentrates primarily on what is built.

A second sub-role focuses on serving a class of people and their needs. Paul Davidoff [1965] described "advocacy planning" as the active support of the poor, racial and ethnic minorities, and others who are disadvantaged in urban politics. He deplored the prevailing ethos in the profession that claimed objective neutrality but by default served the ends of a power structure dominated by the already advantaged. He urged planners in government and nonprofit agencies to integrate this role with their professional aims. One who practiced this was Edward Kirschner in Berkeley, California, a leader in the citizens' movement of the 1970s that advocated greater collective control over the community's land and economy. His coalition won most elective offices and dominated that city's politics until 1981 [Clavel 1986, ch. 4].

Howell Baum [1983, xiii–xvi] surveyed a sample of professional planners and learned that most of them have little grasp of bureaucratic structures and decision-making processes. They tend to see themselves not as power wielders but as specialized problem solvers, quite autonomous of their constituents. This model of the profession, in his view, is entirely inappropriate to the roles which planners actually have to play in allocating social and economic values.

Citizen planning commissions have also had varying relationships to the dominant coalitions. Often, their members are chosen from their ranks or are known to support the growth-oriented planning policies. Thus, they are expected to evaluate only the technical features of the proposals before them. In more pluralistic cities and counties, the commissions are broadly representative bodies—perhaps one black, one realtor, one Hispanic person, one banker, a resident from each of the major neighborhoods, and so on. Often they are selected because they bring resources for influence with them from their outside affiliations. In such cases, they can reflect more accurately the political diversity and controversies of the community as a whole. But lacking elected authority or any other real base of power, planning commissions can at most function as appendages to governing coalitions, influential only when acting in harmony with their purposes.

Many portraits of urban power structures could be painted with the information presented here. As they pertain to land use planning and development, two features have nonetheless become clear. First, major choices can only emerge from the commitments that leading investors and top public officials jointly make. As Elkin [1987, ch. 3] maintains, developers' need for legal approval and financial support and politicians' need for projects that give them a progressive and dynamic image draw them together symbiotically, though this does not lead to automatic approval of whatever either partner proposes. This nexus gives the various elitist interpretations the most support.

On the other hand, many planning choices that a city or county must routinely make have smaller stakes or involve a delicate balance of interests. The Reichmann brothers probably could not care less what is built in the South Bronx. Influentials in such cases have only a neighborhood base. In San Diego, the moratorium advocates mobilized voters who cared about La Jolla Valley but were willing to leave downtown renewal to the big developers. Power structures appear quite segmented when viewed from this angle, and certainly are more open to the expansion of conflicts.

Stalemates can also result when no one clearly has the upper hand. A group that can keep an unwanted issue off the public agenda or prevent action on it also has power of sorts. Delays serve the interests that are tied to the status quo. Growth coalitions inherently seek change, but they do not sponsor all changes. While Warren, New Jersey, makes a hesitant response to the Mount Laurel decisions, other communities wait to see what happens. In such cases, no one can describe the power structure with confidence.

If planning is inherently future oriented, then it matters what images of futures its practitioners hold. These images consist of expectations of what would come about if they did nothing, of what could happen if they made choice A or plan B, and above all of what ideals guide their actions. The next chapter addresses the trends that are creating urban futures and the options that planners and political leaders have before them to respond to, and if necessary, alter.

QUESTIONS FOR DISCUSSION

1. How can one recognize who has how much power when viewing actual planning events?
2. What causes the power of individuals and groups to grow and decline over time?
3. What factors link local power structures with powerful entities on the metropolitan, state, national, and global levels?
4. What determines the distribution of power between the governmental and business participants in public-private partnerships?
5. Are there system biases other than growth that influence planning goals and choices?
6. What is the most appropriate means for holding professional planners accountable to the larger society and political system?

9 | PLANNING IN AND FOR THE FUTURE

9.1 IMAGES OF URBAN FUTURES

Imagine a reborn Daniel Burnham sitting down at his drawing board, 80 years after beginning work on his Comprehensive Plan of Chicago. Once again his assignment is to plan for the Chicago metropolitan area—a very different place than he viewed in 1908. What should he include in his designs this time? Is it even possible to set forth a coherent vision for that incredibly diverse region? He does have the dubious advantage of seeing what happened to his first grand plan for Chicago: except for the peripheral forest preserves and parts of the lakefront, the city's development proceeded just as if he had never put pen to paper. Most likely he would ask what use it would be to plan anyway, if the planning process doesn't actually control urban development.

How should modern planners answer Burnham's questions? Could Mayor Sawyer tell him, "Yes, go ahead and make big plans—we have great needs in our city and we intend to strike out in new directions!"? Would suburban political leaders accept any "Chicago planner" telling them how to design their communities? All through this book we have assumed that planning really does make a difference, and indeed, there is evidence that much of it has. At the

218

same time, though, there are many plans that have done no more than gather dust on a shelf. The difference between effective and ineffective planning is, more often than not, politics. But plans also call for *vision* to be successful.

Planning is about futures and the paths by which we reach them. It cannot lead to a single future because urban society is too complex to be contained within one unitary design. Its objectives, defined through a continual process of cooperation and conflict, must be pluralistic enough to satisfy the needs and demands of a diverse population. A healthy downtown or growing suburban retail/office ring cannot alone define a metropolitan area; the working-class homes and shopping areas, the inexpensive single-room residences, the railyards and waste management sites—all have rightful places in plans. Burnham focused on the esthetic and functional values in his 1909 vision for Chicago's future, but he could not be so limited today. Justice and community have to be planned for as well.

All planners and governmental decision makers, in all of their plan-making enterprises, carry in their minds images of pasts, presents, and futures that influence their choices. That is, they hold memories of what has been before, which they may judge to be good, bad, or neutral—something to restore, eliminate, obtain, or avoid. The landmarks in the American planning memory presented in section 2.6 are collective images that can be treated in the same way.

In viewing the present, planners often assess its beneficial and negative characteristics. What is on the ground provides advantages to some groups of people and disadvantages to others. Esthetically, it may please some and offend others. Central to the planning process is the identification and definition of problems, often conceived as the discrepancy between "what is" and "what ought to be." How one defines the problems sets the purposes and themes of the plans. It is tempting, and often politically irresistible, to perceive only the problems that one wants to solve or is able to solve. Burnham and his sponsor, the Commercial Club of Chicago, saw the city's ugliness and incredible traffic congestion as the main problems to be solved; the unsafe and unhealthful conditions of the working class appeared to be of low priority to them.

Equally important are planners' images of expected and desired futures. Some may be explicit and deliberately chosen, while others are implicit in their minds, perhaps accepted with little or no thought. They comprise the ideals, goals, and operational purposes that guide them in their choices, large and small. Some of these images may be utopian—ideals that are impossible to realize in real cities but which offer directions in which to progress.

One such utopia was proposed by the architect Frank Lloyd Wright in 1958. His Broadacre City is based on the central principle of the free individual living in harmony with beneficent nature. He carries Ebenezer Howard's Garden City ideal one step further, integrating the "country" into the "city" and allowing at least one acre of land to every inhabitant. Each building would take on the nature and character of the ground on which it stood. His plan intersperses high-rise office buildings and "organic" single-family homes with grain fields and orchards, sports stadiums and markets, lakes and forests. All of these are connected by wide boulevards that enable one to travel quickly and enjoyably. Within this community, citizens can pursue learning, sports, the creative arts, and even true religion [Wright 1963]. His influence on actual plans has been small, but the ideals he set forth still stir many imaginations.

Other images of the future are more specific and realizable. One may dream of a downtown anchored with a new convention center that draws in thousands of free-spending visitors annually, or a revived ethnic neighborhood with atmosphere-rich restaurants and picturesque festivals. A community organization just organized in an economically depressed neighborhood might adopt images of resident-owned business enterprises that both provide jobs and reinvest the profits in the area. Such images may not be fully achieved, but they supply hope that motivates the necessary hard work and risk taking.

Of course, some may hold images of the future that simply reflect the status quo. Planners are sometimes hired to play a protective role, even to prevent threatened change. This is most common in very affluent communities, such as Palm Beach, Florida, that fear intrusion of the "wrong" kind of people or activity [Babcock & Siemon 1985, ch. 3].

These images of past, present, and future can exist on several levels. They may be purely personal, unique to one's own experiences, perceptions, and values and not necessarily linked to those of anyone else. Groups have collective images as well; those of the construction industry may clash sharply with the growth-limitation and historic preservation lobbies. Finally, there can be community-wide images—those shared by a broad spectrum of a local population. Prior to the San Diego moratorium vote described in chapter 1, a strong consensus had taken root in that city that unchecked growth would do more harm than good. This supported the adoption of a comprehensive management program in 1979, six years before that vote [Shirvani & Stepner 1986].

The political process has a major role to play in building such community images of pasts and futures. Public policy, to be fair and effective, must be founded on broad goals rather than parochial group and personal aims. While politics often institutionalizes self-ishness, it has the potential, where conducted through a democratic process, to reconcile many conflicting parts to form a reasonably coherent whole. This requires sensitive leadership, widespread participation, free flow of information, and time for a consensus to form.

9.2 PLANNING AS ANTICIPATION

Planning must begin with anticipation, which is the process of looking ahead, of "wide-angle foresight." Those who anticipate what is to come often distinguish *probable* from *possible* futures. Probable futures are those human-chosen situations judged most likely to come about, viewed from the present. They can be perceived as near-inevitable or, if the confidence level is a bit lower, as a 75 or 60 percent probability. Probable futures need only the continuation of present choices and trends to be realized. They can, of course, be disrupted by a decision outside the particular urban realm, such as a cutoff of Middle East oil imports or an earthquake on California's San Andreas Fault.

Possible futures are those with a less-than-likely chance of happening, requiring a different pattern of choices than now prevails. A 40 percent possible future might need only a small redirection, while a future with a 1 percent likelihood would call for radical change in present trends. The South Bronx would prosper once again if middle- and upper-class households find it desirable or necessary to depart from their Scarsdales and Warrens and relocate to that blighted area. But that would require a drastic reorientation of both personal values and economic conditions to bring about.

To conceive of possible futures has an additional value: they are a reminder that "probable" is not "inevitable." When a likely future is not attractive—continued decay in an inner-city neighborhood, for example—residents can anticipate what could result if they chose means to alter that trend. Examples of realized possible community futures abound, from Southeast Baltimore to East Los Angeles (see section 4.4). To realize that renewal is possible at all can spur people to search for ways to increase its likelihood.

What planners have to anticipate are not individual futures, however. Possible and probable futures occur in clusters and sequences, each linked with others. Each decision, each forecast condition, spills over to make others more or less likely. Planners now contemplating expansion of the San Francisco area's rapid transit system must assess several trends and uncertainties. For example, if suburban commercial growth outpaces that in downtown San Francisco, ridership patterns will change accordingly. Likewise, fuel costs rising or falling sharply will affect both of the above. Fixed-rail transit systems lack flexibility to meet unanticipated growth patterns, but they can also influence those patterns more strongly than bus lines. Some of these contingencies are under their control, others are decided by different specialists; yet others are subject to no government's direct choices.

Planners rely heavily on recognizing trends. A *trend* is a sequence of related events that, on the basis of experience, can reasonably be projected forward. Trend analysis, to be most reliable, requires hard data and sound interpretation of those data. However, intuitive trend perceptions are often used when data are lacking, as with changes in public values and life-styles. To a degree, all trend analysis is subjective, for it requires selection of some data as more significant than others. To forecast the demand for industrial land, for example, one must make a judgment on which kinds of industry are likely to grow in a rapidly changing national and global economy.

Environmental scanning (or external scanning) is an increasingly used technique for systematically surveying and identifying issues and trends likely to impinge on an organization's choices. Used widely by business corporations, it is also being practiced by the Toledo Area Council of Governments, Hennepin County, Minnesota, and the Florida Office of Planning and Budgeting, among many. Scanners are assigned to monitor specific issues in which change occurs, such as technological innovations, shifts in financial markets, and demographic trends. Each scanner reports to a clearing house where others can analyze and report the data to decision makers. Two students of this process concluded that external scanning can provide the planner with useful qualitative insights that can be synthesized into more comprehensive frameworks [Pflaum & Delmont 1987].

Those who study trends must also realize that the "shape" of each one can vary. Some projections are straight lines—that is, the rate of change will remain constant for the foreseeable future. For example, a city may project its growth to be 1,000 residents per year for the next decade. Another trend picture may portray acceleration: traffic levels increasing 5 percent in year one, 10 percent in year two, 15 percent in year three, and so on. Or there may be growth up to a limit: planners may foresee that a city can accommodate no more than ten percent growth within its present boundaries, and stability or slow decline will follow that. If planners assume one shape of a trend and another shape emerges, their efforts may be frustrated. Also, one trend can counteract another: San Francisco found that the general movement of central city dwellers to the suburbs has been overtaken by the inflow of Asian and Hispanic immigrants with their large families, who have increased the city's population.

Four major trend categories stand out as most salient for urban planners. The first is the prospect for *new technologies* for energy and resource use. In the late 1970s, when oil prices were high, much effort went into devising new energy sources and means of conservation. The interlude of the late 1980s, in which energy prices dropped, is unlikely to last long, and planners will again have to be sensitive to energy production and consumption. Anticipating this, the city of Austin, Texas, installed, early in 1987, a $3 million, 300-kilowatt solar electricity generator. With sufficient research and development, solar power can soon become economically competitive with fossil fuel generation in some parts of the country, even if oil prices remain near present levels [Bronstein 1987]. Should solar (or other forms of renewable energy) gain widespread use, it will certainly affect building design and location. Some cities now have zoning ordinances protecting solar energy collectors from being shaded by new buildings.

Resource recycling is a second example of technological trends. Many metropolitan areas will run out of landfill space to deposit their wastes in the next decade, and must find alternatives. Reducing the volume of wastes by recycling valuable items is one answer; burning it to produce electricity is another. Both methods require planning to deal with their spillovers. Recycling also is taking place with waste water, treating it so thoroughly it can be reused immediately for irrigation or injected into the ground to recharge aquifers. Itasca, Illinois, in suburban Chicago, has a model treatment system of this kind. These require planning not only for the surface sites but also for the subterranean "landscape" to protect ground water from pollution. Chemical wastes, now nearly always deposited in the ground, can also be neutralized or reprocessed, but careful planning is required in locating and overseeing the facilities for this.

Socioeconomic trends make up a second broad category which planners must anticipate. First, demographers have traced the aging of the public: in 1986, about 28 million Americans were over 65, nearly 12 percent of the population. Reasonable forecasts project 65 million over that age in 2030, 21 percent of the whole [Hey 1986]. Most will be in the "young old" category of 65–85, and will be relatively healthy and capable of productive or service pursuits. Some communities have much experience with the elderly now, but this shift will particularly affect the suburbs, which up to now have been child oriented. Overall, this trend demands careful planning for transportation, recreation, and social service facilities as well as housing.

As society continues its shift away from the stable two-parent nuclear family toward a variety of household forms and smaller household sizes, housing demands will alter in several directions. The U.S. Census Bureau reported in 1987 that the average household had declined in size to 2.67 persons (compared with 3.14 in 1970). Basically, each household requires a separate living unit. The townhouse or condominium with only two bedrooms, but abundant amenities, is one response, and these are rising in self-contained clusters in many communities. At the same time, single parents with low incomes require safe, inexpensive quarters in which to raise their children. The typical city or county must plan for a wide variety of home types, and invest public funds where necessary to secure an adequate supply of each.

Children are increasingly at risk in less stable family environments, and planners must include care providers for them in their designs. These range from the corporate franchise operations and Montessori-type schools to the one woman in her home caring for children under a city or county license. Increasingly, employers are taking responsibility for their workers' children, and future industrial and office parks are likely to incorporate day-care facilities. Another possible future is suggested by Centura Parc in Coconut Creek, Florida, the first community planned specifically for young families whose parent(s) work outside the home. Now accommodating 374 homes, it is distinguished by several modern child-care centers [Gardner 1986].

American cities have always been places of great ethnic diversity; in this decade the immigrants are seldom Polish, Italian, or Irish but more often Mexican, Cambodian, Iranian, Haitian, and Ethiopian. Urban neighborhoods can change drastically in a short time—for better or for worse—as new immigrants enter. Some groups are noted for business entrepreneurship: a deteriorated three-block stretch of Argyle Street on Chicago's North Side blossomed with restaurants, grocery stores, and other shops when Southeast Asian groups located there recently. The Cuban community in Miami offers another example of this. Such enterprise cannot be planned for fully, but can strongly shape the outcome of neighborhood renewal efforts.

Ethnic diversity can have its less happy side as well. Rapid turnover in a neighborhood from a white to black majority has led not only to social conflict but also to physical deterioration, as white landowners failed to maintain their properties. Planners must continue to be sensitive to such transitional areas where housing quality and other amenities can decay, harming not only the new residents but also the city as a whole.

A further socioeconomic change with major implications for the planning system is the sharpening separation between rich and poor in metropolitan areas. This dichotomy has a residential dimension with deep roots: the poor clustered in the least desirable inner-city homes and neighborhoods (and scattered low-status suburbs), and the upper-income households occupying the high-amenity suburbs and those gentrified inner-city districts they find most attractive. Recent studies have documented the rapid growth of a highly isolated "underclass" in New York, Chicago, Detroit, and Philadelphia. The neighborhoods in which they are concentrated present complex challenges, not only for social service agencies but also for planners concerned for their housing, employment opportunities, and prospects for renewal generally [Wilkerson 1987].

Increasingly, however, this racial split has an employment dimension as well. Few of the new jobs that enterprises are creating in cities benefit the poor.

> New York City, for example, gained 239,000 jobs from 1980 to 1986, a rise of 7 percent. . . . Manufacturing jobs, which in the past provided entry-level work for millions of poor immigrants, declined 108,000, or 22 percent, to 390,000, while service jobs, led by those in information processing that require higher levels of skills and education, increased 183,000, or 21 percent.

[Herbers 1986]. This is a particularly oppressive fact of life with which the South Bronx renewal groups must cope.

The spatial location of the jobs within urban regions is also socioeconomically significant. Retail and manufacturing employment is growing fastest in suburban areas, where very few of the poorest live and which are poorly served by public transportation. In fact, booming Gwinnett and Cobb Counties, on the fringe of the Atlanta metropolitan area, reject any form of public transportation, including the MARTA rapid rail system, to discourage blacks from finding either homes or jobs there. The poor face linguistic, racial, and geographic barriers to greater opportunity. Since these barriers are entrenched in the American culture and marketplace, planners will not be able to remedy them in the short run, but can attack pieces of the problem if they are sensitive to it. For example, they can plan transit service to new industrial developments and secure suburban locations for modest-cost homes.

A more narrowly economic trend but with definite social impacts is the prospect for the American economy in a global context and the resulting distribution of resources between the private and governmental sectors. During the 1980s, the United States has become the world's leading debtor nation. While this is a demonstration of the confidence that other nations' investors have in our economy, it also means that they have increasing control of our productive resources. Further, tens of billions of dollars must go overseas annually to pay their profits and interest. As a consequence, an increasing share of investment in urban development will come from foreign sources.

The fact that the federal government's record deficits have coincided with this trend toward international debt also reduces sharply the funds available for its investment in urban areas that marked the 1960s and 1970s. State and local tax resources are not great enough to fill the gap, and when they borrow, they must compete on the same bond market as private corporations. The public-private partnerships discussed earlier are vital as sources of funds, but as government's ability to finance projects declines, the agenda will be determined more and more by the prospects for profit than by social need.

A third group of trends occurs in the *physical environment* as impacted by human activity. This has many facets: the accumulation of wastes in the ground and water, increased air pollution due to automobiles and coal burning, and the loss of open space, woods, and wetlands to urban growth, to name only three. In the past two decades, many public policies have been enacted to deal with these, but the problems often appear to outpace the solutions. Many more chemicals with potentially toxic effects will be on the market, and more automobiles will be on the streets to pollute the air, even though control devices reduce the amount of emissions per car. While acid rain is a widespread problem, many others, such as toxic waste dumps, affect very specific locations.

A longer term environmental trend widely accepted by scientists is the rising sea level. The warming of the atmosphere is expected to raise oceans by one foot in the next 30–40 years, and 3 to 5 feet over the century. That would move many shorelines inward by hundreds or thousands of feet and threaten billions of dollars of investments. Some beaches in Long Island, New York, are retreating at the rate of one foot per year. A major storm that coincides with a high tide can do much more damage now than in past years. Water supply, drainage, sewage treatment, and recreational facilities would also be affected. Planners in such communities must decide whether to "retreat" from the shorelines by banning development in vulnerable areas, or "harden" what is located there to protect it from the waves. Since the serious problems are farther in the future than most others, and many citizens are not certain that they will appear at all, the political obstacles to advance regulation and spending might prevent such plans from being implemented [Eckholm 1986].

What *political* trends are likely to accompany these changes? The entire history of twentieth century cities has been one of increasing pluralism. Not only have new racial and ethnic groups claimed shares of power, but diverse economic and social interests have insisted on both attention and services from their governments.

There is no reason for this trend not to continue. This will affect many metropolitan suburbs, as well, whose populations are both aging and becoming more like those of the central cities. Intergroup conflict can erupt more easily over issues related to any of the above trends, and this demands a greater capacity to form coalitions to achieve the cooperative settlements of those conflicts.

Another political imperative is the need for local and state politicians and planners to think strategically. Since World War II, they have focused their attention on getting aid from Washington and thus oriented their policies to win support from Congress and the President. But with the decline in the resilience of the federal budget, they must take greater initiative for themselves. This includes development of foreign trade, long-term investment in their growth and infrastructures, and building up their own human resources through education and training. To do this well, the coalitions that negotiate policy choices must be able to create or obtain the resources to implement them over the long run.

9.3 ANTICIPATING URBAN FUTURES

What will be the combined effects of these trends for the form and function of urban areas? What can planners and politicians expect to result if they do not alter or reverse those trends? Futurists often use *scenarios,* verbal pictures, to portray holistic images of what could come about. The best ones are realistic enough to enable readers to "get inside" them and evaluate their realism and desirability.

Eldredge [1974] catalogued 15 alternative urban futures and ranked them according to the likelihood of their coming about. In the "almost certain to continue" group he cited the extension of the existing patterns: the large megalopolis, the metropolitan central city and its suburbs, and a network of smaller cities in the hinterlands around it. Much less likely are vast megastructures that would house and employ tens of thousands of people under one roof, and floating cities like that proposed in the 1970s for Tokyo Bay to relieve overcrowding on land. He conceded that "more of the same" will mark urban growth for the rest of this century and much of the next. But for this reason, it is imperative to build diverse social and physical possibilities to accommodate the life-styles likely to emerge in the next decades. There should be minimal standards for essentials of living, but beyond these there should be no arbitrary limit to options. Perhaps the complex spread metropolis would be the best option if it can supply those possibilities and the freedom for groups to create more.

Recall the four urban sectors that were introduced in section 7.2: the growth centers, the inner transition zones, the stable established areas, and the outer transition zones. Each can have a distinctive scenario, and those which follow embody the major trends identified in the preceding section.

For major command and control cities, the growth centers can be found both in the old downtowns and in the suburban rings and radii. The former will house the networks of "face-to-face" professionals, along with government centers, while the less location-dependent offices are free to spread to the fringes and expand into the outer transition zones. The radial freeways and rapid transit systems such as BART are vital links between those centers. But many other cities, especially the old industrial hubs of the Northeast, will lack growth stimuli for their downtowns, which may continue to decay. What growth or renewal they experience will consist of smaller retail and office facilities scattered about their fringes.

Smaller cities, not part of metropolitan areas, can enjoy a measure of growth where regional or local economies prosper. Even for them, however, activity is not likely to concentrate in their traditional centers but on the fringes that have the best highway access and lowest land costs.

The stable established areas of large and small urban areas will prosper as long as their homeowners are employed. Where funds are available to invest, decay can be held off and older structures rehabilitated. But planners must be sensitive to social and economic forces that can quickly render an area undesirable. It is easy to neglect this zone as long as no obvious deficiencies appear and its residents and business owners do not complain.

The inner transition zones face the greatest uncertainty. These suffer most from the concentration of investment in the central and suburban growth centers. In older cities, they have been expanding since the clearance of unused structures has outpaced the infill with new ones. To stand on the top of Chicago's Sears Tower or fly over central St. Louis and observe the hundreds of newly vacant acres is to be impressed both with the great potential for new development and the lack of present demand for it. Economically healthy cities— Boston and San Francisco at present—have smaller inner transition zones than Detroit and perhaps quicker transitions as well. Small cities will have such zones, also, though perhaps only a few blocks in extent, and they present as much a challenge to local resources as the extensive areas in Chicago.

The outer transition zones represent a different kind of challenge in their shift from rural to urban use. Suburban growth centers can expand into them, particularly where they are traversed by freeways. Other areas face the challenge of residential development, as urbanites seek multiacre lots with trees and privacy. But many of the new residents also want sewers, city water, and paved roads, and wish that the farmer next door would get rid of his cows and pigs. Unless there is strict protection of agricultural lands and rural amenities, the new suburbanites will politically overwhelm the current residents. Of course, the latter may find their land worth so much that they gladly sell it for development.

These scenarios could be called, from today's viewpoint, "surprise free." That is, they are entirely foreseeable with trends and conditions that can be observed now. Yet, implementation of any public policy has rarely lacked for surprises, and some unintended conditions or consequences have prevented its objectives from being achieved. For example, highway planners did not anticipate how quickly automobile traffic would grow once their new freeways were open. In California, they were shocked to find that some roads' maximum vehicle capacity was reached in the first months or year. Perhaps they should have foreseen it, along with the suburban growth explosions that would accompany the freeways, but their horizons were too limited by their experience.

To guard against surprises, one must realize that there are different kinds of uncertainty, with varying effects on planning. Friend and Jessop [1969, 88–89] proposed three types:

> Class UE: uncertainties in knowledge of the external planning environment including all uncertainties relating to the structure of the world external to the decision making system. . . . Class UR: uncertainties as to future intentions in related fields of choice including . . . other fields of discretion beyond the limited problem which is currently under consideration. . . . Class UV: uncertainties as to appropriate value judgments.

Uncertainties of class UE require more information on what conditions exist or could come about in the area planned for, and a greater basis for confidence in saying, "If we do X, then Y will result." Many public housing programs failed due to ignorance of how specific living environments actually affect poor families and of how they respond to them. Often, planners (not being poor themselves) assumed that they would respond to their new homes in a familiar middle-class manner. They did not even realize that they needed more information.

UR-type uncertainties grow out of the fact that no plan can be implemented in isolation. Decisions of politicians, landowners, employers, and individual homeowners can parallel and possibly greatly affect its success. A program to rehabilitate homes in one block of a large blighted area like the South Bronx can fail if landlords in adjoining blocks let their buildings deteriorate or if the crime rate in the neighborhood soars. The ideal solution to this type of uncertainty is better coordination of relevant decisions—but urban political systems are not so well organized as to bring this about in most cases.

Finally, uncertainties of value grow out of inadequate policy making or unresolved conflict over which of several values shall prevail in the situation. Federal, state, and local legislation usually embody compromises and a typical law may require both "reasonable opportunities for development" and "protection of environmentally sensitive areas." For this dilemma, the proper solution is policy that leaves no doubt on value choices. But as with the two preceding uncertainties, pragmatic and partial resolution is more achievable. A dispute between developers and conservationists over one site may be settled with some kind of compromise, but it does not necessarily influence how a different contest will end nor impose a rigid set of values on every case.

Planners must be sensitive to the various roles they can play in situations of uncertainty. Where the goal of the planning effort is agreed upon but the technology for reaching it is not known (for example, to reduce traffic congestion in a newly developed suburban commercial center), they could well function as researchers, experimenters, or innovators. On the other hand, when the goals themselves are not agreed on, as with providing for the homeless, planning participants have to be more pro-active as advocates, bargainers, or shapers of public opinion [Christensen 1985]. In the first case of uncertainty, technical choices will dominate, while in the second, political power makes the difference. To the extent that goal and value choices are also imbedded in the technological decisions (and they often are), politics is likely to steer them also.

The mazes of uncertainty are compounded with a dilemma that Wachs [1985, 563] described: "We want to know what the future will be like so that we can act, yet actions will determine what the future will be, and may negate the forecast. Because of this circularity, rarely may the accuracy of a forecast made in the public policy arena be literally verified." For this reason, forecasters must be in close touch with administrators, ready to update their anticipations with each new set of results. Thus, an economic development plan that depends for success on closely linked actions and outcomes has to be revised frequently to account for unexpected events that alter its context.

Planners also need means to foresee the overall impacts of any projected change in a particular site. One means of doing this is provided by the Environmental Simulation Laboratory of the University of California. During the 1983–84 controversy over a new downtown plan for San Francisco, the laboratory built a detailed model of the area and then filmed it from many angles and in different light conditions to show how proposed buildings would affect their surroundings. These were shown to the planning commission, board of supervisors, and general public who were then able to make more informed decisions. Sponsors of proposed structures are now required to place their models into this system for filming and evaluation [Myer 1986].

Another tool of anticipation increasingly used by both governmental and private-sector planners is computer-aided drafting and design. Beginning with a current map, one can experimentally add roads, buildings, and other features, and examine the result. More sophisticated yet is a program used by Design Workshop of Aspen, Colorado, that generates a three-dimensional representation of a site plan that can be rotated to show all perspectives. It was used by a developer in the design of a 14,000-unit residential community south of Denver in which a major concern was to preserve its environmental amenities and mountain views. It should soon be possible to produce a video from the computer that will simulate a drive through the development [Zotti 1987a]. When these techniques are available to all interested participants, they promise to increase the competence of both decision makers and those who seek to influence them.

To give some coherence to all of these planning efforts, *strategic planning* emerged in the 1980s as a major foresight effort in both private and public organizations. Basically, it integrates several elements in a single vision: the essential purposes or mission of the agency or company: the stakeholders who are involved, whether citizens, customers, or employees; identification of its internal strengths and weaknesses and of its external opportunities and threats relative to achieving its mission; and finally the strategic decisions necessary to accomplish its goals amid these conditions. Many local governments, including their planning departments, have adopted such strategic planning efforts, but it remains to be seen after longer experience what real difference it will make in land use policies and outcomes [Bryson & Roering 1987; Kaufman & Jacobs 1987]. Good planning efforts had already included these things before they were so named.

Scenario-building and strategic planning are as much political processes as they are technical. Since the data used in forecasting must be selected and interpreted, there is much room for subjectivity. The desire to gain power or to secure a prechosen outcome can easily shape one's use of data. A democratic political process can be an asset to anticipation, however. First, when decision-making coalitions are open and competitive, they cast a wide net for information and responses from stakeholders. Many neighborhood redevelopment schemes were begun, especially in the early years of urban renewal, without participation by either the would-be beneficiaries or the ones to be displaced by it. Recent programs in many cities that used such participation, as in Pittsburgh (see section 8.3), have more accurately forecast the prospects for neighborhood renewal [Ahlbrandt 1986].

But "politics" can also seriously bias anticipation. Highways, transit systems, industrial parks, and sewage facilities are high-stake projects, and certain groups and political figures may seek them only because of the private benefits they will provide. The assumptions on which any forecast must be based (e.g., future demand, benefits, costs, feasibility) leave room for subjectivity, which opens the door to political influence. Often, studies have been produced to justify a conclusion that was selected beforehand. The forecast then becomes a weapon of the advocates to secure approval of the project. This occurred in the case of San Francisco's BART system. From this, Wachs [1985, 567] concluded,

> The example of BART illustrates an age-old problem in forecasting the demand for and the cost of public works. If demand for a water supply system, bridge, or port facility is overestimated and cost is underestimated, the benefits of the project can easily be made to seem to outweigh the costs. Once the decision to build the project has been made, and expenditures of public monies have taken place, the realization that initial cost estimates were too low will rarely kill the project.

Politicians may also resist long-range foresight due to their short terms of office, one-year budget cycles, and pressures for immediate benefits from programs. They may be properly skeptical, since they realize how unreliable forecasts can be. But to the extent that they foresee trouble to come rather than happy times, that can reduce their appeal to voters and make them appear powerless in the face of the inevitable. Thus, many will ignore the need to prepare for rising ocean levels with the attitude that any response to it will cost a great deal and produce no benefits for a long time, if ever.

9.4 PLANNING AS A VALUE ENTERPRISE

The final task of this book is to survey the values that are available to guide the future of urban planning. Chapter 2 presented those values which have been embodied over the years in plans and urban policies and thus enshrined in the American planning memory. Essentially, a *value* was there defined as a quality that one seeks in an object or situation, something good that can be obtained from it. Thus, city parks were established because they provided residents with beauty, fresh air, recreation space, and contact with nature—all goods that had significant value to their planners and users.

All planning is value-guided. Any time one makes a deliberate choice, the object sought thus becomes a value. Naturally, perceptions of "good" differ between individuals, places, and times. L'Enfant selected a pattern of diagonal boulevards for Washington, D.C. to bestow an aura of grandeur on that capital city; designers of most other cities selected the grid street pattern because it simplified subdivision and development. Politics typically enters planning choices because of a lack of consensus on which values (and whose) shall control them. A democratic political process maximizes the potential for value conflict, because it can inject a wider variety of values into a choice situation.

A widely cited value in public policy is the *public interest*. This hazy term is an attempt to identify choices that would be of the greatest good to the greatest number of citizens, if one follows a utilitarian perspective, or upholds a standard of justice and rightness, to take a less relativistic approach. To use this term implies that there is indeed some kind of good that transcends the particular wants and interests of those who happen to be influential. Often, the term serves as a necessary myth in debates, since we need to believe that it exists and we can determine what it is.

Debates over the meaning and identity of the public interest can take several tracks. One is simply that it doesn't exist. There are only "interests"—private, conflicting, and often irreconcilable. A choice to benefit one set of interests inevitably harms another, and the best one can hope for, in this view, is to balance public policies over time so that no one is left without some benefits. Thus, no downtown renewal program is possible that would be to the entire city's benefit; the only way to compensate for that is to provide additional programs that serve the interests of the other areas.

A second and more hopeful view is that the preeminent public interest is a democratic process which can discover or create agreements that can be beneficial to all. If there is a controversy over a particular redevelopment effort, open negotiation should formulate a program that integrates a package of benefits. The public interest is nonexistent before the process begins, and must be remade and reconfirmed at each step. The incremental and transactive planning styles, identified in section 5.1, generally depend on this process-oriented concept.

Others hold substantive concepts of the public interest which they insist should be at the heart of all public policies. They are not negotiable nor should they be set aside even by democratic agreement. Advocates of racial or social justice are in this category, arguing that urban designs and policies that benefit the least advantaged of the population actually serve the entire community by maximizing their opportunity to contribute to the whole. Here we find the adherents of the advocacy and radical approaches to planning.

A fourth concept of the public interest is held by some planners and administrators who perceive it to be whatever is in the laws and ordinances. They were hired, they respond, to carry out the law, and not to question it or substitute their own judgment for it. Even if a program were enacted that contradicted their own values, they believe themselves bound to it as long as their employment lasts. This "I just work here" attitude has a certain administrative logic, but also frees its holders from any uncertainties on this issue. The synoptic style of planning, also described in section 5.1, can assume this concept.

In real controversies the concepts become intermixed. In a classic case of public housing location in Chicago, the city's housing authority sought to serve a unitary concept of the public interest by reducing racial segregation in public housing and locating its buildings in white neighborhoods as well as black. The city council, which vigorously rejected this purpose, held to an individualistic concept that defined the two races' interests as separate and often contradictory. Both sides used the public interest terminology, but since they pointed in totally different directions, no synthesis was possible [Meyerson & Banfield 1957]. In that instance, speaking of the public interest hindered discussion more than helped it.

For this reason, it is usually more constructive to consider substantive values to pursue in planning choices. Lynch [1984, 54–56] proposes five categories of planning values, based on the degree to which they are consciously pursued and visible in the built environment. First, *strong values* are "objectives of city form policy which are frequently and explicitly cited, whose achievement is detectable and is clearly dependent some significant degree on city form, and which can be achieved in practice." Among these he cites meeting housing and access needs, reducing pollution, improving safety and health, and maintaining property values.

Second, Lynch cites *wishful values,* which are "often cited, detectable, and probably linked to city form" yet are rarely achieved to the satisfaction of many. Perhaps more idealistic than the first group, they include improving equity, supporting families, and conserving resources.

Lynch's third set consists of *weak values,* which are "aims whose dependence on city form is doubtful or not proven, or whose achievement is very difficult to detect or measure." These include increasing social integration and stability, improved mental health, and crime reduction. They are not less important or desirable but are too complex to be implemented by a few specific steps in a plan. It is clear, however, that particular neighborhood designs do influence the likelihood of crime, for example.

A fourth category of values are *hidden* in the sense that they are as strong as the first but not often expressed because they might arouse unwanted controversy. Among these are maintaining political control, making profits, and removing unwanted people or activites from a location. Most planners, politicians, and developers carry with them such hidden values but have learned how to cover them with statements that are more in tune with community ideals.

Finally, Lynch suggests that there are *neglected values* that appear more obscure, vague or unconnected to the built environment, among which he cites "the fit of environment to human biology and function" and "the quality of the symbolic and sensory experience of cities." Their neglect could be ended if they were more clearly defined or if a particular group chose to campaign for them. The sponsorship of a more humane form of architecture would be an example of this. Indeed, each of these values depends for its impact less on its relevance to citizens' lives than on the support it receives from politically powerful groups.

We can obtain a more systematic view of alternative value futures by returning to the four value categories in chapter 2— esthetic, functional, moral, and social—and asking about the prospects for their development in years to come.

First, the *esthetic* values are based on the visual and sensual properties of the urban environment and their effects. Whereas these have traditionally been identified with beauty in architecture, open spaces, and vegetation, future concepts are likely to be more holistic. Lynch [1984, 131] uses the term *sense* to represent these ideals. "By the sense of a settlement, I mean the clarity with which it can be perceived and identified, and the ease with which its elements can be linked with other events and places in a coherent mental representation of time and space. . . ." A person who has such a sense can form an identity with a place, find personal meaning in it, and find one's way around in it. Every community needs to have certain distinctives that can be seen and felt; thus Boston could never be mistaken for Los Angeles. Decaying industrial areas and chaotic strip shopping centers are often repulsive enough to weaken one's identity with the place and violate the sense of beauty and order. Planning for esthetic values should therefore enhance the desirable distinctives, whether in architecture, natural water front-ages, street patterns, or neighborhoods.

The harmonizing of human society with nature is a second theme in modern esthetics. This is no longer just a matter of big urban parks and boulevard trees, but of preserving open spaces of all kinds amid rapidly sprawling metropolitan areas. Spirn [1984, 268–275] envisions a "celestial city" of the future in which every residence and workplace has a garden on the ground, balcony, or rooftop, flowing water passes in many channels through outdoor public places, wildflowers and forests line major highways, and wild areas stand as islands separating the residential and industrial areas. Each grove of trees and body of water serves not only to please the eye and refresh the spirit but also to cleanse the environment and conserve soil.

To do these grand things within a fragmented and pluralistic urban governance system is not easy, as we have already seen. Yet there are many examples of governments, citizen groups, and busi-nesses taking small steps in their own communities to create green spaces, control surface waters, improve air quality, recycle wastes, and moderate wind speeds. More than ever, it is obvious to them that action (or lack of it) in one sphere affects other spheres; where wastes are carelessly deposited in air, water, or soil, no other part of the biosphere can remain untouched. This has provided a strong incentive to comprehensive planning and action.

The esthetic quality of a city is also rooted in time. But historic preservation is no longer simply the collecting of museum pieces. More and more, "active history" is in demand, fully integrated with the lives of people. For example, residents of New Orleans' Vieux Carre—the "French Quarter"—are concerned that rising land values and increased catering to affluent tourists will drive out many of its 7,000 residents and the small businesses that serve them. At present, the Vieux Carre Commission, a local design review agency, regulates such matters as building heights, signs, and colors to protect that ambiance. Future efforts must aim at preserving an historic consciousness as well as structures. Visitors to the French Quarter should gain some awareness of who once lived there and what they accomplished. The site of a slave market must compete successfully for public attention with a popular jazz bar because they both constitute the heritage of New Orleans and the nation as a whole.

Functional values have also undergone change in passing into the last fifth of the twentieth century. The profit motive has been expanded to include the city and county governments; the political system itself has become an entrepreneur. Peterson [1981, 22] signaled this, as described in section 7.1: communities competing for economic advantage much as an individual company does in its market. Functional values that are increasingly dominant are those which maximize this local potential: attractive sites for private investors, airports and freeways, convention centers and facilities serving large gatherings, electronic information services, and residential communities that can draw the people who make the greatest entrepreneurial contributions. Slater [1984, 4] asserts that a central role for local government planning and management is now "to define the required return on investment prior to planning for the level of service or type of land use to be accommodated." Thus they would define profits for individual businesses as a goal of public policy to the extent that they expand the economy of an entire city or region.

The field of *moral* values still gives the ideal of justice a central place. However, a society that is increasingly sensitive to the advantages and disadvantages that various groups experience is often forced to rethink its means of pursuing justice. John Rawls' *A Theory of Justice* [1974] is highly relevant to planning values. He is concerned with the distribution of benefits and burdens in society generally, and with the standards to evaluate whether one person should have more of the world's goods than another. Clearly, cities are tangible representations of such distribution, particularly where one can view some of their most and least affluent neighborhoods within a walk of five minutes. Their spatial arrangements in themselves distribute benefits and burdens (such as residential amenities) and at the same time stand as evidence of how the society and economy as a whole benefit some and impose hardships on others.

Rawls' concept of justice assumes the fundamental value of equality and can be stated in two basic principles. First, "each person is to have an equal right to the most extensive total system of equal basic liberties compatible with a similar system of liberty for all." Second, "social and economic inequalities are to be arranged so that they are both: (a) to the greatest benefit of the least advantaged . . . and (b) attached to offices and positions open to all under conditions of fair equality of opportunity" [Rawls 1974, 302].

These principles have many applications to urban planning. A redevelopment project in an inner transition zone that eliminates the homes of a thousand lower income persons will allocate considerable benefits to the developers, business operators, and other participants. Rawls might declare that the project could be just only if the displaced were fairly compensated from the profits with new homes at reasonable cost and possibly better employment. Basically, Rawls would admonish the planner to "first seek those programs and policies that maximize benefits for the *very* least advantaged socioeconomic group in the community" [Beatley 1984, 462]. This calls for a professional sensitivity to human needs as they are cumulated in groups and affected by land use decisions.

The *social* values are closely linked with each of the above and also need to be viewed more holistically. Lynch [1984, 203] proposes two values that fall into the social realm: *access* and *control.* Access is basically the ability to travel to what a person wants and needs: employment, health care, recreation, friends, information, goods and services. "Access is one fundamental advantage of an urban settlement, and its reach and distribution are a basic index of settlement quality." While there is a technological dimension to it (vehicles by which to travel, for example), the larger problem for many people is socioeconomic. A person confined to a wheelchair can be imprisoned in a tiny world without mobility. To live without a car in an inner-city poor neighborhood prevents one from reaching suburban jobs. Traffic congestion, cost of travel, and social discrimination are additional barriers to access. While one can argue that some of the social barriers that existed in 1900 are gone, and widespread car ownership has improved access for most, the hindrances which remain are just as oppressive for those who experience them. Lynch [1984, ch. 10] suggests several ways in which access can be improved by judicious planning and use of governmental power.

Control, to Lynch [1984, 118], is "the degree to which the use and access to spaces and activities, and their creation, repair, modification, and management are controlled by those who use, work, or reside in them." As a social value, it first acquired a priority in the 1960s; yet many professional planners and most elected politicians did not take mandated citizen participation very seriously. But in the 1970s, a second generation of citizen organizations appeared, whose dynamic came from within the neighborhoods and grassroots associations. Their impact was reviewed in section 4.4 and elsewhere.

For citizen control to be effective, it must play a central role in plan making and implementation. Often such groups are on the periphery: after plans are prepared and elected officials have made some commitment to them, they are presented to citizen advisory boards for review and comment. Rarely have their comments made any real difference. But when their contribution begins with stating anticipations and asserting their values and goals, and continues with creating planning options, then control as Lynch defines it can be a reality. A community that values mutual responsibility among its citizenry can enhance it in such a holistic involvement in planning decisions.

These four clusters of values represent a broad sample, though not necessarily complete, of current public expectations of urban life. They are also interdependent to an important extent; to increase the supply of one should also increase the chances of achieving most others. To think of *community* profitability rather than that of individual or corporate gain assumes that opportunity for employment and personal growth will be spread more widely. Justice, however one conceives of it, is likely to be stronger where the built environment encourages mutual responsibility among citizens. They, in turn, can see themselves as guardians of the natural environment as well.

Finally, one other set of values deserves attention here: those set forth by the planning profession in its code of ethics and professional conduct. The American Institute of Certified Planners adopted these in 1981 to state "the aspirational standards that require conscious striving to attain," not just the evils that planners should avoid. The code's principles "derive both from the general values of society and from the planning profession's special responsibility to serve the public interest" [cited by Wachs 1985, 335].

Of special interest in the political context is the code's calling for special attention to the "long range consequences of present actions" and "the interrelatedness of decisions." Planners must strive to "expand choice and opportunity for all persons," and in so doing supply full and accurate information on issues and "give citizens the opportunity to have a meaningful impact on the development of plans and programs." Substantively, they should seek to protect the "integrity of the natural environment," work for "excellence of environmental design," and "conserve the heritage of the built environment" [cited by Wachs 1985, 336].

A 1973 statement of the American Institute of Planners succinctly expressed the moral and social values of the profession: "A planner shall seek to expand choice and opportunity for all persons, recognizing a special responsibility to plan for the needs of disadvantaged groups and persons, and shall urge the alteration of policies, institutions, and decisions which militate against such objectives" [cited by Wachs 1985, 346]. Over the years, the profession has expanded its ethical vision in response to society's widening definitions of justice and social responsibility.

There is a limit to which professional planners have internalized these ethical standards, however. One third of the respondents to a study by Baum [1983, 150–151] in the early 1980s conceived of ethics solely in terms of the technical principles and procedures that they should follow. Of the remaining two thirds who also referred to desired outcomes, many cited service to clients' interests as a high value. Overall, the planners surveyed rarely referred to the professional code cited above, and were generally uncomfortable in dealing with ethical principles. Baum concluded that their statements "fail to offer any consistent response to public concerns about the ethics of practitioners claiming expertise in dealing with important social problems."

Political executives and legislators have no equivalent statement of ethics, but they are bound to obey state and federal laws as interpreted by the courts. Like codes of ethics, the laws may be broad and open to many interpretations, yet unlike them, the laws can result in definitive, enforceable rulings by state and federal judges. These officials also are formally and directly accountable to the citizens for their conduct, which planners are not. As we have seen, however, the public lacks consistent standards for such accountability, particularly in the informal and weakly publicized arenas of local government.

9.5 THE END OF THE MATTER

Endings often return to beginnings. The first two questions asked in this book called attention to those who are building our cities, whether few or many, and to whether what they are building is making us more or less humane, secure, prosperous, sociable, or just. What answers have we discovered to these questions?

This entire book is a set of answers. But what has really been said, in capsule form? Cities are built according to clusters of discrete choices. Rarely, in the United States, has a city been designed according to a unitary vision and actually built in that way. Rather, they reflect a plurality of visions that extend across time and value communities. New York City is a set of layers of development that began with the Dutch founders of New Amsterdam in 1626; the 1988 layer consists of choices made by groups as diverse as Bronx homeowners and Times Square redevelopers.

This plurality of participants should not hide the prevalence of dominant coalitions in these choices, however. Choices of Types 2, 3, and 4 are seldom mass efforts. In all of the cases cited here, the initiative was taken by a few. In most cases, the approval of a larger body was needed to ratify it, at times even the whole electorate of a community, which had an undeniable veto power. Yet, the developers, government planners, and political decision makers had the power to initiate the changes and set forth the choices to which the public had to respond.

Where a few act on behalf of the many to change the conditions of their lives, politics becomes vital to a democratic society. We have viewed instances where the system of democratic accountability has given citizens a meaningful influence, and others where it has not. Where a particular political process has failed, it demonstrates all the more why it needs to work properly.

What have our cities done to us? To be sure, they display great extremes of wealth and poverty, of security and disorder, of beauty and ugliness. They portray, and perhaps magnify, the contradictions that are in humanity itself. Any serious theory of urban planning must rest on some concept of human nature, whether optimistic or pessimistic. Planning, as it evolved into a discipline at the turn of the twentieth century, shared in the optimism of that age; well-planned cities would, along with social and political reforms and the new technologies, elevate humanity to unprecedented heights. Since the world wars, the Depression, and failure of so many of the reformers' bright hopes, more sober expectations have replaced them.

Some people are indeed better off, and others probably worse. Those who live in the new developments enjoy better housing, while those who have been repeatedly displaced by renewal projects and cannot afford the new homes do not. Residents of suburbs like Warren, New Jersey, generally have benefited from the trends of the past half century, while most who are still in the South Bronx lack the opportunities that a suburb-dominated metropolitan area offers.

The planning community and the political community share responsibility, both for the extent of democratic participation in planning decisions and for their impact on the lives of citizens. Their unique yet interdependent roles have been outlined throughout this book. Each must ask, what concerns and values must be considered here? which have been neglected? whose views and interests are dominating? whose ought to receive more attention? Each can supplement and possibly correct the other. Thus, planners should not think like politicians nor vice versa. Planners should think like planners, but welcome the worldly wisdom inherent in political cooperation and conflict.

QUESTIONS FOR DISCUSSION

1. In what ways have images of ideal cities changed during the twentieth century? why?
2. How should planners respond to their inability to make reliable forecasts of cities 20 years hence?
3. What role do planners have in reducing the disparity in income and opportunities between social groups in cities? what specific actions can they take toward this end?
4. To what extent is it possible for planning to be "value free"?
5. What trends other than those mentioned here should planners and political leaders be alert to?

APPENDIX

CASE STUDIES IN PLANNING POLITICS

Students who seek a realistic, "how things happen" look at planning politics do well to examine the good case study literature in the field. The following 25 citations (publishers of the books are listed in the References section) contain much of this literature. Some books consist of a single case, while others offer a collection of cases from one or several cities. They also provide some interpretation of the case(s), often within one of the conceptual frameworks that have been discussed in this book. There is, of course, a difference beween the "facts" of a case and their interpretation, even though the choice of facts can be guided by one's interpretive stance. Students who read both the case and the analysis can spark their imagination by seeking some alternative explanations.

The following books do not exhaust the list of good case study literature. They do supply a variety of interpretive viewpoints: elitist, pluralist, neo-Marxist, and others less easily classifiable. They also cover different policy areas, from housing and transportation to comprehensive planning and suburban growth limitation. This list does not include cases published in the professional and scholarly periodical literature, some of which are also of high quality and have been cited in the text. Occasionally a national newspaper such as the *New York Times* presents a useful case; see Gottlieb [1984] for an example.

Alan A. Altshuler, THE CITY PLANNING PROCESS [1965]. Four planning cases, two each from Minneapolis and Saint Paul, emphasize the political context in which planners must operate, and which they must understand if they would be successful.

Richard F. Babcock and Charles L. Siemon, THE ZONING GAME REVISITED [1985]. Eleven cases from around the country, all describing political and legal conflicts over land use regulation. The authors, who are attorneys themselves, played a personal role in most of them.

Edward C. Banfield, POLITICAL INFLUENCE [1961]. Six cases from Chicago, all but one concerning land use. The author argues a pluralist viewpoint: that influence in a big metropolitan area is exerted by many, and government is the process of concerting that influence.

Robert A. Caro, THE POWER BROKER [1974]. A sequence of projects in the life of Robert Moses, powerful planner of public improvements in the New York City region, whose expansive vision and deep-seated biases were equaled only by his political astuteness.

Matthew Crenson, THE UNPOLITICS OF AIR POLLUTION: A STUDY OF NON-DECISION MAKING IN THE CITIES [1971]. Why Gary and East Chicago, Indiana, were unable to deal with their air pollution problem; a chronicle of the political obstacles put up by the big steel companies to consideration of that issue.

Mario Cuomo, FOREST HILLS DIARY: THE CRISIS OF LOW-INCOME HOUSING [1974]. The struggle to locate a housing project in a middle-class Queens neighborhood, by the present Governor of New York. He was then an attorney who was asked by the mayor to mediate the dispute.

Robert A. Dahl, WHO GOVERNS? DEMOCRACY AND POWER IN AN AMERICAN CITY [1958]. The classic pluralistic analysis of decision making in New Haven, including its large scale urban renewal programs of the 1950s.

G. William Domhoff, WHO REALLY RULES? [1978]. A reexamination of Dahl's work in New Haven, concluding that his evidence on the urban renewal programs better supports an elitist model than pluralism.

Susan S. Fainstein et al., RESTRUCTURING THE CITY: THE POLITICAL ECONOMY OF URBAN REDEVELOPMENT [1983]. Cases from New Haven, Denver, New Orleans, Boston, and San Francisco that demonstrate the interpenetration of governments and capitalist economic enterprises in determining the use and reuse of central-city land.

Bernard J. Frieden, THE ENVIRONMENTAL PROTECTION HUSTLE [1979]. The politics of growth limitation programs in several San Francisco area suburbs: their built-in biases and effects on housing supply and costs.

Mark Gottdiener, PLANNED SPRAWL: PRIVATE AND PUBLIC INTERESTS IN SUB-URBIA [1977]. The forces stimulating and steering urban growth in one township in Long Island, New York.

Chester W. Hartman, THE TRANSFORMATION OF SAN FRANCISCO [1984]. The conflict between city planners, redevelopment entrepreneurs, resident groups, and other participants over the rebuilding of a low-income neighborhood on the edge of downtown.

Bryan D. Jones and Lynn W. Bachelor, THE SUSTAINING HAND: COMMUNITY LEADERSHIP AND CORPORATE POWER [1986]. Conflicts over the siting of automobile plants in Detroit, Flint, and Pontiac, Michigan, which demonstrate the restricted latitude which public officials have in making industrial location decisions.

Dennis R. Judd and Robert E. Mendelson, THE POLITICS OF URBAN PLANNING: THE EAST ST. LOUIS EXPERIENCE [1973]. Struggles between professional planners and local political forces to reverse the steady decline of this poor, predominantly black city, showing the futility of traditional planning in this context.

Harold Kaplan, URBAN RENEWAL POLITICS: SLUM CLEARANCE IN NEWARK [1963]. A successful effort at clearing slums and replacing them with new homes in the 1949–63 period, in which cooperation prevailed over conflict.

Roscoe C. Martin et al., DECISIONS IN SYRACUSE [1965]. Governmental and public-private decisions, several of which concern land use, affecting the larger metropolitan area and involving participants from more than one jurisdiction.

Eugene J. Meehan, THE QUALITY OF FEDERAL POLICYMAKING: PROGRAMMED FAILURE IN PUBLIC HOUSING [1979]. The many federal and local governmental choices that led to both the failure of the Pruitt-Igoe housing project in St. Louis and the relative success of several other projects.

Martin Meyerson and Edward C. Banfield, POLITICS, PLANNING, AND THE PUBLIC INTEREST [1957]. The struggle between the Chicago Housing Authority and the City Council to locate public housing projects in various sites around the city, including middle-class white neighborhoods.

Mollenkopf, John H., THE CONTESTED CITY [1983]. The national-local coalitions that sponsored extensive inner-city rebuilding since the New Deal era, and their specific impacts on Boston and San Francisco.

Jeffrey L. Pressman and Aaron Wildavsky, IMPLEMENTATION, 2d ed. [1979]. Efforts by federal and local officials to stimulate economic development in Oakland by funding job-creating projects, and the reasons for their near-complete failure.

Peter Rossi & Robert A. Dentler, THE POLITICS OF URBAN RENEWAL [1961]. The interplay of public officials and neighborhood residents in a largely successful effort to conserve and upgrade the Hyde Park-Kenwood area of Chicago.

Sandra P. Schoenberg and Patricia L. Rosenbaum, NEIGHBORHOODS THAT WORK: SOURCES FOR VIABILITY IN THE INNER CITY [1980]. Five neighborhoods in St. Louis that achieved some measure of renewal through citizen action, with analysis of the factors in their successes and shortcomings.

Clarence N. Stone, ECONOMIC GROWTH AND NEIGHBORHOOD DISCONTENT: SYSTEM BIAS IN THE URBAN RENEWAL PROGRAM OF ATLANTA [1976]. An alternative view of urban power structures, based on 20 years of urban renewal that favored the central business district, disrupted low-income neighborhoods, and neglected residential areas in general.

Todd Swanstrom, THE CRISIS OF GROWTH POLITICS: CLEVELAND, KUCINICH, AND THE CHALLENGE OF URBAN POPULISM [1985]. The interwoven impacts of political and economic forces on finance and community development in Cleveland, further complicated by the ambitions of an unusual mayor.

J. Allen Whitt, URBAN ELITES AND MASS TRANSPORTATION: THE DIALECTICS OF POWER [1982]. The successful effort to build the San Francisco area's rapid transit system (BART) and the lack of success in doing so in the Los Angeles region, analyzed from the elitist, pluralist, and neo-Marxist perspectives.

HOW TO RESEARCH AND WRITE A CASE STUDY IN PLANNING POLITICS

The learning advantages from reading and analyzing other scholars' case studies can be multiplied by researching and writing one's own. Here are a few guidelines on how to do this in the study of planning politics.

First, find a "case." Decision-making events in urban planning are continuous, and in a larger city or region many controversies may present themselves. The best ones, however, are those that illustrate the major themes in this book: the planning cycle, the allocation of values, goal setting, one or more of the planning decision types, implementation of policy, and the interplay of conflict and cooperation over land use choices. In some, the political action will be clear and vivid, while in others it will be in muted tones and require more sensitive perception.

The second step is to discern the key issues at stake in the case. These usually exist at several levels: some more obvious and public, and others subtle and not readily admitted. They can be legal, environmental, economic, social, or personal—usually several of these wrapped together. Within these issues are one or more basic values, as chapter 2 demonstrated.

Third, it is necessary to identify the participants in the case and their goals and interests. Chapters 3 and 4 catalogued the most common groups, but it is not an exclusive list. Again, a student must take care to pick out the less obvious ones as well as those "out front."

Then the major events must be chronicled. They can initially be listed in order, just as they occurred. But it is also useful to arrange them as steps in the planning cycle outlined in chapter 1, or in the decision-making stages proposed in section 8.4. These offer means to analyze as well as describe what happened.

Last, the outcomes of the case demand explanation. Even if it has not been concluded at the time of writing, one can still analyze its progress up to that point. This explanation can be in theoretical terms—elitism versus pluralism, for example. Or it can approach the outcome in terms of the organizational forces or economic imperatives at work. Political factors can also supply insights, such as strong leaders, partisan rivalries, or election prospects. Most cases offer latitude for two or more reasonable explanations.

What information sources are most useful for this enterprise? Data are where one finds them, but not all data are equally valid or useful. Generally, one needs more than one source in order to be confident of their reliability. Newspapers and other periodicals often report events from a "here and now" perspective, helpful to a chronology, but often lacking in depth and comprehensiveness. Documents and reports, such as minutes of city council meetings, are more official but tend to exclude political factors. Statistical analysis may be useful where the debate concerns measurable factors, such as land values or housing units.

In many situations, the researcher needs to supplement the above with more personal sources—interviews with participants, surveys of residents, and on-site observations of key events in the case. Some excellent cases have been produced by persons who have been participants themselves, as interns, citizen activists, or journalists. Students must decide for themselves what their opportunities are and how much time they can devote, and set their research priorities accordingly. In all methods of inquiry, but particularly those in this paragraph, the student must have the questions clearly in mind and a sense of what data will be most important to obtain.

Case study authors also need to decide how objective they will be about their work. Scholarly dicta call for scrupulously factual analyses, not seeking to justify or condemn the outcome or any of the participants. Yet it is possible to hold and express preferences and still do honest work. That very perspective can bring out a valuable dimension of the case. Harder to deal with are the biases and differing perceptions which the participants express; objectivity may thus have to travel one path rather than another, and the author must choose which one.

GLOSSARY

The definitions are the author's, chosen for their utility in the context of this book. However, many incorporate standard definitions from the scholarly and professional literature. The section(s) of the text in which the term is most fully covered is given in parentheses.

Authority: (a) the legal power to make decisions, vested in a public office (1.4, 8.1); (b) a form of special purpose government or a subunit of a general purpose government with legal power to act on its given functions, such as the Port Authority of New York and New Jersey or the Chicago Housing Authority (3.3).

Citizen participation: the formal and informal means by which persons not in official roles can take part in or influence governmental decision making (4.4).

Command and control centers: major metropolitan areas in which the strategic economic and political decisions are made which affect the rest of the nation (7.2).

Comprehensive plan: holistic portrayal of the development policies of a city, county, or region, with applications to specific parcels of land (5.3)

Developer: Private entrepreneur that plans and undertakes development of land. Typically profit making, although nonprofit developers exist (4.2).

Elite: Small group of persons, typically in upper socioeconomic class, who control the majority of public decisions in their own interests (8.2).

Elite negotiation: method of decision making by bargaining among a small group of those most closely involved and who can deny entry to others (5.3).

Esthetic values: those related to the visual and sensual properties of the built environment and their impact on city inhabitants (2.2).

Fiat: method of decision making by public officials without bargaining or conflict (5.3).

Functional values: those related to the accumulation of wealth and the means to carry on productive enterprises (2.3).

General purpose government: unit of local government with broad powers in public services and regulations, including land use control. Includes cities, villages, boroughs, counties, towns, and townships (3.2).

General obligation bonds: means of governmental borrowing of funds by which bonds are guaranteed by the full tax base of the unit (7.3).

Grant-in-aid: transfer of funds from the national government to a state or local government for a specific purpose. Includes housing, urban renewal, community development, highway, and mass transit funding. May also be provided by a state to its local governments (3.6).

Historic preservation: Maintenance or restoration of structures and districts of historic significance; legal provisions encouraging investment in these and restricting alteration (6.5).

Implementation: Process by which policies and decisions are carried out in order to achieve their objective (5.4).

Manager: Title of chief administrative officer in cities and counties which have the council-manager form of government. Employed by the legislative body and held responsible for all implementation of its policies (3.2).

Metropolitan area: Contiguous urbanized region that includes one or more central cities, the county(ies) in which they are located, and any surrounding counties that are urbanized and linked with the core city (1.3).

Moral values: those related to the personal character of citizens and to the fair distribution of benefits, costs, and responsibilities in urban society (2.4).

Neighborhood: residential area within a governmental unit that has some distinct identity to its inhabitants and observers (4.4).

New town: Urban settlement built according to a unitary plan that incorporates housing, business, employment, transportation, parks, and other functional elements. May be sponsored by government or private enterprise (6.6).

Open negotiation: method of decision making by bargaining in which no party clearly dominates and new participants may freely enter (5.3).

Partnership (public-private): Development enterprise in which government and one or more private parties share the planning, financing, and/or construction (1.3, 8.3).

Planner: a person who has professional education and credentials in the planning field and/or is employed in a public agency or private firm that specializes in urban planning (3.1).

Planning: the process of making and implementing decisions about land use and space-dependent social and economic policies (1.3).

Planning commission: board composed of nonspecialist members and/or elected officials who study the planning choices to be made by their local government and advise its lawmakers on them (3.2).

Politics: the process of authoritatively allocating values for a society, which is marked by conflict and cooperation and the use of authority, power and influence (1.4).

Power: the effort by which one person or group secures an action or outcome in a situation that would not otherwise come about (8.1).

Public policy: a course of action taken by government that defines the authoritative allocation of a value (1.5).

Social values: those related to solidarity, identity, and mutual responsibility among citizens and the means by which they take part in decisions affecting their lives and neighborhoods (2.5).

Special purpose government: unit of local or regional government that is responsible for one or a few related functions and is independent of the general purpose governments in its area. May be called district, board, commission, or authority (3.3).

Urban place: a nonagricultural settlement of sufficient size, density, and heterogeneity to pose regular choices about the use of land (1.3).

Zoning: classification of permitted and prohibited land uses, applied to each parcel of land (5.4).

REFERENCES

Advisory Commission on Intergovernmental Relations. 1979. CITIZEN PAR-
TICIPATION IN THE AMERICAN FEDERAL SYSTEM. Washington: U.S. Gov-
ernment Printing Office.
Ahlbrandt, Roger S. Jr. 1986. Public-private partnerships for neighborhood
renewal. ANNALS OF THE AMERICAN ACADEMY OF POLITICAL AND SOCIAL
SCIENCE 488 (November): 120–134.
Alperin, Davida. 1983. Community politics and the St. Paul Port Authority.
Unpublished dissertation, University of Minnesota.
Altshuler, Alan. 1965. THE CITY PLANNING PROCESS. Ithaca: Cornell University
Press.
Altshuler, Alan. 1979. THE URBAN TRANSPORTATION SYSTEM: POLITICS AND
POLICY INNOVATION. Cambridge: MIT Press.
Anderson, Jane. 1984. Savannah. CHRISTIAN SCIENCE MONITOR, May 31 & June
7.
Appleyard, Donald. 1981. LIVABLE STREETS. Berkeley: University of California
Press.
Armstrong, Scott. 1985. Minimalist mass transit in Hartford, Conn. CHRISTIAN
SCIENCE MONITOR, July 9.
Aronson, J. Richard & John L. Hilley. 1986. FINANCING STATE AND LOCAL
GOVERNMENTS, 4th ed. Washington: Brookings Institution.
Babcock, Richard F. and Charles L. Siemon. 1985. THE ZONING GAME RE-
VISITED. Boston: Oelgeschlager, Gunn & Hain.
Bachelor, Lynn. 1985. Evaluating the implementation of economic develop-
ment policy: lessons from Detroit's Central Industrial Park project. POLICY
STUDIES REVIEW 4 (May): 601–612.
Bachmann, Geraldine. 1987. Attleboro Mall: risky business under Section 404.
URBAN LAND 46 (February): 2–5.
Bachrach, Peter & Morton Baratz. 1963. Decisions and nondecisions: an
analytical framework. AMERICAN POLITICAL SCIENCE REVIEW 57 (Septem-
ber): 632–642.

255

Banfield, Edward C. 1961. POLITICAL INFLUENCE. New York: Free Press.

Barnett, Jonathan. 1982. AN INTRODUCTION TO URBAN DESIGN. New York: Harper & Row.

Baum, Howell. 1983. PLANNERS AND PUBLIC EXPECTATIONS. Boston: Schenkman.

Baumbach, Richard O. Jr. & William E. Borah. 1981. THE SECOND BATTLE OF NEW ORLEANS: A HISTORY OF THE VIEUX CARRE RIVERFRONT EXPRESSWAY CONTROVERSY. University, Ala.: University of Alabama Press and the National Trust for Historic Preservation.

Beatley, Timothy. 1984. Applying moral principles to growth management. JOURNAL OF THE AMERICAN PLANNING ASSOCIATION 50 (Autumn): 459–469.

Belsie, Laurent. 1984. Playskool closing may change the way cities woo firms. CHRISTIAN SCIENCE MONITOR, December 28.

Berger, Joseph. 1986. Church seeks end to status as landmark. NEW YORK TIMES. September 3.

Boyer, M. Christine. 1983. DREAMING THE RATIONAL CITY: THE MYTH OF AMERICAN CITY PLANNING. Cambridge: MIT Press.

Branch, Melville C. 1985. COMPREHENSIVE CITY PLANNING. Chicago: American Planning Association.

Bronstein, Scott. 1987. Coming soon: competitive solar power. NEW YORK TIMES. February 11.

Bryson, John M. & William D. Roering. 1987. Applying private-sector strategic planning in the public sector. JOURNAL OF THE AMERICAN PLANNING ASSOCIATION 53 (Winter): 9–22.

Buder, Stanley. 1967. PULLMAN: AN EXPERIMENT IN INDUSTRIAL ORDER AND COMMUNITY PLANNING 1880–1930. New York: Oxford University Press.

Burnham, Daniel H. & Edward H. Bennett. 1970. PLAN OF CHICAGO. New York: Da Capo Press. (Original edition published by Commercial Club of Chicago, 1909)

Butler, Kent S. & Dowell Myers. 1984. Boomtime in Austin, Texas: negotiated growth management. JOURNAL OF THE AMERICAN PLANNING ASSOCIATION 50 (Autumn): 447–58.

Callies, David. 1981. Public participation in the United States. TOWN PLANNING REVIEW 52 (July): 286–96.

Caro, Robert A. 1974. THE POWER BROKER: ROBERT MOSES AND THE FALL OF NEW YORK. New York: Random House.

Catanese, Anthony J. 1984. THE POLITICS OF PLANNING AND DEVELOPMENT. Beverly Hills: Sage Publications.

Cervero, Robert. 1986. Unlocking the suburban gridlock. JOURNAL OF THE AMERICAN PLANNING ASSOCIATION 52 (Autumn): 389–406.

Chavez, Lydia. 1987. From the ashes of ruin, the Bronx sees a future. NEW YORK TIMES. June 14.

Chicago Department of Development and Planning. 1966. THE COMPREHENSIVE PLAN OF CHICAGO.

Chicago Urban League. 1968. THE RACIAL ASPECTS OF URBAN PLANNING: CRITIQUE OF THE COMPREHENSIVE PLAN OF THE CITY OF CHICAGO. Chicago: Urban League.

Christensen, Karen S. 1985. Coping with uncertainty in planning. JOURNAL OF THE AMERICAN PLANNING ASSOCIATION 51 (Winter): 63–73.

Clavel, Pierre. 1986. THE PROGRESSIVE CITY: PLANNING AND PARTICIPATION. New Brunswick: Rutgers University Press.

Collins, Richard C. 1980. Changing views on historical conservation in cities. ANNALS OF THE AMERICAN ASSOCIATION OF POLITICAL AND SOCIAL SCIENCE 451 (September): 86–97.

Corden, Carol. 1977. PLANNED CITIES: NEW TOWNS IN BRITAIN AND AMERICA. Beverly Hills: Sage Publications.

Crenson, Matthew A. 1971. THE UNPOLITICS OF AIR POLLUTION: A STUDY OF NON-DECISION MAKING IN THE CITIES. Baltimore: Johns Hopkins Press.

Crenson, Matthew A. 1983. NEIGHBORHOOD POLITICS. Cambridge: Harvard University Press.

Cunningham, James V. & Milton Kotler. 1983. BUILDING NEIGHBORHOOD ORGANIZATIONS. Notre Dame: Notre Dame University Press.

Cuomo, Mario. 1974. FOREST HILLS DIARY: THE CRISIS OF LOW-INCOME HOUSING. New York: Random House.

Dahl, Robert A. 1958. WHO GOVERNS? DEMOCRACY AND POWER IN AN AMERICAN CITY. New Haven: Yale University Press.

Danielson, Michael N. & Jameson W. Doig. 1982. NEW YORK: THE POLITICS OF URBAN REGIONAL DEVELOPMENT. Berkeley: University of California Press.

Davidoff, Paul. 1965. Advocacy and pluralism in planning. JOURNAL OF THE AMERICAN INSTITUTE OF PLANNERS 31 (November): 331–38.

Davidson, Jeffrey L. 1979. POLITICAL PARTNERSHIPS: NEIGHBORHOOD RESIDENTS AND THEIR COUNCIL MEMBERS. Beverly Hills: Sage Publications.

Davies, Stephen. 1985. Managing downtown public spaces. TECHNOLOGY REVIEW 88 (August-September): 18–25, 60–61.

DeSeve, G. Edward. 1986. Financing urban development: the joint efforts of governments and the private sector. ANNALS OF THE AMERICAN ACADEMY OF POLITICAL AND SOCIAL SCIENCE 488 (November): 58–76.

Domhoff, G. William. 1978. WHO REALLY RULES? NEW HAVEN AND COMMUNITY POWER REEXAMINED, New Brunswick, N.J.: Transaction Books.

Downs, Anthony. 1985. THE REVOLUTION IN REAL ESTATE FINANCE. Washington: Brookings Institution.

Dunlap, David W. 1984. Battle of St. Bart's goes to New York landmarks agency. NEW YORK TIMES. February 1.

Easley, Gail. 1984. Performance controls in an urban setting. URBAN LAND 43 (October): 24–27.

Easton, David. 1953. THE POLITICAL SYSTEM. New York: Alfred A. Knopf.

Eckholm, Erik. 1986. Significant rise in sea level now seems certain. NEW YORK TIMES. February 18.

Eldredge, H. Wentworth. 1974. Alternative possible urban futures. FUTURES 6 (February): 26–41.

Elkin, Stephen L. 1987. CITY AND REGIME IN THE AMERICAN REPUBLIC. Chicago: University of Chicago Press.

Elkin, Stephen L. 1985. Twentieth century urban regimes. JOURNAL OF URBAN AFFAIRS 7 (Spring): 11–27.

Fainstein, Susan S. et al. 1983. RESTRUCTURING THE CITY: THE POLITICAL ECONOMY OF URBAN REDEVELOPMENT. New York: Longman.

Fasenfest, David. 1986. Community politics and urban redevelopment: Poletown, Detroit, and General Motors. URBAN AFFAIRS QUARTERLY 22 (September): 101–123.

Fawcett, James A. 1986. Redefining local government power: the influence of informal powers in challenging joint implementation of a state coastal plan. POLICY STUDIES REVIEW 6 (November): 330–339.

Feiss, Carl. 1985. The foundations of federal planning assistance. JOURNAL OF THE AMERICAN PLANNING ASSOCIATION 51 (Spring): 175–184.

Finnell, Gilbert L. Jr. 1976. Florida's State Land Use Laws and the ALI Model Land Development Code. Richard Cowart, ed., LAND USE: PLANNING, POLITICS, AND POLICY. Berkeley: University of California Extension Publications, pp. 35–54.

Fischer, Michael L. 1985. California's coastal program: larger-than-local interests built into local plans. JOURNAL OF THE AMERICAN PLANNING ASSOCIATION 51 (Summer): 312–321.

Fishman, Robert. 1977. URBAN UTOPIAS OF THE TWENTIETH CENTURY. New York: Basic Books.

Foster, Richard W. 1983. In downtown Denver, a civic group calls the shots. PLANNING 49 (January): 18–21.

Frank, Michael J. 1982. Performance zoning: how it's doing in the place where it began. URBAN LAND (December): 21–23.

Freeman, Linton C. 1968. PATTERNS OF LOCAL COMMUNITY LEADERSHIP. Indianapolis: Bobbs-Merrill.

Frieden, Bernard J. 1979. THE ENVIRONMENTAL PROTECTION HUSTLE. Cambridge: MIT Press.

Friedland, Roger. 1983. POWER AND CRISIS IN THE CITY: CORPORATIONS, UNIONS, AND URBAN GROWTH. New York: Schocken Books.

Friend, J. K. & W. N. Jessop. 1969. LOCAL GOVERNMENT AND STRATEGIC CHOICE. London: Tavistock Publications.

Gallion, Arthur B. & Simon Eisner. 1985. THE URBAN PATTERN: CITY PLANNING AND DESIGN, 5th ed. New York: Van Nostrand Reinhold.

Gardner, Marilyn. 1986. Children in an aging society. CHRISTIAN SCIENCE MONITOR. September 18.

Gold, John R. & Jacquelin Burgess, 1982. On the significance of valued environments. VALUED ENVIRONMENTS. London: George Allen & Unwin, pp. 1–9.

Goodwin, Michael. 1983. City's tax incentive panel is called slipshod. NEW YORK TIMES. May 4.

Gottdiener, Mark. 1977. PLANNED SPRAWL: PUBLIC AND PRIVATE INTERESTS IN SUBURBIA. Beverly Hills: Sage Publications.

Gottlieb, Martin. 1984. Redevelopment proposal for Times Square a lesson in politics and power in New York. NEW YORK TIMES. March 9 & 10.

Greenhouse, Steven. 1986. Chicago does its job-hunting at home. NEW YORK TIMES. November 30.

Haar, Charles M. 1977. LAND-USE PLANNING: A CASEBOOK ON THE USE, MISUSE, AND RE-USE OF URBAN LAND, 3d. ed. Boston: Little, Brown.

Hale, George E. and Marian Lief Palley. 1981. THE POLITICS OF FEDERAL GRANTS. Washington: Congressional Quarterly Press.

Hall, Derek. 1982. Valued environments and the planning process: community consciousness and urban structure. John R. Gold & Jacquelin Burgess, ed. VALUED ENVIRONMENTS. London: George Allen & Unwin, pp. 172–188.

Hall, Peter. 1980. GREAT PLANNING DISASTERS. Berkeley: University of California Press.

Hanley, Robert. 1987. Housing the poor in suburbia: a failed vision in New Jersey. NEW YORK TIMES. June 1.

Hanson, Royce (ed.). 1983. RETHINKING URBAN POLICY: URBAN DEVELOPMENT IN ADVANCED ECONOMY. Washington: National Academy Press.

Harrigan, John J. & William C. Johnson. 1978. GOVERNING THE TWIN CITIES REGION: THE METROPOLITAN COUNCIL IN COMPARATIVE PERSPECTIVE. Minneapolis: University of Minnesota Press.

Hartman, Chester W. 1984. THE TRANSFORMATION OF SAN FRANCISCO. New York: Rowman & Allanheld.

Henderson, Keith. 1985. Bay area farms: an endangered species? CHRISTIAN SCIENCE MONITOR. November 26.

Herbers, John. 1986. New jobs in cities little aid to poor. NEW YORK TIMES. October 22.

Hey, Robert P. 1986. Suburbs will have to change to accommodate older population. CHRISTIAN SCIENCE MONITOR, December 30.

Howard, Ebenezer. 1965. GARDEN CITIES OF TOMORROW. London: Faber & Faber.

Hoyt, Homer. 1939. THE STRUCTURE AND GROWTH OF RESIDENTIAL NEIGHBORHOODS IN AMERICAN CITIES. Washington: U.S. Government Printing Office.

Hudson, Barclay M. 1979. Comparison of current planning theories: counterparts and contradictions. JOURNAL OF THE AMERICAN PLANNING ASSOCIATION 95 (October): 387–398.

Hunter, Floyd. 1963. COMMUNITY POWER STRUCTURE. Garden City, N.Y.: Doubleday.

Johnson, William C. 1984. Citizen participation in local planning in the U.K. and U.S.A. PROGRESS IN PLANNING 21: 149–221.

Johnston, Robert A. et al. 1984. Growth phasing and resistance to infill development in Sacramento County. JOURNAL OF THE AMERICAN PLANNING ASSOCIATION 50 (Autumn): 434–446.

Jones, Bryan D. 1983. GOVERNING URBAN AMERICA: A POLICY FOCUS. Boston: Little Brown.

Jones, Bryan D. & Lynn W. Bachelor. 1986. THE SUSTAINING HAND: COMMUNITY LEADERSHIP AND CORPORATE POWER. Lawrence: University Press of Kansas.

Judd, Dennis R. & Robert E. Mendelson. 1973. THE POLITICS OF URBAN PLANNING: THE EAST ST. LOUIS EXPERIENCE. Urbana: University of Illinois Press.

Judd, Dennis R. 1984. THE POLITICS OF AMERICAN CITIES, 2d ed. Boston: Little Brown.

Kaplan, Harold. 1963. URBAN RENEWAL POLITICS: SLUM CLEARANCE IN NEWARK. New York: Columbia University Press.

Kaufman, Jerome L. & Harvey M. Jacobs. 1987. A public planning prospective on strategic planning. JOURNAL OF THE AMERICAN PLANNING ASSOCIATION 53 (Winter): 23–33.

Keating, W. Dennis. 1986. Linking downtown development to broader community goals: an analysis of linkage policy in three cities. JOURNAL OF THE AMERICAN PLANNING ASSOCIATION 52 (Spring): 133–141.

Lasswell, Harold D. 1958. POLITICS: WHO GETS WHAT, WHEN, HOW. New York: Meridian Books.

Louv, Richard. 1985. AMERICA II. New York: Penguin Books.

Lueck, Thomas J. 1985. Princeton corridor split on pace of development. NEW YORK TIMES. April 21.

Lueck, Thomas J. 1987. Not just football booming in Jersey Meadows. NEW YORK TIMES. January 11.

Lupo, Alan, Frank Colcord, & Edmund P. Fowler. 1971. RITES OF WAY: THE POLITICS OF TRANSPORTATION IN BOSTON AND THE U.S. CITY. Boston: Little Brown.

Lynch, Kevin. 1972. WHAT TIME IS THIS PLACE? Cambridge: MIT Press.

Lynch, Kevin. 1984. GOOD CITY FORM. Cambridge: MIT Press.

Lynd, Robert & Helen Lynd. 1929. MIDDLETOWN. New York: Harcourt, Brace & World.

Marris, Peter. 1982. COMMUNITY PLANNING AND CONCEPTIONS OF CHANGE. London: Routledge & Kegan Paul.

Martin, Roscoe et al. DECISIONS IN SYRACUSE. Garden City, N.Y.: Doubleday.

May, Clifford D. 1986. L.I. roads cope with congestion. NEW YORK TIMES. October 7.

McHarg, Ian. 1971. DESIGN WITH NATURE. Garden City, N.Y.: Natural History Press.

Meehan, Eugene J. 1979. THE QUALITY OF FEDERAL POLICYMAKING: PROGRAMMED FAILURE IN PUBLIC HOUSING. Columbia: University of Missouri Press.

Meislin, Richard J. 1987. Long-delayed Times Square plan is taking more new twists. NEW YORK TIMES. April 3.

Meyerson, Martin & Edward C. Banfield. 1957. POLITICS, PLANNING AND THE PUBLIC INTEREST. New York: Free Press.

Miller, Delbert C. 1974. LEADERSHIP AND POWER IN THE BOS-WASH METROPOLIS: ENVIRONMENT, ECOLOGY, AND URBAN ORGANIZATION. New York: John Wiley.

Mollenkopf, John H. 1983. THE CONTESTED CITY. Princeton: Princeton University Press.

Molotch, Harvey. 1976. The city as a growth machine: toward a political economy of place. AMERICAN JOURNAL OF SOCIOLOGY 82 (September): 309–332.

Moore, W. John. 1988. Bond voyage. NATIONAL JOURNAL. January 23.

Mouat, Lucia. 1984. How James Rouse shapes cities. CHRISTIAN SCIENCE MONITOR. August 31.

Myer, Chuck. 1986. Cities in 3-D. PLANNING 52 (May): 31–37.

Nadel, Mark V. 1975. The hidden dimension of public policy: private governments and the policy making process. JOURNAL OF POLITICS 37 (February): 2–34.

Olson, Richard Stuart. 1985. The political economy of life-safety: the city of Los Angeles and 'hazardous structures abatement,' 1973–1981. POLICY STUDIES REVIEW 4 (May): 670–679.

Ottensmeyer, Edward J., Craig R. Humphrey, and Rodney A. Erickson. 1987. Local industrial development groups: perspectives and profiles. POLICY STUDIES REVIEW 6 (February): 569–583.

Park, Robert E., Ernest W. Burgess, & Roderick D. McKenzie. 1967. THE CITY. Chicago: University of Chicago Press.

Peirce, Neal R. 1987. Hope—without a hitch—for nation's slums. NATIONAL JOURNAL. March 28: 779.

Perrenod, Virginia M. 1986. SPECIAL DISTRICTS, SPECIAL PURPOSES: FRINGE GOVERNMENTS AND URBAN PROBLEMS IN THE HOUSTON AREA. College Station, Tex.: Texas A & M University Press.

Perry, Clarence A. 1924. Planning a city neighborhood from the social point of view. PROCEEDINGS OF THE NATIONAL CONFERENCE OF SOCIAL WORK. Chicago: University of Chicago Press.

Peterson, Paul E. 1981. CITY LIMITS. Chicago: University of Chicago Press.

Pflaum, Ann M. & Timothy J. Delmont. 1987. External scanning—a tool for planners. JOURNAL OF THE AMERICAN PLANNING ASSOCIATION 53 (Winter): 58–68.

Phillips, Stephen. 1986. Small bank revives urban area. NEW YORK TIMES. January 30.

Popper, Frank J. 1987. The environmentalist and the LULU. Robert W. Lake, ed. RESOLVING LOCATIONAL CONFLICT. New Brunswick, N.J.: Center for Urban Policy Research, pp. 1–13.

Porter, Douglas R. 1986. Downtown San Francisco's new plan. URBAN LAND 45 (February): 34–35.

Porter, Douglas R. 1987. Financing infrastructure with special districts. URBAN LAND 46 (May): 9–13.

Powell, John Duncan. 1985. Assault on a precious commodity: the local struggle to protect groundwater. POLICY STUDIES JOURNAL 14 (September): 62–69.

Pressman, Jeffrey L. & Aaron Wildavsky. 1979. IMPLEMENTATION, 2d ed. Berkeley: University of California Press.

Rapoport, Amos. 1977. HUMAN ASPECTS OF URBAN FORM. Oxford: Pergamon Press.

Ravetz, Alison. 1980. REMAKING CITIES: CONTRADICTIONS OF THE RECENT URBAN ENVIRONMENT. London: Croom Helm.

Rawls, John. 1971. A THEORY OF JUSTICE. Cambridge: Belknap Press of Harvard University Press.

Reinhold, Robert. 1984. Houston tries to rein in its sprawl. NEW YORK TIMES. September 9.

Rider, Robert W. 1982. Local government planning: prerequisites of an effective system. URBAN AFFAIRS QUARTERLY 18 (December): 271–280.

Rivkin, Malcolm D. 1986. Negotiating with neighborhoods: managing development through public/private negotiations. URBAN LAND 45 (January): 15–19.

Roberts, Sam. 1984. Battle of the Westway: bitter 10-year saga of a vision on hold. NEW YORK TIMES. June 4.

Roberts, Sam. 1987. Charlotte Street: tortured rebirth of a wasteland. NEW YORK TIMES. March 9.

Rohe, William M. & Lauren B. Gates. 1985. PLANNING WITH NEIGHBORHOODS. Chapel Hill: University of North Carolina Press.

Rosenbaum, Nelson. 1978. Growth and its discontents: origins of local population controls. Judith V. May & Aaron B. Wildavsky, ed. THE POLICY CYCLE. Beverly Hills: Sage Publications, pp. 43–61.

Rossi, Peter & Robert A. Dentler. 1961. THE POLITICS OF URBAN RENEWAL. New York: Free Press.

San Diego, City of, Planning Department. 1986. BACKGROUND SUMMARY: CITY OF SAN DIEGO GROWTH MANAGEMENT PROGRAM.

Savitch, H. V. 1979. URBAN POLICY AND THE EXTERIOR CITY: FEDERAL, STATE, AND CORPORATE IMPACTS UPON MAJOR CITIES. Elmsford, N.Y.: Pergamon.

Sawers, Larry. 1984. New perspectives on the urban political economy. William K. Tabb & Larry Sawers, ed. MARXISM AND THE METROPOLIS, 2d ed. New York: Oxford University Press, ch. 1.

Sayre, Wallace S. & Herbert Kaufman. 1965. GOVERNING NEW YORK CITY. New York: W. W. Norton.

Scardino, Albert. 1985. College's growth has old Savannah in an uproar. NEW YORK TIMES. November 29.

Schattschneider, E. E. 1960. THE SEMI-SOVEREIGN PEOPLE. New York: Holt, Rinehart and Winston.

Schmalz, Jeffrey. 1987. New York reaches accord on housing. NEW YORK TIMES. December 27.

Schmidt, William E. 1985. Cities place new fees on developers. NEW YORK TIMES. October 31.

Schoenberg, Sandra P. & Patricia L. Rosenbaum. 1980. NEIGHBORHOODS THAT WORK: SOURCES FOR VIABILITY IN THE INNER CITY. New Brunswick: Rutgers University Press.

Schwartz, Lisa. 1986. Mutual housing associations: promise for affordable housing. URBAN LAND 45 (May): 17–21.

Scott, Mel. 1969. AMERICAN CITY PLANNING SINCE 1890. Berkeley: University of California Press.

Seley, John E. 1983. THE POLITICS OF PUBLIC-FACILITY PLANNING. Lexington: D. C. Heath Lexington Books.

Shirvani, Hamid. 1985. THE URBAN DESIGN PROCESS. New York: Van Nostrand Reinhold.

Shirvani, Hamid & Michael Stepner. 1986. San Diego's environmental planning process ten years later. JOURNAL OF THE AMERICAN PLANNING ASSOCIATION 52 (Spring): 212–219.

Silver, Christopher. 1985. Neighborhood planning in historical perspective. JOURNAL OF THE AMERICAN PLANNING ASSOCIATION 51 (Spring): 161–174.

Simmons, Tom. 1984. A quest for 'open space' near bustling Silicon Valley. CHRISTIAN SCIENCE MONITOR. August 3.

Sinclair, Upton. 1906. THE JUNGLE. New York: Doubleday, Page.

Slater, David C. 1984. MANAGEMENT OF LOCAL PLANNING. Washington: International City Management Association.

Spencer, James A. 1979. Planning agency management. Frank S. So, ed. THE PRACTICE OF LOCAL GOVERNMENT PLANNING. Washington: International City Management Association, ch. 3.

Spirn, Anne Whiston. 1984. THE GRANITE GARDEN: URBAN NATURE AND HUMAN DESIGN. New York: Basic Books.

Stepner, Michael (Assistant Planning Director, City of San Diego). Interview by author, December 30, 1986.

Sternleib, George. 1986. PATTERNS OF DEVELOPMENT. New Brunswick, N.J.: Rutgers University Center for Urban Policy Research.

Stokvis, Jack R. 1987. Making downtown competitive again. URBAN LAND 46 (April): 7–11.

Stone, Clarence N. 1976. ECONOMIC GROWTH AND NEIGHBORHOOD DISCONTENT. Chapel Hill: University of North Carolina Press.

Stone, Clarence N. 1987. The study of the politics of urban development. Clarence N. Stone & Heywood T. Sanders, ed. THE POLITICS OF URBAN DEVELOPMENT. Lawrence: University Press of Kansas, 3–22.

Swanstrom, Todd. 1985. THE CRISIS OF GROWTH POLITICS: CLEVELAND, KUCINICH, AND THE CHALLENGE OF URBAN POPULISM. Philadelphia: Temple University Press.

Teltsch, Kathleen. 1987. Aiding housing in the Bronx wins respect for a group. NEW YORK TIMES. October 30.

Thompson, Wilbur. 1965. A PREFACE TO URBAN ECONOMICS, Baltimore: Johns Hopkins Press.

Tuan, Yi-Fu. 1974. TOPOPHILIA. Englewood Cliffs, N.J.: Prentice-Hall.

Ventriss, Curtis & Robert Pecorella. 1984. Community participation and modernization: a reexamination of political choices. PUBLIC ADMINISTRATION REVIEW 44 (May–June): 224–31.

Wachs, Martin. 1985. ETHICS IN PLANNING. New Brunswick, N.J.: Rutgers University Center for Urban Policy Research.

Wald, Matthew L. 1983. Saving aging housing: a costly city takeover. NEW YORK TIMES. November 27.

Walsh, AnnMarie H. 1978. THE PUBLIC'S BUSINESS: THE POLITICS AND PRACTICES OF GOVERNMENT CORPORATIONS. Cambridge: MIT Press.

Warner, Sam Bass, Jr. 1968. THE PRIVATE CITY: PHILADELPHIA IN THREE PERIODS OF ITS GROWTH. Philadelphia: University of Pennsylvania Press.

Warren, Elizabeth. 1979. CHICAGO'S UPTOWN: PUBLIC POLICY, NEIGHBORHOOD DECAY, AND CITIZEN ACTION IN AN URBAN COMMUNITY. Chicago: Loyola University Center for Urban Policy.

Warson, Albert. 1986. The Canadian trio who turned flooring into a real estate empire. CHRISTIAN SCIENCE MONITOR. March 7.

Webber, Melvin W. 1976. The BART experience—what have we learned? THE PUBLIC INTEREST 45 (Fall): 79–108.

Whitt, J. Allen. 1982. URBAN ELITES AND MASS TRANSPORTATION: THE DIALECTICS OF POWER. Princeton: Princeton University Press.

Wikstrom, Nelson. 1977. COUNCILS OF GOVERNMENT: A STUDY OF POLITICAL INCREMENTALISM. Chicago: Nelson-Hall.

Wildavsky, Aaron. 1964. LEADERSHIP IN A SMALL TOWN. Totowa, N.J.: Bedminster Press.

Wilkerson, Isabel. 1987. Growth of the very poor is focus of new studies. NEW YORK TIMES. December 20.

Williams, Oliver P. & Charles R. Adrian. 1963. FOUR CITIES. Philadelphia: University of Pennsylvania Press.

Wirt, Frederick M. 1974. POWER IN THE CITY: DECISION MAKING IN SAN FRANCISCO. Berkeley: University of California Press.

Wirt, Frederick M. 1985. The dependent city? External influences upon local control. JOURNAL OF POLITICS 47 (February): 83–112.

Wirth, Louis. 1938. Urbanism as a way of life. AMERICAN JOURNAL OF SOCIOLOGY 44 (July): 1–24.

Wolman, Abel. 1965. The metabolism of cities. SCIENTIFIC AMERICAN 213 (September): 179–205.

Wong, Kenneth K. & Paul E. Peterson. 1986. Urban response to federal program flexibility: politics of Community Development Block Grant. URBAN AFFAIRS QUARTERLY 21 (March): 293–309.

Woodhams, Mark. 1983. Victory in the Hamptons. PLANNING 49 (November): 16–20.

Wrenn, Douglas M. & Ronald W. Case. 1984. Cooperative planning in Long Beach: SEADIP. URBAN LAND 43 (May): 20–23.

Wright, Frank Lloyd. 1963. THE LIVING CITY. New York: New American Library.

Yates, Douglas. 1977. THE UNGOVERNABLE CITY: THE POLITICS OF URBAN PROBLEMS AND POLICY MAKING. Cambridge: MIT Press.

Zotti, Ed. 1987a. CADD takes hold. PLANNING 53 (January): 22–24.

Zotti, Ed. 1987b. Design by committee. PLANNING 53 (May): 22–27.

INDEX

Accessibility, 167, 240
Activists, 76
Adams-Morgan Commission, 93
Advisory Committee on Intergovernmental Relations, 92, 93
Advocacy tradition, 102
Ahlbrandt, Roger S., Jr., 233
Airports, 146, 168
Alinsky, Saul, 91
Allocation, 15–17
Alperin, Davida, 57
Altshuler, Alan, 110, 142, 147, 205
Ambler Realty Company, 27
American Civil Liberties Union, 82
American Institute of Certified Planners, 241–42
American Institute of Planners, 70
Appleyard, Donald, 146
Army Corps of Engineers, 65
Aronson, J. Richard, 171
Atlanta, Georgia, 41, 71, 145, 196, 207, 226
Attorneys, 82
Austin, Texas, 127, 223
Authoritative value allocation, 15–16

Babcock, Richard F., 73, 82, 89, 105, 113, 114, 185, 185, 200
Bachelor, Lynn, 4, 86, 176, 201
Bachmann, Geraldine, 65
Bachrach, Peter, 192, 194
"Back to nature" movement, 25–26
Baltimore, Maryland, 44, 71, 72, 90, 145, 222

Southeast Community Organization (SECO), 92, 198
Banana-Kelly Community Improvement Association, 141
Banfield, Edward C., 138, 203, 236
Baratz, Morton, 192, 194
Barnett, Jonathan, 157
Bartholomew, Harland, 43
Bathgate Industrial Park, 6, 59, 178
Battery Park City, 80, 139
Baum, Howell, 216, 242
Baumbach, Richard O., Jr., 69
Bay Area Rapid Transit System (BART), 7, 19, 77, 84, 95, 114–15, 167
  evaluation of, 129–31
  planning of, 111–12, 209, 234
Beatley, Timothy, 240
Belsie, Laurent, 179
Bennett, Edward H., 36, 37
Berger, Joseph, 154
Berkeley, California, 215–16
Berman v. Parker, 44
Bicycle travel, 146
Bixby Ranch Company, 116
Boca Raton, Florida, 126
Bonds to finance urban development, 169, 171–72
Borah, William E., 69
Borough government, 53
Borrowing, *see* Bonds
Boston, Massachusetts, 139, 143, 164–65, 213, 230
Boyer, M. Christine, 25, 26, 39, 41, 43
Branch, Melville, 122, 125, 153

Broadacre City, 220
Bronx, *see* South Bronx, New York
Brown v. Board of Education of Topeka, 31
Bryson, John M., 233
Bucks County, Pennsylvania, 124
Buder, Stanley, 36
Burgess, Ernest W., 165
Burgess, Jacquelin, 47
Burnham, Daniel, 36, 37, 142, 212, 218, 219
Bus transportation, 145
Butler, Kent S., 127

Cabrini-Green project, 137
California, 58, 63, 135, 152, 170, 230
California Coastal Commission, 116
Callies, David, 95
Carbone, Nicholas, 184
Caro, Robert A., 26, 59, 215
Carter, Jimmy, 141
Case, Ronald W., 116
Cases of planning politics, 2–7
Catanese, Anthony J., 31, 81, 128, 214–15
Centralized Retail Management (CRM) program, 183
Centura Parc, 225
Cervero, Robert, 143, 144, 182
Chavez, Lydia, 6
Census Bureau, 8, 224
Charlotte Gardens, 6, 16
Chicago, Illinois, 35–37, 71, 82, 83, 96, 138, 145, 155, 164, 165, 178, 179, 198, 225, 230
    Department of Development and Planning, 104, 105, 142
    1909 Comprehensive Plan for, 36–37, 142, 212
    1966 Comprehensive Plan for, 31, 36, 104–105, 1–2
    power structure in, 197, 202–203
Chicago Housing Authority, 105, 236
Chicago Urban League, 31–32
Choices, making specific planning, *See* Decision making
Christensen, Karen, 231
Churches, 86–87
Church of St. Paul and St. Andrew, 154
Citizen participation, 87–97
    in land use planning, 30–31
    in neighborhood renewal planning, 33, 71–72
    planning commissions, 216
City Beautiful movement, 24–25, 28, 35, 36, 88, 155
City government, 53, 54–55
City of Eastlake v. Forest City Enterprises, 95

City of Renton v. Playtime Theatres, 73
Civic League of St. Louis, 32
Civic Ventures Inc., 84
Civil rights movement, 31, 67
Clavel, Pierre, 184, 216
Clean Air Act, 151
Clean Water Act, 64–65
Cleveland, Ohio, 43, 70
    Fine Arts Committee, 57
Coalitions, 212–14
    formations of, 79
    planning by, 206–210
    role of planners in, 214–17
    types of, 207–208
Colcord, Frank, 148
Columbia, Maryland, 81, 157
Commission form of local government, 55
Communication of planning decisions, 127–28
Community Development Block Grants, 70, 72, 93, 94, 172
Comprehensive plans, 103, 105–109
Computer-aided drafting and design, 232
Concentric zone model, 165
Conflict, *see* Cooperation/conflict
Contemporary City (Ville Contemporaine), 41–42
Contemporary values, 44–48
Control, 240
    planning and, 9
    see also Power to plan
Cooperation/conflict, 2, 14, 20, 208
    authoritative value allocation and, 15–16
    cases of, 2–7
    between government units, 47–48
    industrial development and, 178–79
    private sector versus public interests, 10–11
COPS (Communities Organized for Public Service), 88–89, 91
Corden, Carol, 158, 159
Corruption, 30, 126
Councils of Government (COGs), 61
County government, 53–55
Courts in urban planning, 72–74, 115, 170
    see also New Jersey Supreme Court; Supreme Court
Crenson, Matthew, 90
Crow, Trammel, 80, 112
Cultural aspects of planning, 153–56
Cumulative zones, 117–20
Cunningham, James V., 92, 94, 198

Dahl, Robert, 196–97, 199–200, 213
Daley, Richard, 197, 203
Danielson, Michael N., 59, 202
Davidoff, Paul, 215

Davidson, Jeffrey L., 77
Davies, Stephen, 155
Decision making:
  elite/mass competition for, 5
  by elite negotiation, 115, 210
  by fiat, 2, 20–21, 115, 210
  by open negotiation, 115–16, 210
  in planning cycle, 10, 110–16
  planning for economic development and, 185–89
  power structures and, 196–200
Delmont, Timothy J., 223
Democratic process in urban planning, 20–21, 78, 235
Demonstration Cities and Metropolitan Development Act, 61, 67
Denver, Colorado, 82, 84, 150
Denver Partnership, 84
Department of . . ., see U.S. Department of
DeSeve, G. Edward, 203
Design review board, 56–57
Design Workshop, 232
Detroit, Michigan, 3–4, 13, 15, 16, 19, 54, 115, 165, 168, 176, 225, 230
  Community Economic Development Department, 3
Developers, 80–82
Development fees, 170
Discrimination, 31, 44
  zoning and, 41
  see also Moderate-income housing
Districts, special purpose local, 58–60
Doig, Jameson W., 59, 202
Domhoff, G. William, 196, 199–200
Downs, Anthony, 82, 173, 175
Downtown/uptown development, politics of, 180–85
Dunlap, David W., 87
Du Pont Circle Commission, 93

Easements, public, 124–25
Easley, Gail, 124
East Brooklyn Churches, 87
East Hampton, New York, 54
East Los Angeles Community Union, 91
Easton, David, 14
Eckholm, Erik, 227
Economic Development Administration, 178
Economics of urban planning, politics and, 161–90
  downtowns and uptowns, 180–85
  economic goals, 161
  engines of the urban economy, 166–68
  high stakes and hard choices of, 185–89
  industrial development, 176–80

  promotion of economic growth, 19
  sources of capital, 65–72, 82–83, 168–75
Effectors, 76
Eisner, Simon, 135
Elderly, housing for, 19
Eldredge, H. Wentworth, 228
Electoral politics:
  initiative, 95
  intervention in, 78–79
  referendum, 4, 50, 54, 95, 111, 113, 116, 171, 184
Elitists, 5, 78, 196–97, 206, 207
  decision making by negotiation of, 115, 210
Elkin, Stephen L., 212, 216
Employment opportunities, promotion of, 19, 161
Enterprise Development Company, 80–81
Enterprise Foundation, 86
Enterprise zones, 172–73
Environmental determinism, 24
Environmental impact statement (EIS), 152–53
Environmental issues, 19, 88, 89, 202
  planning involving, 149–53
  trends in, 227
Environmental Protection Agency (EPA), 65
Environmental scanning, 222–23
Erickson, Rodney A., 179
Esthetic values and urban planning, 24–26, 149, 237–38
Euclid, Ohio, 27
Exactions, 170
Exclusive zones and zoning, 120, 122
External scanning, 222–23

Fainstein, Susan S., et al., 183, 188
Faneuil Hall, 81
Fasenfast, David, 4
Fawcett, James A., 63
Federal government, see National government
Federal Housing Authority, 71
Federal National Mortgage Association (Fannie Mae), 173
Feedback, planning, 10, 128–32
Feiss, Carl, 66
Fiat, choice by, 2, 20–21, 115, 210
Financing of urban development, 65–72, 82–83, 168–75, 226–27
Finnell, Gilbert L., Jr., 63
First English Evangelical Lutheran Church v. County of Los Angeles, 73, 125
Fischer, Michael L., 63
Fishman, Robert, 41

Florida, 58, 63
Forest Hills Gardens, 38
Foster, Richard W., 84
Fowler, Edmund P., 148
Frank, Michael J., 124
Freeman, Linton C., 76
Friedland, Roger, 85, 180, 181, 204
Friend, J. K., 230
Fulton County, Georgia, 170
Functional planning, 133–60
Functional values in urban planning, 26–29, 238–39
Future, planning in and for the, 218–44

Gallion, Arthur B., 135
Garden City Association of America, 38
Garden City movement, 37–38
Gardner, Marilyn, 225
Gates, Lauren B., 116
Gautreaux v. Chicago Housing Authority, 105
General Motors, 3–4, 13, 16, 19, 50, 54, 85–86, 163, 168, 176, 201
    Poletown and, 3, 15, 17, 115, 162, 166, 167, 167, 186, 195
General obligation bonds, 171
Gentrification, 141–42
Glossary, 251–53
Goal-setting stage of planning, 9–10, 103–10
Gold, John, 47
Goodwin, Michael, 170
Gottdiener, Mark, 81, 83
Gottlieb, Martin, 112, 113
Gould, Elgin R. L., 30, 38
Government National Mortgage Association (Ginnie Mae), 173
Government planning, 10–11, 23–24, 47–74
    partnership with private sector, 10–14, 203, 227
    responsibilities of, 18–20, 30
    types of decisions in, 11–14
    see also Local governments; National government; State government
Greenbelt Congress, 89
Greenhouse, Steven, 177
Growth, 210–14
    industrial, 3–4, 176–80
Growth centers, 166, 229
Growth limitation, 126–27
    case of, 4–5
Growth rate, limitation of, 126–27
Guernsey Dell, 177

Haar, Charles M., 9
Habitat for Humanity, 141

Hackensack Meadowlands Development Commission, 159–60
Hale, George E., 70
Hall, Derek, 46
Hall, Peter, 7, 129
Handicapped, housing for, 19
Hanley, Robert, 5
Hanson, Royce, 164, 165
Harborplace, 81, 182
Harrigan, John J., 62
Hartford, Connecticut, 30–31, 147–48, 184–85
Hartman, Chester W., 57
Hawkins v. Town of Shaw, 31
Henderson, Keith, 89
Herbers, John, 226
Hey, Robert P., 224
"Highest and best use" principle, 27, 162
Highways, 67, 71, 168, 202
Highway service strip, 182
Hilley, John L., 171
Historic preservation, 153–55, 238
    tax credits for, 172
Historic Preservation Act, 153
Home versus housing, 46
Housing, 23–24, 30, 134–42
    home versus, 46
    moderate-income, *see* Moderate-income housing
    policy goals, 136–37, 139
    public, 43–44, 71, 134, 137–38, 236
    urban renewal, 42–44, 65, 71, 139–42
Housing and Community Development Act, 67
Housing legislation, federal, 66, 135, 138, 158
Houston, Texas, 82, 121
Howard, Ebenezer, 37–38, 102
Hoyt, Homer, 165
Hubert H. Humphrey Metrodome, 85
Hudson, Barclay M., 102
Humphrey, Craig R., 179
Hunter, Floyd, 192, 196, 207

Implementative participation, 79
Implementing planning goals and choices, 10, 117–28
Improvement assessment, 170
Incentive zoning, 124
Incremental tradition, 102, 103, 235
Incumbent upgrading, 142
Industrial Areas Foundation, 91
Industrial growth, 176–80
    case of, 3–4
Industrial revenue bonds, 171
Industrial towns, planned, 35
Informal consultation, 78

Initiative, 95
Inner transition zones, 166, 229–30
Insider relationships, 77, 78
Institutional leaders, 76
Itasca, Illinois, 224

Jacobs, Harvey M., 233
Jessop, W. N., 230
Johnson, William C., 62, 79, 84
Johnston, Robert A., et al., 127
Jones, Bryan D., 4, 86, 176, 195, 201
Judd, Dennis R., 67
Jungle, The (Sinclair), 37

Kaufman, Herbert, 78, 98–99
Kaufman, Jerome L., 233
Keating, W. Dennis, 139
King, Martin Luther, Jr., 31
Kirschner, Edward, 215–16
Kotler, Milton, 92, 94, 198
Labor unions, 85–86
La Jolla Valley, San Diego, 4, 16
Land availability, 167
Landmarks in urban planning, 34–44
Land speculators, 83
Land use, planning of, 18
  citizen participation in, 30–31
  corruption in, 30
  see also Zoning
Largo, Florida, 124
Lasswell, Harold D., 17, 193
Lawsuits, 79
Leagues of Women Voters, 89
Le Corbusier, 41–42, 102
Lee County Commission, 113
Letchworth, England, 38
Legislature, local, 54
L'Enfant, Pierre, 35, 234
Lindsey, 4
LISC (Local Initiatives Support Corpora-
  tion), 140–41
Living amenities, 167
Local governments, 11, 47, 175
  federal grants to, 65–72, 172
  general purpose, 52–57
  special purpose, 58–60
  state grants to, 172
Local industrial development group
  (LIDG), 179–80
Long Beach, California, 116
Los Angeles, California, 152, 164, 198,
  222, 307–308
Los Angeles County Regional Planning
  Commission, 60
Lower income housing, *see* Moderate-in-
  come housing

Lueck, Thomas J., 54, 160
LULUs (Locally Unwanted Land Uses),
  178–79
Lupo, Alan, 148
Lynch, 45, 153, 236–37, 240, 241
Lynd, Helen, 196
Lynd, Russell, 196

McCormick Place, 202–203
McHarg, Ian, 150
McKenzie, Roderick D., 165
Maps:
  comprehensive guide plan, 105–107
  zoning, 117, 118–19, 120, 125
Marris, Peter, 9, 188
Martin, Roscoe, et al., 199
Mass transit, 143, 144–45, 168, 182, 226
  see also Bay Area Rapid Transit System
Mayors, 54, 55
Meadowlands, New Jersey, 159–60
Media, 84–85, 128
Meehan, Eugene J., 47, 134, 138
Meislin, Richard J., 112
Metropolitan Life Insurance Company, 44
Metropolitan planning agencies, 60–62
Metropolitan Statistical Area, 8
Meyerson, Martin, 138, 236
Miami, Florida, 145
Mid-Bronx Desperadoes, 6, 86
Miller, Delbert C., 199
Milton Bradley Company, 179
Milwaukee, Wisconsin, 72
Minneapolis-Saint Paul region, 140, 145,
  205
    Citizens League, 89
    Metropolitan Council, 62, 148
Minneapolis Star and Tribune Company,
    85
Minnesota, 62, 63, 145, 172
Minnesota Department of Transportation,
    62
Mitchell Energy and Development Corpo-
    ration, 159
Model Cities program, 33, 71, 93
Moderate-income housing, 16, 19, 82, 94,
    136–42
  case of, 5–6
  displacement of, for downtown renewal
    projects, 183–84, 186, 239–40
Mollenkopf, John H., 213
Molotch, Harvey, 211
Moore, W. John, 172
Moral values in urban planning, 29–32,
    239–40
Mortgages, 173
Moses, Robert, 26, 59, 215
Mouat, Lucia, 81, 86

Mount Laurel cases, 5, 72, 94, 122
Mutual Housing Association, 138
Myer, Chuck, 232
Myers, Dowell, 127

Nadel, Mark V., 18
National Association for the Advancement
    of Colored People, 72
National Defense Highway Act of 1956, 67
National Environmental Protection Act,
    152
National government, 11, 47, 64–72, 137,
    172, 175
National League of Cities, 69
National Planning Conference of 1931, 43
National Research Council, Committee on
    National Urban Policy, 164
Negotiation:
  elite, 115, 120
  open, 115–16, 210
Nehemiah Project, 87
Neighborhood(s):
  definition of, 90
  downtown, 180–85
Neighborhood groups, 90–92, 198, 214
Neighborhood redevelopment:
  case of, 6
  citizen participation in, 33
  in South Bronx, 6, 13, 15–17
Neighborhood Reinvestment Corporation,
    140
New Haven, Connecticut, 183, 196–97,
    200, 213
New Jersey, 16, 19, 21, 58, 72, 94, 122, 136
  Council for Affordable Housing, 5
New Jersey Supreme Court, 5, 15, 72
New Orleans, 56–57, 69, 238
New York City, New York, 70, 99, 139,
    145, 164, 202, 225, 226
  Housing Authority, 43
  Industrial and Commercial Incentive
    Board, 170
  as landlord of last resort, 140
  Times Square area, 112–13, 115
  zoning in, 39–40, 212
New York State, 44
Nollan v. California Coastal Commission,
    170
Nongovernmental participants, 75–100
Nonprofit institutions, 85–87
Norris, Tennessee, 158

Oakland, California, 7, 149, 178
  see also Bay Area Rapid Transit System
Oak Ridge, Tennessee, 157, 158
Oberlin, Ohio, 198

Olmsted, Frederick L., 26
Olson, Richard Stuart, 152
Olympia & York Enterprises, Ltd., 80
Open negotiation, 115–16, 210
Ottensmeyer, Edward J., 179–80
Outer transition zones, 166–67, 230
Outsider relationships, 77, 78, 79
Overlap districts, 122

Palley, Marian Lief, 70
Palm Beach, Florida, 220
Park, Robert E., 165
Parks, 26, 149–50
Parks, Rosa, 31
Partnership of public and private sector,
    10–14, 203, 227
Pecorella, Robert, 91, 198
Pedestrian travel, 146
Peirce, Neil R., 141
Penn, William, 34
People for Open Space, 89
Performance zoning, 122–24
Perrenod, Virginia M., 60
Perry, Clarence, 32–33, 38
Petaluma, California, 126–27, 212
Peterson, Paul E., 72, 162, 163, 211, 239
Pflaum, Ann M., 223
Philadelphia, Pennsylvania, 34, 225
Phillips, Stephen, 83
Phoenix, Arizona, 149
Pittsburgh, Pennsylvania, 204, 233
Place, 45–46, 47
Planned unit development (PUD), 122, 123
Planners, 205
  definition of, 50–51
  in the power structure, 214–17
  values of, 241–42
Planning:
  control and, 9
  functional, 133–60
  in the future, 218–44
  governments' role in, see Government
    planning
  power to plan, 191–217
  in public policy, 17–21
  steps in the cycle of, 9–10, 101–33, 209–
    10
  evaluation and feedback, 10, 128–32
  implementing goals and choices, 10,
    117–28
  making specific choices, 10, 110–16
  setting of goals and criteria, 9–10, 103–
    10
  types of decisions, 11–14
  power structures and, 200–206
  value allocation and, 22–48
  the vocabulary of, 8–14

Planning commission, local, 55–56, 216
Playskool Corporation, 179
Pluralists, 78, 197, 206, 212
Poletown, Michigan, 3, 15, 17, 50, 115, 162, 166, 167, 186, 195
Police power of government, 51
Polikoff, Alex, 82, 105
Political party machine, 197
Political values and city building, 22–24
Politics, 2, 20–21, 49–50
  economics of urban planning and, 161–90
  government participants, 47–74
  nongovernmental participants, 75–100
  planning for the future and, 233–34
  political trends, 227–28
  in specialized planning, 156–60
  the vocabulary of, 14–17
Pontiac, Michigan, 201
Popper, Frank J., 151, 178, 179
Port Authority of New York and New Jersey, 59, 60
Porter, Douglas R., 58, 131
Powell, John Duncan, 152
Power to plan, 191–217
  in the community, 195–200
  growth as ends of power, 210–14
  planners in the power structure, 214–17
  planning by coalitions, 306–10
  power structure in planning choices, 200–206
  sources of, 194
  views of, 192–94
Power structures, 195–200
  planners in, 214–17
  in planning choices, 200–206
Pressman, Jeffrey L., 178
Private sector, 10–11, 17–18, 23, 24
  financing from, 173, 174
  partnership with public sector, 10–14, 203, 227
Profit-making participants, 80–85
Project for Public Spaces, 155
Property values, preservation of, 27, 28
Pruitt-Igoe homes, 47, 134, 138
Public interest, 235–36
Public opinion, influencing, 79
Public policy, planning in, 17–21
Pullman, George, 35–36
Pullman, Illinois, 35–36, 157
Pyramid Companies, 65

Quincy Market, 182

Radburn, New Jersey, 38
Radical tradition, 102

Rapoport, Amos, 46
Ravetz, Alison, 46
Rawls, John, 239
Reagan, Ronald, 67–68, 138
Redevelopment, see Neighborhood redevelopment
Redlining, 83
Referendum, 4, 50, 54, 95, 111, 113, 116, 171, 184
Reichmann brothers, 80, 81
Reinhold, Robert, 121
Religious institutions, 86–87
Renton, Washington, 73
Research, 108–109
Resident survey, 109
Revenue bonds, 171
Revenue sources, 65–72, 82–83, 168–75, 226–27
Rider, Robert W., 109
Rivkin, Malcolm D., 116
Roberts, Sam, 6, 147
Robert Taylor Homes, 42, 137
Rockefeller, John D., 202, 215
Roering, W. D., 233
Rohe, William M., 116
Roosevelt, Franklin D., 43
Rosenbaum, Nelson, 109, 126
Rosentraub, 85, 108
Rouse, James, 80–81, 86

Sacramento County, California, 127
Safe Drinking Water Act, 151–52
Safety of life and property, 19
St. Bartholomew's Episcopal Church, 86–87
St. Croix National Wild and Scenic Riverway, 124
Saint Paul, Minnesota, 57, 62, 94, 97, 120, 155, 156
  Planning Department of, 205
San Diego, California, 4, 14, 16, 19, 21, 50, 54, 95, 127, 143, 145, 155, 212, 221
San Francisco, California, 7, 21, 34, 57, 71, 131, 139, 145, 164, 184, 213, 230
  planning for the future, 222, 223
  see also Bay Area Rapid Transit System
San Francisco Redevelopment Agency, 57
Sanibel Island, Florida, 113–14, 115, 116
Santa Monica, California, 139
Savannah, Georgia, 154, 155, 157
Savitch, H. V., 163
Sawers, Larry, 187
Sayre, Wallace S., 78, 98–99
Scardino, Albert, 155
Scenarios, 228–30
Schattschneider, E. E., 49, 50, 75, 76, 208
Schmalz, Jeffrey, 139

Schmidt, William E., 170
School districts, 58
Schwartz, Lisa, 139
Scientific Management movement, 39
Scott, Mel, 30, 31, 32, 37, 38, 40, 43, 44, 60, 65–66, 70, 88
Sector model, 165–67
  kinds of sectors, 166–67
Segregation, 31, 236
Seley, John E., 151
Shared-ride facilities, 144
Shirvani, Hamid, 122, 124, 221
Shoreview, Minnesota, 108
Siemon, Charles L., 73, 82, 89, 105, 113, 114, 185, 220
Sierra Club, 4, 88
Silver, Christopher, 33
Simmons, Tom, 150
Sinclair, Upton, 37
Sioux City, Iowa, 184–85
Slater, David C., 239
Social Gospel movement, 29
Social values in urban planning, 32–33, 240–41
Socioeconomic trends, 224–27
Sohio Tower, 57
South Bronx, New York, 6, 13, 15–17, 21, 59, 77, 86, 116, 139, 141, 166, 178, 185, 188, 214
South Bronx Development Corporation, 6
Southern Burlington County N.A.A.C.P. et al. v. Township of Mount Laurel, 72
South Shore Bank, 83
Space, 45–46
Specialty retail centers, 182–83
Spencer, James A., 55
Spirn, Anne Whiston, 238
"Spot zoning," 125
Spring Hill, Tennessee, 163
Stable, established areas, 166, 229
Stakeholders, 75–76
State government, 11, 47, 62–64, 172, 175
  federal grants to, 65–72
Stepner, Michael, 4, 221
Sternlieb, George, 135, 137
Stokvis, Jack R., 183
Stone, Clarence, 188–89, 208
Strategic planning, 233
Stuyvesant Town, 42, 44
Subdivision regulations, 121–22
Suburbs:
  case of, 5–6
  moderate-income housing in, 16, 19
  new downtowns of, 181–82
Suffolk County, New York, 81, 83
Supreme Court cases, 27, 31, 44, 73, 95, 125, 127, 170
Synoptic tradition, 102, 103, 236

Syracuse, New York, 199
System bias, 210–11

Tax abatement, 169–70
Tax credits, 172
Tax Reform Act of 1986, 171–72, 173
Tax increment financing, 169
Tax revenues as funding source, 169, 226–27
Taylor, Frederick, 39
Technologies, new, 223–24
Teltsch, Kathleen, 6, 86
Tenements, 30, 37
  regulation of, 28, 29
Testimony to exert influence on decision makers, 78
Texas, 58
Theory of Justice, A (Rawls), 239
Thompson, Wilbur, 161
Times Square area, New York City, 112–13, 115
Town/township government, 54
Traditional downtown, 180–81
Transactive tradition, 102, 103, 235
Transfer of development rights, 125
Transportation, metropolitan, 19, 28, 67, 71, 142–48, 168
  case of, 7
  see also specific forms of transportation
Trends, analysis of, 222–28
"Trickle-down" view, 187, 188
Trolley Square, 182
Trump, Donald, 80
Tuan, Yi-Fu, 45

Uncertainties, types of, 230–32
United Auto Workers, 85–86, 207
United Neighborhood Organization (UNO), 91
U.S. Bureau of the Budget, 61
U.S. Census Bureau, 8, 224
United States Conference of Mayors, 69
U.S. Congress, 61, 64, 65, 66, 67, 68
U.S. Department of Housing and Urban Development, 67, 69, 129, 158, 183
U.S. Department of Transportation, 129, 148
U.S. Economic Development Administration, 178
University of Chicago, Environmental Simulation Laboratory, 232
Uptown/downtown development, politics of, 180–85
Urban, definition of, 8
Urban design, concept of, 157

Urban Development Action Grant (UDAG) program, 67
Urban Development Corporation, 112, 113
Urban enterprise zones, 68
Urban Mass Transit Administration, 183
Urban renewal, 42–44, 65, 71, 139–42, 204, 239–40

Value allocation:
  authoritative, 15–16
  urban planning as, historical and contemporary view of, 22–48
Valued environment, 46–47
Values, 14–15, 23, 234
  in urban planning, 22–48, 234–42
    contemporary, 44–48
    esthetic, 24–26, 149, 237–38
    functional, 26–29, 238–39
    moral, 29–32, 239–40
    of planners, 241–42
    planning landmarks, 34–44
    political, 22–24
    social, 32–34, 240–41
Vehicle movement sector, 143–44
Vehicle storage sector, 144
Ventriss, Curtis, 91, 198
Vieux Carre Commission, 56, 238
Village government, 53
Village of Euclid v. Ambler Realty Co., 27

Wachs, Martin, 232, 234, 241, 242
Wagner-Steagall Housing Act, 23, 44, 65, 66
  Section 701 of, 65, 66
Wald, Matthew, 140
Walsh, AnnMarie H., 59–60
Warner, Sam Bass, Jr., 212

Warren, Elizabeth, 96, 198
Warren, R., 85, 108
Warren, New Jersey, 5–6, 17, 54
Warson, Albert, 80
Washington, Harold, 208
Washington, D.C., 34–35, 93–94, 145, 234
Waste management, 19–20, 65, 71, 150–52, 223–24
Webber, Melvin, 130, 131
Westway, 80, 146–47
Whitt, J. Allen, 7, 84, 112
Wikstrom, Nelson, 61
Wildavsky, Aaron, 178, 198
Wilkerson, Isabel, 225
Williams, Oliver P., 104
Wirt, Frederick M., 200, 206–207, 208
Wirth, Louis, 8
Witchita, Kansas, Midtown Citizens Association, 91–92
Wolman, Abel, 149
Wong, Kenneth K., 72
Woodhams, Mark, 54
Woodlands, Texas, 157, 159
World's Columbian Exposition in 1893, 26
Wrenn, Douglas M., 116
Wright, Frank Lloyd, 220

Yates, Douglas, 197–98
Young, Coleman, 3, 4, 54, 168, 195

Zoning, 27, 38–41, 54, 117–26, 212
  industrial development and, 177
Zoning board, local, 56
Zoning map, 117, 118–19, 120, 125
Zoning ordinance, 117–20
Zotti, Ed, 57, 232